Rosalie
Natchez, Mississippi

Pond Store
Pond, Mississippi

Fine Dining
Mississippi Style

Signature Recipes from Mississippi's
Restaurants and Bed & Breakfast Inns

Fine Dining Mississippi Style

Signature Recipes from Mississippi's Restaurants and Bed & Breakfast Inns

by John M. Bailey

QUAIL RIDGE PRESS

Preserving America's Food Heritage

Library of Congress Cataloging-in-Publication Data

Bailey, John M.. 1936-
    Fine dining Mississippi style : signature recipes from Mississippi's restaurants and bed & breakfast inns / by John M. Bailey
       p. cm.
    ISBN 1-893062-55-4
    1. Cookery. 2. Cookery—Mississippi. I. Title.

TX714.B15613 2003
    641.59762—dc22   2003058628

ISBN 1-893062-55-4

Front cover photo by John Bailey.
Design by Cynthia Clark.
Manufactured in the United States of America.

QUAIL RIDGE PRESS
P. O. Box 123 • Brandon, MS 39043 • 1-800-343-1583
email: info@quailridge.com • www.quailridge.com

Dedication

Dedicated to my wonderful wife and best friend
Ann
A great cook in her own right!

Table of Contents

Table of Contents

Introduction

In my many years traveling across the state of Mississippi entertaining clients at various restaurants, I developed a great love for Mississippi's fine food. At the same time, as an amateur photographer, I compiled quite a portfolio of photographs featuring state landmarks. After my retirement in 1997, I decided to put my love of food and my photographs to use by creating my first cookbook, the original *Fine Dining Mississippi Style*.

Now six years later, there are two new editions in the FINE DINING SERIES, *Fine Dining Tennessee Style* and *Fine Dining Louisiana Style,* and the first Mississippi cookbook has sold out. So many new restaurants have made Mississippi home that the decision to create an all-new *Fine Dining Mississippi Style* was an obvious choice.

After putting a few more miles on my car and enjoying heaping helpings of great food, I present to you nearly 300 recipes from eighty-five of the finest chefs, restaurants and bed & breakfast inns in Mississippi. With detailed instructions, these culinary delights can now be prepared and enjoyed in your own home. Most are signature recipes from fine restaurants including savory Panéed Soft-Shell Crab from Nick's and decadent Irish Coffee Balls from Mary Mahoney's Old French House Restaurant. Others are the most requested dishes from popular, casual dining establishments including down-home Chicken and Dumplings from Jim's Café and traditional Chicken Salad from Phill It to the Brim Café. This time around, I have included some of my own personal favorite recipes in a special "Bailey House" section (see page 149) where you can try recipes contributed by my friends and family. My favorites, like cheesy Italian Spinach and rich, luscious Hot Fudge Pie, are sure to become your favorites, too.

As with the first book, the restaurants and recipes are categorized into the various regions of the state: Hills, Delta, Capital/River, Pines, and Coastal. In this way, *Fine Dining Mississippi Style* will serve not only as a food guide but also as a travel guide to the fine dining available throughout Mississippi. If you are looking for a particular restaurant while you are traveling through the Delta, for instance, *Fine Dining Mississippi Style* can lead you there with not only an address and telephone number, but a description of the restaurant itself. If you are interested in the cuisine of a certain area, just turn to that section and start cooking! Plus, you can visit each area vicariously through a full-color photograph section and through the collection of pen and ink drawings by Martha Miller and Bill Williams, Jr., that are scattered throughout the book. Whether it's the best Mississippi restaurant food you seek or the need to visit the state without leaving the comfort of your own home—*Fine Dining Mississippi Style* is sure to satisfy your cravings no matter how you look at it.

My hope is that you will enjoy your culinary adventures through the state of Mississippi as much as I have. Enjoy!

John Bailey

Acknowledgments

I would like to extend my sincerest gratitude to all the great Mississippi chefs
who so generously shared their signature recipes.

To all the local chapters of the Mississippi Chamber of Commerce,
I thank you for your help in locating the best restaurants.

My thanks as well to the Mississippi Department of Tourism
for the use of historical information and descriptions.

To Bill Williams, Jr., AIA, and Martha Miller Designs,
thank you for the use of your wonderful pen and ink drawings.

Finally, I would like to thank the following for their help on this project:
W. Jett Wilson; attorney Ed Neal, CPA;
and Miles McMath, owner of Timbeaux's Restaurant,
for providing the crab cake dish for the cover.

JMB

About the Author

John Bailey, author of *Fine Dining Mississippi Style, Fine
Dining Tennessee Style,* and *Fine Dining Louisiana Style,* is
a graduate of the University of Mississippi. He is an associate member of the American Culinary Federation and a
member of the Southern Foodways Alliance. In his spare
time, John enjoys photography, cooking and collecting cookbooks. A native of Mississippi, he and his wife Ann reside in
Germantown, Tennessee.

The Hills Region

In picturesque northeastern Mississippi, beautiful, rolling hills stretch from the Mississippi River Delta to the foothills of the Appalachian Mountains. If you listen carefully you might hear Civil War gunshots ringing out in Corinth, the clip-clop of horse hooves trotting to a stately antebellum home in Holly Springs, or the voice of Elvis Presley singing in his church choir in Tupelo. Literary greats like William Faulkner and John Grisham called Oxford home. There you'll also find the University of Mississippi and the Center for the Study of Southern Culture and Blues Archive. The Hills are truly alive with the soul of Mississippi.

Map labels: Nesbit, Olive Branch, Corinth, Hernando, Holly Springs, Booneville, New Albany, Oxford, Batesville, Tupelo, Grenada

The Hills Region Menu

The Hills Region Menu

BOONIE MAE'S
Restaurant and Catering

102 Hwy 51 South
Batesville, MS 38606
662 578-9300

Sheila Pounders, owner/manager, specializes in major event planning and works throughout Mississippi and into Tennessee and Arkansas. Her catering events range from 20 to 700 people! Boonie Mae's has been featured in *Southern Living, Mid-South Living, Delta Business Journal, Art and Soul* and *Ole Miss Alumni Review.*

New Potatoes with Cold Sauce

2 pounds (size B) new
  potatoes, boiled until
  tender
1 pound bacon, fried
  crisp

1 cup shredded sharp
  cheese
1 cup finely chopped
  green onions

Layer all ingredients in a glass baking dish and bake at 350° for 30 minutes.

COLD SAUCE:
1 cup buttermilk
1 cup mayonnaise
1 cup sour cream

1 package Hidden Valley
  Salad Dressing Mix
  (dry)

Mix all ingredients, then refrigerate. Pour over hot new potatoes.

Baked Tomatoes

1 medium onion
1 bell pepper
3 tablespoons real butter
4 (14½-ounce) cans Del
  Monte diced tomatoes
  with juice
3 teaspoons light brown
  sugar
2 teaspoons
  Worcestershire sauce

3 dashes of Tabasco sauce
¼ teaspoon Tony's
  Creole Seasoning
Salt and pepper to taste
2 cups Pepperidge Farm
  dry stuffing mix
  (in a bag)
1 cup shredded mild
  Cheddar

Chop onion and bell pepper. Sauté in butter. Add remaining ingredients (except cheese). Put into 9x13-inch casserole dish. Top with cheese. Cook 30 minutes at 350°. Serves 8.

Whole Summer Squash

2 pounds whole summer
  squash, ends trimmed
1 yellow onion

Monterey Jack cheese,
  shredded
Real butter

Boil whole squash with yellow onion. Drain water from squash; let squash drain for 1 to 2 hours to remove water. Place whole squash in a glass baking dish that has been rubbed with butter. Place shredded Monterey Jack cheese and butter pats on top of squash. Bake at 350° for 30 minutes.

Beef Tenderloin
Stuffed with Lobster

1 beef tenderloin
1 lobster tail
1 garlic

Lemon juice
Lemon pepper

Trim all fat from beef tenderloin. Split lengthwise and lay lobster tail meat down the middle. Rub with fresh garlic, lemon juice and lemon pepper. Grill at 350° for 1 hour.

Cold-Marinated Vegetables

Fresh asparagus
Whole baby carrots
Whole green beans

Artichoke hearts
Roma tomatoes

Combine amount of vegetables necessary for number of servings needed.

VEGETABLES SAUCE:

2 cups Hellmann's or homemade mayonnaise
1 cup red wine vinegar
1 cup fresh chopped chives
4 hard-boiled eggs, chopped

1 tablespoon Tabasco sauce
1 tablespoon fresh-ground garlic

Whisk ingredients together with a wire whisk. Pour over vegetables; refrigerate for 1 to 2 hours before serving.

BETHANY GUEST HOUSE
"Home of the European Breakfast"

350 CR 7000
Booneville, MS 38829
662-728-1772

Hosts: Bill and Shirley Knighton

Candlelight Dinners
Private Dinner Parties
Anniversaries and Honeymooners

Bethany's Nut Pastries

1 package yeast
¼ cup warm water
1 cup butter-flavored Crisco

4 cups plain flour
1 can evaporated milk
2 eggs
¼ teaspoon salt

Dissolve yeast in warm water. Cut shortening into flour. Add remaining ingredients. Chill dough. Divide dough into portions the size of pie crust. Roll out into circle in sugar (not flour). Sprinkle with cinnamon and chopped pecans. Cut into 8 wedges. Roll into crescents. Bake at 350° for 15 minutes, until golden.

THE GENERALS' QUARTERS
Bed and Breakfast Inn

924 Fillmore Street
Corinth, MS 38834
662-286-3325

This beautifully restored, two-story Victorian structure built in 1872 with many of the original features still intact is located in the historic district of this old Civil War town. Grounds are beautifully landscaped with a lovely pond, magnolias, roses and azaleas. Shiloh National Military Park and Pickwick Lakes are located nearby. Luke and Charlotte Doehner own this lovely bed and breakfast inn.

Chef Luke Doehner has honed his culinary skills by attending the Cordon Bleu in Paris and the Tuscany Cooking School in Sienna. Charlotte and Luke have started cooking classes at the inn this year and have added some of the wonderful ingredients that they learned about in France and Italy!

Sweet Onion and Artichoke Salad with Oliveda Dressing

1 small head leaf lettuce	6 ounces artichoke hearts,
1 small head romaine	packed in water or fresh
lettuce	
1 medium-size Vidalia	
onion (or Mayan white)	

Rinse all lettuce extremely well and pat dry. Tear leaves to desired size (about 1-inch square) and place in large salad bowl. Discard any brown or wilted pieces. Toss both kinds of lettuce together to blend. Evenly distribute into 4 smaller bowls. Peel onion and slice into $\frac{1}{4}$-inch rings. Place 3 onion rings on top of each bowl in a heart shape. Chop artichoke hearts into $\frac{1}{4}$-inch strips. Sprinkle over top of onion rings. Top with Oliveda Dressing. Serves 4.

OLIVEDA DRESSING:

1 teaspoon salt	8 teaspoons vegetable oil
2 teaspoons sugar	2 tablespoons green
2 teaspoons red wine	olive tapenade
vinegar	$\frac{1}{2}$ teaspoon crushed
4 teaspoons balsamic	garlic
vinegar	$\frac{1}{4}$ teaspoon dry mustard
4 teaspoons virgin olive oil	(double refined)

Mix ingredients together in a salad oil cruet or a glass jar with a lid. Set aside until ready to serve. Do not refrigerate. When ready to serve salad, shake jar or stir ingredients in cruet briskly to blend together. Distribute evenly over each of the four salads.

Collards with a "Touch" of Rome

4 cups water	1 clove fresh garlic,
1 pound collard greens,	finely chopped
thoroughly washed	$\frac{1}{2}$ teaspoon salt
$\frac{1}{4}$ cup lightly salted	$\frac{1}{2}$ teaspoon ground
butter	black pepper

In a 9-quart pot, add 4 cups water. Bring to a boil, then add washed collard greens. Cook on high for 5 minutes. Remove collards and drain well. Place a medium-size skillet on stove. Set to medium heat. Place butter in skillet and allow it to melt and brown slightly. Add garlic and sauté for about two minutes. Add salt and pepper, then collards. Sauté the collards for about 4 to 5 minutes. Serve immediately. Serves 4.

Hot and Spicy
Grilled Tenderloin Medallions

2 teaspoons paprika
1 teaspoon chili powder
1 teaspoon ground cumin
1 teaspoon ground
  coriander
1 teaspoon sugar
1 teaspoon salt
½ teaspoon dry mustard
½ teaspoon dried thyme
  leaves
½ teaspoon curry
  powder
½ teaspoon cayenne
  pepper
4 beef tenderloin
  medallions (about 4
  ounces each)
Olive oil for basting

In a large mixing bowl, combine all ingredients except beef. Once thoroughly mixed, add the 4 beef medallions. Cover the medallions with spices and roll them around for a good coating. Remove the coated medallions from the spice mixture. Gently brush off any excess. Place them on a tray and refrigerate for at least one hour.

Heat your barbecue grill to high. Place medallions on hot grill over high heat. Turn frequently. Baste the medallions with olive oil. Remove from grill when cooked to your liking. (Recommend rare to medium rare.) Serve with Coriander Cucumber Sauce. Serves 4.

CORIANDER CUCUMBER SAUCE:

½ large fresh cucumber,
  peeled, seeded and diced
  (about 4 tablespoons)
3 tablespoons sour cream
2 tablespoons fresh
  chopped coriander
  (cilantro)
½ teaspoon grated
  lime peel
4 drops Tabasco sauce
¼ teaspoon salt
⅛ teaspoon black pepper

Place ingredients in a blender and blend until smooth. Refrigerate until needed.

"Southern" Gelato
with Peach Nappage

½ quart heavy whipping
  cream
3 tablespoons ice water
4 tablespoons granulated
  sugar
3 tablespoons vanilla
  extract
½ gallon French vanilla
  ice cream

In a large mixing bowl that has been in the refrigerator for at least two hours, add heavy whipping cream. Turn on mixer to medium speed. Add ice water, granulated sugar and vanilla extract. As whipping cream begins to thicken, increase speed of mixer to high and whip until peaks form. Slow mixer to medium speed, and add French vanilla ice cream by large spoonfuls. Combine entirely. Pour into large plastic or metal bowl; cover with plastic wrap and place in freezer. Freeze for at least 4 hours. When ready to serve, prepare the Peach Nappage.

PEACH NAPPAGE:

1 (6-ounce) jar of your
  favorite peach preserves
1 ounce French cognac
Mint leaves
Strawberries, sliced

In a saucepan set on medium heat, place the peach preserves and cognac. Cook on medium to reduce to about ⅔ of original volume. Remove from the heat and allow to cool to room temperature. Place a large scoop of gelato mixture into a glass ice cream dish. Drizzle Peach Nappage over top and garnish with a sprig of mint and some sliced strawberries. Serves 8.

TIMBEAUX'S
On the Square

333 Losher
Hernando, MS 38632
662-429-0500

Miles Timothy McMath
Chef/Owner

Mustard Crusted Grouper
with Warm Lobster Potato Salad
Finished with Sage Brown Butter

1/2 cup butter, melted, divided	2 cups sliced red potatoes, cooked
2 (8- to 10-ounce) pieces grouper	1/4 cup sour cream
2 teaspoons Creole seasoning, divided	1/4 cup mayonnaise
1/4 cup prepared mustard	1 tablespoon chopped tarragon
1 cup seasoned fish fry	1/2 cup green onions
1 cup diced raw lobster tail	1/2 cup garlic butter
	1/4 cup chopped fresh sage

Preheat oven-proof skillet on medium with 1/4 cup melted butter. Season fish with 1 teaspoon Creole seasoning. Coat top of fish with mustard. Dip fish into fish fry (mustard side only). Place fish mustard-side-down into hot skillet. Cook for about 3 minutes until golden brown. Turn fish over and cook in a 350° oven for about 10 minutes. While fish is cooking, preheat another oven-proof skillet on medium heat. Add remaining melted butter. When hot, add lobster and sauté for 2 minutes. Add potatoes, sour cream, mayonnaise, tarragon, green onions and remaining 1 teaspoon Creole seasoning. Place in a 350° oven and bake for 10 minutes until hot and bubbly. Remove fish from skillet and add garlic butter and sage. Cook butter until golden brown. Place potato salad on a plate and top with grouper, then add sage brown butter. Serves 2.

Shrimp and Grits

12 (16 to 20 count) shrimp, peeled	1/4 cup sherry wine
Creole seasoning to taste	1/2 cup shrimp stock
1/2 cup sliced tasso ham	3 tablespoons garlic butter
2 Portobello mushrooms, sliced	2 cups cooked grits
1/4 cup sliced green onions	1 tablespoon parsley for garnish

Preheat cast-iron skillet. Season shrimp with Creole seasoning and add to hot skillet. Cook for about 2 minutes. Add ham, mushrooms and green onions. Cook for about 3 minutes and add sherry and shrimp stock. When shrimp are cooked, add garlic butter and remove from heat. Pour over grits and garnish with parsley. Serves 2 to 3 people.

Peppercorn Crusted Rack of Elk
with Sage Mashed Potatoes Finished with a 10-Year-Old Tawny Port and Local Grown Blackberry Demi-Glace

2 (12- to 14-ounce) elk chops	2 cups prepared mashed potatoes
1 teaspoon salt	1/2 cup fresh blackberries
2 tablespoons fresh-cracked pepper	1/4 cup tawny port wine
1 teaspoon butter	1 cup demi-glace
1 tablespoon chopped fresh sage	

Preheat cast-iron skillet on high heat. Season elk with salt and cracked pepper. Melt butter in skillet and sear elk for 2 minutes on each side. Once seared, place elk in a 400° oven and roast for about 8 to 10 minutes. While elk is cooking, fold chopped sage into cooked mashed potatoes. Once elk has cooked, remove it from hot skillet and add blackberries, port wine and demi-glace, and cook for 2 minutes on medium heat. Place a scoop of potatoes on a plate and top with elk; pour sauce over elk. Serves 1.

Blackened Red Snapper with Pontchartrain Butter

2 (8- to 10-ounce) snapper
   fillets
Creole seasoning
6 (16 to 20 count) shrimp,
   peeled
1 cup artichoke hearts
1 cup mushroom quarters
¼ cup brown gravy
¼ cup shrimp stock
Juice from 1 lemon
¼ cup sherry
½ cup garlic butter
¼ cup green onions
1 tablespoon fresh parsley

Preheat cast-iron skillet on high. Coat fillets with Creole seasoning. Add to skillet and cook on each side for 3 to 4 minutes. Remove fish from skillet and reduce heat to medium. Add shrimp, artichokes, and mushrooms and sauté for about two minutes. Add brown gravy, shrimp stock, lemon juice and sherry. Simmer for about 3 minutes, then add garlic butter and green onions. Remove from heat and serve over fish. Top with fresh parsley. Serves 2.

FITCH FARMS

Galena Plantation
P. O. Box 610
Holly Springs, MS 38635
662-252-8855

W. O. Fitch, Owner

Duck with Grand Marnier Sauce

4 ducks
1 apple, quartered
3 stalks celery, sliced
3 onions, sliced
3 oranges, peeled and
   sectioned, divided
4 tablespoons Grand
   Marnier, divided
12 slices bacon
Lemon-pepper seasoning
Lawry's Seasoned Salt

In a large roaster (with rack), loosely place foil on bottom and sides, leaving enough to loosely wrap duck. Place apples, celery, onions, and some of the orange sections in cavity of ducks. Press remaining orange sections between breasts. Being gentle (not to tear), lift up skin and put 2 tablespoons Grand Marnier under skin; season to taste. Place ducks in roaster and lay bacon on top of ducks. Place remaining 2 tablespoons Grand Marnier around the ducks and loosely seal. Bake at 250° for 7 hours.

GRAND MARNIER SAUCE:

¾ cup Grand Marnier
1 (8-ounce) jar orange
   marmalade
¼ pound butter
1 (16-ounce) can whole
   cranberry sauce

In a saucepan, bring Grand Marnier, marmalade, and butter to a boil, then add cranberry sauce. Serve as a side with the ducks.

Quail in Wine Sauce
Served with Wild Rice Casserole

6 to 8 quail	1 bunch green onions
Buttermilk	1 green bell pepper
Poultry seasoning	1 cup white wine
Flour	1 large can sliced
½ cup butter or	mushrooms
margarine	

Soak quail in buttermilk overnight; rinse and towel dry. Rub birds with poultry seasoning; dredge in a small amount of flour. Brown birds in butter and set aside. In same pan, melt ½ cup butter and sauté onions and green pepper. Add wine and slowly simmer birds for 30 minutes. Add mushrooms just before serving.

WILD RICE CASSEROLE:

½ cup chopped onion	1 can beef consommé
½ cup chopped green	1 cup saffron rice
bell pepper	½ cup wild rice
½ cup butter or	½ cup brown rice
margarine	1 large can sliced
White wine	mushrooms

Sauté onion and peppers in butter. Add enough white wine to beef consommé to make 2 cups. Add and mix in remaining ingredients; bake at 325° for 1 hour. If casserole begins to lose moisture, add additional consommé, water and wine. Serve with the quail in wine sauce. Serves 6 to 8.

BONNE TERRE
Country Inn and Café

4715 Church Road West
Nesbit, MS 38651
662-781-5100

Max Bonnin, Owner

Bonne Terre is located on 100 beautifully manicured acres of rolling land in Nesbit. The Inn has twelve rooms and a two-room suite. It also features a reception and conference center called Ashley Hall, wedding chapel, and riding stable, as well as two clear spring-fed lakes. Bonne Terre was featured in the September 1998 issue of *Southern Living* magazine. Bonne Terre has been featured several times on the "Mid-South Gardens" television show.

Anthony P. Field, Executive Chef

Chef Field was born in South Port, England. He has had extensive culinary work experiences in Maryland, the West Indies, Bermuda and Memphis. He is a 1995 honors graduate of the Culinary Institute of America. Chef Field is a member of the Confrerie del la Chaine des Rotisseurs.

Andrew Steele, Pastry Chef

Chef Steele was born in Colchester, England. He attended the School of Hotel and Catering Studies at Colchester Institute in England. Chef Steele won numerous awards in England including "Best Young Chef U.K. 1997" which was presented by Prince Phillip. He worked at The Stafford Hotel in London (a 2 Michelin Star hotel) 1998-1999. Chef Steele started at Bonne Terre in 2001.

Sweet Mashed Potatoes

1 pound sweet potatoes	1 tablespoon vanilla
1/2 pound Yukon Gold	extract
potatoes	2 tablespoons honey
3 ounces heavy cream	Salt and pepper to taste
2 ounces butter	1 teaspoon cinnamon

Boil sweet and Yukon potatoes till tender. Heat cream and butter, but don't boil. Strain potatoes and push through food mill. Add vanilla, cream, butter and honey. Season with salt, pepper and cinnamon, and mix.

Anthony P. Field, Executive Chef

Crab Cakes

1 egg	1 yellow bell pepper,
1 tablespoon Dijon	diced small
mustard	1 bunch scallions, sliced
2 teaspoons Tabasco sauce	3 tablespoons Sea Food
1 cup mayonnaise	Magic
1 pound jumbo lump	1 teaspoon black pepper
crabmeat	2 teaspoons Kosher salt
1 red bell pepper, diced	2 cups Japanese bread
small	crumbs

Combine all wet ingredients and mix. Pick crabmeat from shells. Don't break up too much. Add vegetables, seasonings and crabmeat to wet mixture, then fold in bread crumbs. Let rest for 1 to 2 hours in refrigerator. Shape in cakes (about 3½ ounces each). Yields 6 entrée (2 per person) portions.

Anthony P. Field, Executive Chef

Andouille Cream Sauce

2 tablespoons olive oil	2 cups white wine
4 ounces small diced	1 sprig fresh thyme
andouille sausage	2 cups heavy cream
3 tablespoons finely	1/2 pound butter, cut
diced shallots	in cubes
1 tablespoon finely	Salt and pepper to taste
chopped garlic	
1/4 cup finely chopped	
celery	

Sweat andouille with shallots, garlic and celery. Add white wine and thyme sprig. Reduce by 2/3, then add heavy cream. Reduce by 1/2, then gradually add butter cubes, stirring constantly. Season with salt and pepper. Yields 4 portions.

Anthony P. Field, Executive Chef

Country French Bread and Butter Pudding

1 vanilla bean	1 French baguette
1 quart heavy cream	1/2 pound butter,
1 cup sugar	softened
1 cup egg yolks	1 fresh nutmeg
1 cup dried cherries	Brown sugar

Split and seed vanilla bean and place into cream. Mix and bring cream and sugar to a boil. Let sit for approximately 10 minutes. Pour onto egg yolks, whisking constantly. Strain. Place dried cherries into each ramekin. Cover with a little egg mix. Cut bread into nice-size pieces. Rub bread with soft butter and soak in egg mix. Put approximately 3 bread pieces into each ramekin. Top with freshly grated nutmeg.

To cook, put raw puddings into a shallow tray. Pour in warm water (half filling the tray). Cover with foil and bake for approximately 50 minutes at 325° to 350°. Turn tray halfway through cooking. Remove foil when done. Sprinkle with brown sugar. Caramelize in oven prior to serving.

Andrew Steele, Pastry Chef

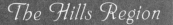

Cinnamon Shortbread Cookies

¹/₂ pound unsalted butter
1 cup confectioners' sugar
1¹/₂ cups cornstarch, sifted
1¹/₂ cups all-purpose flour, sifted

Pinch salt
4 ounces cinnamon powder
Water, as needed

Cream butter and sugar together until light. Gradually add cornstarch, flour, salt and cinnamon to form dough. Some water may be needed to make the dough workable. Roll out on lightly floured work surface to ¹/₄-inch thickness. Start out with desired shape cutter. Refrigerate for 30 minutes to firm up before baking.

Preheat oven to 350°. Bake on sheet tray for approximately 20 minutes until edges of cookies are golden. The scraps can be re-rolled (with water added) and used to make more cookies.

Andrew Steele, Pastry Chef

Chocolate Mousse

28 ounces chocolate
10 egg yolks
2 whole eggs

1¹/₂ cups sugar, divided
1¹/₂ quarts heavy cream

Melt chocolate in bowl over a pan with simmering water (a bain-marie). Set aside. In a large bowl, whip eggs and ¹/₂ sugar until soft peaks form. Set aside.

Whip cream and remaining sugar until soft peak forms. Add melted chocolate to egg mixture and beat in well until evenly dispersed, then add whipped cream. Again mix very well. Put mousse in desired glasses or cups and refrigerate until set.

Andrew Steele, Pastry Chef

VILLAGE CAFÉ and JAVA STOP

108 West Bankhead Street
New Albany, MS 38652
662-534-6565

The Village Café and Java Stop has been in existence since February of 1994. James Vigeant (known to everyone as VEEG) and his wife Susan Finch have been offering a high-quality dining experience to New Albany since their opening. James has enjoyed cooking since his college days at the University of Massachusetts. After 14 years in the corporate world, James left that environment and he and his wife changed their lifestyles and turned to something that they really enjoyed doing—cooking! Some Village Café recipes have been published in a local cookbook called *Worth Savoring*.

Village Café
Creole Barbeque Shrimp with Grilled Onions and Peppers

16 jumbo shrimp
1 cup bell peppers (green, yellow and red)
1 cup sweet Vidalia onions
¼ cup Creole seasoning
¼ cup brown sugar
2 cups basmati rice
1 healthy pinch salt
½ stick butter, divided
¼ cup extra virgin olive oil, divided
¼ cup semi-dry white wine
4 sprigs of fresh dill

Peel and devein shrimp. Set aside and keep chilled. Slice peppers and onions and also set aside. Blend Creole seasoning, brown sugar and salt in a bowl and set aside. Prepare basmati rice according to instructions on package. When rice is almost finished, melt ½ the butter and ½ the olive oil in a large skillet over medium heat, and sauté the peppers and onions until they are tender, yet still crisp. Remove peppers and onions from skillet, leaving drippings in pan. Add remaining butter and olive oil to skillet and bring back to temperature. Completely cover shrimp with dry Creole brown sugar mixture. Place shrimp into hot oil butter and cook 1 to 2 minutes on each side. Do not overcook shrimp; they are ready when you see them turn pink-coral colored. Try not to toss shrimp. When shrimp are done, remove from pan and keep warm. Return peppers and onions to skillet and gently toss as you deglaze pan with white wine.

For presentation, place a healthy serving of basmati rice in center of plate and create a nest. Scoop a portion of peppers and onions into nest and place 4 shrimp on top. Garnish each plate with a sprig of fresh dill. Finish the remaining bottle of wine with your meal. Unless, of coarse, you live in a dry county, then add an extra bottle of wine.

Cajun Grinder

A New England Oven Baked Sandwich with a Southern Style! This sandwich has an interesting story about its origin. Folk lore has it that when the New England rock quarry grinders, as they were known, would set up a site in the quarry, they would chisel out a hole in the rock face wall and start a fire in the hole to create an oven. The men would bring bread, cured meats, vegetables and cheese into work because it was not possible for them to leave the depths of the quarry during the workday. They would prepare sandwiches and other dishes and would cook them in these chiseled-out ovens.

4 (6-inch) European hoagie rolls, unsliced
8 slices Cajun-seasoned deli roast beef, sliced thick, divided
1 cup shredded leaf lettuce
½ cup diced white onion
½ cup diced bell peppers
¼ cup olive oil
¼ cup red wine vinegar
2 cups shredded medium white Cheddar cheese
¼ cup chopped fresh basil or oregano

Preheat oven to 425°. Coat a 16x24-inch cookie tray with cooking spray. Slice each hoagie roll from the top, about half way through, making sure to leave enough bread at bottom to support the filling; place on tray. Partially open each roll and insert 2 slices of meat; flap excess over sides of roll like a saddle. In the pocket created between the slices of meat, insert ¼ of the lettuce, onion and peppers into each sandwich. Drip a couple of tablespoons of olive oil and red wine vinegar onto stuffing, like a salad. Cover each sandwich with ¼ of the cheese and sprinkle a good amount of basil on top of the cheese. Cook sandwiches uncovered until the cheese is completely melted, approximately 5 minutes.

For presentation, serve sandwich hot with chips or carrot sticks. Sandwich can be eaten with a fork and knife, or for the brave, when it cools slightly, pick it up and have at it. This sandwich goes well with your favorite beer.

PHILL IT TO THE BRIM CAFÉ

9200 Goodman Road
Olive Branch, MS 38654
662-893-2255

**Phill Martin, owner
Anna Martin, manager**

The café is located in an old, renovated cotton gin in Olive Branch. The restaurant specializes in an affordable Southern casual fine dining atmosphere.

Chicken Salad

2 pounds chicken breasts
¼ cup diced sweet onions
1 cup diced sweet bell peppers
½ cup mayonnaise
1 tablespoon rosemary
1 teaspoon Italian seasoning
1 cup chopped walnuts
¼ cup chopped pecans
1 Granny Smith apple, diced
6 ounces pineapple tidbits, drained
6 ounces pineapple, crushed
Salt and pepper to taste

Boil chicken and shred. Sauté onions and bell peppers. Mix all ingredients together. Serve on toasted croissants or crackers.

Crab Cakes

1 cup diced sweet bell peppers
½ cup diced sweet onions
1 stick butter
2 tablespoons minced garlic
2 cups Japanese bread crumbs, divided
½ teaspoon ground mustard powder
1 teaspoon Creole mustard
2 tablespoons Italian seasoning
Salt and pepper to taste
1 tablespoon pesto
1 cup mayonnaise
½ pound lump crabmeat

Sauté onions and bell peppers in skillet with butter and garlic. Mix 1 cup Japanese bread crumbs, mustard powder, Creole mustard, Italian seasoning, salt, pepper and pesto in bowl. Add sautéed mixture. Fold in mayonnaise. Fold in crabmeat. (You may need to add more bread crumbs to mixture to stiffen to your taste.) Pat out desired-size cakes and bread with 1 cup bread crumbs. Fry or bake patties. Serves 8.

Banana Bread Pudding

1 loaf French bread, cubed
1 quart heavy cream
⅓ cup packed brown sugar
½ cup granulated sugar
4 large eggs
1 tablespoon vanilla extract
1 teaspoon nutmeg
1 tablespoon cinnamon
1 stick of butter, melted
6 bananas, cut in small pieces

Put cubed bread in large mixing bowl and soak in heavy cream for 15 minutes. Mix remaining ingredients, except bananas, in another bowl until smooth. Combine mixtures. Fold in bananas. Spread in a 9x12-inch baking pan. Bake at 350° for 1 hour or until firm. Serve warm with whipped cream and crushed walnuts as toppings. Serves 8.

AJAX DINER

118 Courthouse Square
Oxford, MS 38655
662-232-8880

Mississippi natives Randy Yates and Amy Lott Crockett founded Ajax Diner in 1997. Located on the historic square in Oxford, Ajax Diner specializes in a cuisine that they describe as "upscale, down home cooking." Ajax Diner has been featured on The Food Network's program, "The Best of," and has been acknowledged in publications such as, *Men's Journal,* and *Southern Living.* Noted author, poet, and food writer Jim Harrison chose Ajax Diner to be on the cover of his collection of food writings, "The Raw and the Cooked." Ajax Diner is a yearly participant in the Southern Foodways Alliance's Southern Foodways Symposium held in Oxford every October.

Tamale Pie

CHEESE GRITS:

1 gallon plus 2 cups of water	4 tablespoons Kosher salt
1 (24-ounce) container grits	3 tablespoons Tabasco sauce
½ pound butter	1 teaspoon garlic powder
2 cups grated Cheddar cheese	1 cup Parmesan cheese

In a medium-size saucepan, bring water to a boil and whisk grits in slowly. When grits return to a boil, turn heat down to medium. Continue to whisk grits until they begin to thicken. When the grits are thick, remove from heat and let sit for 10 minutes. Whisk in all other ingredients until cheese is melted and everything is incorporated.

(continued)

(Tamale Pie continued)

MEAT MIXTURE:

2 yellow onions, medium dice	3 tablespoons ground cumin
3 tablespoons garlic purée	3 tablespoons Kosher salt
½ cup butter	2 tablespoons black pepper
4 cups green chopped chiles	2 teaspoons cayenne pepper
4 cups corn (canned or frozen)	4 tomatoes, seeded and chopped
6 cups smoked pulled pork meat	Sliced Pepper Jack cheese
5 tablespoons chili powder	

In a medium-size saucepan, sauté the onions and garlic in the butter over medium heat until onions just become tender. Add the green chilies, corn and meat and continue to sauté for about 5 minutes more. Stir in seasonings, mixing well. Remove pan from heat and add chopped tomatoes.

In bottom of well-buttered, deep baking dish, spread half of Cheese Grits. Layer all of Meat Mixture over grits. Spread other half of Cheese Grits over meat as evenly and smoothly as possible. Bake uncovered in a 375° oven for about 45 minutes. Let mixture sit for at least one hour before cutting. Top with melted Pepper Jack cheese and Salsa Verde. Serves 18.

SALSA VERDE:

40 tomatillos, husked and washed	4 tablespoons chopped jalapeños
4 teaspoons garlic purée	¾ cup chopped cilantro
4 teaspoons honey	2 tablespoons Kosher salt
½ cup sliced scallions	1 tablespoon black pepper
4 tablespoons diced red onion	

Place all ingredients in a food processor, in batches, and process until ingredients are well blended, but not smooth. Taste for salt and pepper. If salsa is too acidic, add a little more honey to taste.

BOURÉ

309 North Lamar
Oxford, MS 38655
662-234-1968

Bouré is John Currence's latest venture. It was named for the Louisiana card game. This restaurant was recently featured in *Southern Living* magazine. John has created a menu and atmosphere that's laid back and family friendly. John also owns the popular fine-dining eatery, City Grocery in Oxford.

Roasted Corn Chowder

1 yellow onion, diced	1 tablespoon salt
1 tablespoon chopped fresh garlic	6 cups roasted corn kernels
2 stalks celery, diced	1 cup white wine
½ cup butter	12 cups chicken stock
5 medium baking potatoes, washed, diced (leave skin on)	3 cups heavy cream
	Salt and white pepper to taste
1 tablespoon cumin seed, toasted, crushed	

Sauté onion, garlic and celery in butter until tender. Stir in potatoes, cumin and salt and combine well. Blend in corn and coat well. Deglaze with white wine and stir in chicken stock. Bring to a simmer over medium heat and simmer until potatoes are tender. Stir in cream and simmer again for 30 minutes. Season with salt and white pepper to taste. Yields 1½ gallons.

White Bean Roasted Garlic Hummus

2 cups well-cooked white beans	½ cup plus 1 tablespoon olive oil
1 cup roasted garlic	1 tablespoon water
6 tablespoons lemon juice	Salt and white pepper to taste
2 tablespoons tahini	

Blend the above ingredients in food processor until smooth. Season lightly with salt and white pepper. Store chilled in tightly covered plastic. Yields 3 cups.

Big Otis Oatmeal Cookies

1 cup butter	2 teaspoons vanilla
1 cup sugar	½ teaspoon cinnamon
1 cup brown sugar	2 cups self-rising flour
2 eggs	2½ cups oatmeal

Beat butter and sugars until creamy. Beat in eggs one at a time. Add vanilla and combine well. Stir in cinnamon, flour and oatmeal and combine completely. Portion into 1½-ounce balls and bake at 350° until just golden around edges. Serve with vanilla ice cream and drizzle liberally with chocolate sauce.

CITY GROCERY

152 Courthouse Square
Oxford, MS 38655
662-232-8080

John Currence
Chef/Owner

Both the restaurant and bar have been hailed coast-to-coast as one of the finest establishments in Mississippi in publications such as *The New York Times, The Atlanta Journal/Constitution, The Los Angeles Times, The London Times, Southern Living, The Memphis Flyer, Seattle Daily, Esquire, USA Today,* etc. Perhaps the finest flattery to be bestowed upon City Grocery was the invitation to cook at the James Beard Foundation in New York City in the summer of 1995. The spring of 1996 saw the filming of "Great Chefs of the South" in the City Grocery kitchen and the City Grocery team returned to the James Beard House in the summer of 1997.

Smoked Catfish and Tasso Savory Cheesecake

CRUST:

1 cup grated Parmesan cheese	$\frac{1}{2}$ cup butter, melted
1 cup bread crumbs	$\frac{1}{2}$ tablespoon Creole seasoning

Combine ingredients in stainless bowl until well blended, and press into a springform pan.

FILLING:

1 tablespoon garlic olive oil	1 teaspoon Creole seasoning
$\frac{3}{4}$ cup chopped yellow onion	$1\frac{1}{2}$ pounds cream cheese, at room temperature
$\frac{1}{2}$ red bell pepper, diced small	$\frac{1}{4}$ cup sour cream
$\frac{1}{2}$ cup chopped tasso	$\frac{1}{2}$ cup heavy cream
1 cup chopped smoked catfish	4 whole eggs, lightly beaten
Salt to taste	$\frac{3}{4}$ cup grated smoked mozzarella
$\frac{1}{2}$ teaspoon cracked black pepper	

Heat oil in pan and sauté onion and red bell pepper until soft. Add tasso and catfish and season with salt, pepper and Creole seasoning. In mixer, beat cream cheese, sour cream, heavy cream and eggs until frothy. Pour over Crust and bake at 350° for $1\frac{1}{2}$ hours or until set. Drizzle with Smoked Tomato Coulis. Makes 1 (10-inch) cake.

SMOKED TOMATO COULIS:

6 tomatoes, cored, halved, seeded	Fresh-cracked black pepper
Pure olive oil	Chopped fresh garlic
Salt	

Drizzle tomatoes with oil and season with salt and black pepper. Sprinkle insides with fresh garlic and smoke over a medium-hot fire until tender. Remove from smoker and allow to cool to room temperature. Remove skins (they will slide off very easily). Place tomato halves in a blender and purée. Season with salt and pepper to taste. Makes about 3 cups.

Duck and Wild Mushroom Pot Pie

3 pounds whole chicken
1 Long Island duckling
Carrots, peeled, diced
  medium
1½ pounds new potatoes,
  NOT peeled, diced
  medium
2 yellow onions, diced
  medium

10 cloves garlic, sliced
1 pound assorted wild
  mushrooms, sliced
1 tablespoon dry thyme
Garlic olive oil
Salt and black pepper
  to taste
8 tablespoons butter
8 tablespoons flour

Salt and pepper outside of chicken and duck, and sear in large roasting pan. Remove from pan and set aside. Combine vegetables and mushrooms in a bowl with dry thyme; toss with garlic olive oil, salt and black pepper to coat. In same roasting pan, caramelize the vegetables. Stir in mushrooms; return foul to pan and roast at 375° for 1½ hours.

Remove and pick chicken and duck when cool; remove roasted vegetables from pan and mix with picked meat. (RESERVE ALL PAN JUICES TO MAKE SAUCE). Make light roux with butter and flour and add reserved pan juices to make sauce; thin with chicken stock, if necessary. Divide mix into soup bowls; cover with sauce, then cover with circles of puff pastry or pie dough. Bake at 475° for 20 minutes. Makes enough for 8 to 10 servings.

Chocolate Chambord Mousse

16 ounces semisweet
  Belgian chocolate,
  chopped
½ cup strong coffee
6 tablespoons Chambord
¾ cup butter, room
  temperature

6 eggs, separated
½ cup powdered sugar,
  divided
1 cup heavy cream

Place chocolate, coffee, and Chambord in double boiler and melt. Stir constantly. Remove from heat and stir in butter until melted. Add yolks one at a time, incorporating each one fully. Set chocolate aside. Whip whites to soft peaks in mixer. Blend in 4 tablespoons of the powdered sugar and finish beating whites to stiff peaks. Fold whites into chocolate and thoroughly combine. Whip cream to soft peaks and add remaining powdered sugar. Fold whipped cream into mousse and combine thoroughly. Pipe into brandy snifters for service. Garnish with Espresso Shortbread, chantilly cream and mint.

ESPRESSO SHORTBREAD:

3 cups flour
1⅓ cups sugar
½ cup cornstarch
1 teaspoon salt

3 tablespoons instant
  espresso powder
1½ cups chilled, cubed
  butter

Combine flour, sugar, cornstarch, salt, and instant espresso powder in processor and blend well. Add butter and pulse until combined. Remove and press into bottom of half sheet pan. Prick dough all over with fork. Bake at 300° until golden, about 40 minutes. Makes about 25 pieces.

CHANTILLY CREAM:

1 cup whipping cream
1 teaspoon sugar

½ teaspoon vanilla
  extract

Combine whipping cream with sugar and vanilla. Whisk until thick, but not stiff (it should be soft and barely able to hold its shape).

DOE'S EAT PLACE

1536 University Ave.
Oxford, MS 38655
662-236-9003

Charles Signa
Chef/Owner

Doe's Quail

12 quail
Salt and pepper to taste
1 cup water
Doe's Seafood Poultry-
  Quail Seasoning,
  if available
$\frac{1}{2}$ pound butter

1 tablespoon fresh
  minced garlic
$\frac{1}{3}$ cup Worcestershire
  sauce
$\frac{1}{3}$ cup fresh squeezed
  lemon juice
10 drops of Tabasco sauce

Place quail in a baking pan; add salt, pepper, water and Doe's Seasoning, if available, then cover. Bake at 375° for 35 minutes. Melt all remaining ingredients in a saucepan. Remove quail from oven and drain juice. Pour melted ingredients over quail. Place quail in oven and broil or brown. Check to make sure quail is tender. Serve with fresh French bread. Serves 6 or more.

Doe's Barbecue Shrimp

2 pounds unpeeled
  (26 to 30 count) shrimp
$\frac{1}{4}$ cup olive oil
$2\frac{1}{2}$ pounds canned
  crushed tomatoes
$\frac{1}{4}$ cup fresh squeezed
  lemon juice

$\frac{1}{4}$ cup Tabasco sauce
1 stem fresh mint
$\frac{1}{4}$ cup Worcestershire
  sauce
Salt and pepper to taste

In a medium saucepan, sauté shelled shrimp with olive oil; cook until all water dissolves. Add all other ingredients to shrimp and cover for 15 to 20 minutes. Serve shrimp with fresh French bread.

Doe's Eggplant Casserole

4 large eggplants, sliced
  diagonally in $\frac{1}{2}$-inch
  slices
2 cups olive oil, divided
1 onion, finely chopped
2 pounds ground chuck
2 tablespoons fresh
  minced garlic

2 ($2\frac{1}{2}$-pound) cans
  crushed tomatoes
1 large stem fresh basil
1 cup grated Parmesan
  cheese
Salt and pepper to taste

Sauté eggplant in skillet with heated olive oil. Place on paper towels to absorb excess oil. Set aside. In a medium size saucepan, sauté onion and ground chuck in olive oil. After ground chuck is brown, drain and set aside. In a medium size saucepan, sauté minced garlic in olive oil; add crushed tomatoes, fresh basil and a little water. Simmer and cook for 20 minutes. Using a 9x13-inch casserole dish, layer alternately, eggplant, meat mixture, tomato sauce and cheese. (This should make two layers of each.) Place in oven and bake for 30 minutes at 350°.

Lyceum at University of Mississippi
Oxford, Mississippi

DOWNTOWN GRILL

110 Courthouse Square
Oxford, MS 38655
662-234-2659

Partners in Downtown Grill:
Patty and William Lewis
Jackie and George Falls
Allison and Louis Brandt

Lee Cauthen, General Manager
Dixie D. Grimes, Chef

Grilled Duck Pasta

1 duck breast	Lemon juice
Extra virgin olive oil	Italian seasonings
Creole seasoning	Julienned tomatoes
1 teaspoon chopped garlic	Kosher salt
6 pieces andouille sausage	Penne pasta, cooked
Sliced mushrooms	Course-ground black
6 quarters artichoke	pepper
hearts	Parmesan cheese
White wine	

First roll duck breast in olive oil and coat with Creole seasoning. Cook on flat grill until medium (needs to be pink on the inside). While duck is cooking, heat sauté pan with olive oil. Throw in garlic, andouille sausage, mushrooms and artichoke hearts. Sauté for a minute, then deglaze with white wine and lemon juice. Add a little more olive oil, Italian seasonings, and Kosher salt, and toss thoroughly with cooked penne pasta. Serve in pasta bowl. Fan sliced duck breast out on top of pasta. Sprinkle coarse black pepper around edge of pasta bowl and place a small amount of Parmesan cheese in center of dish. Serve with julienned tomatoes.

Stuffed Pork Tenderloin

¼ cup butter, divided	Pork tenderloin
3 large Vidalia onions, julienned	12 strips Applewood bacon
4 cups mushrooms	Pepper Jack cheese grits
2 teaspoons sugar	¼ cup wilted fresh
1 teaspoon salt	spinach
1 teaspoon ground black pepper	½ teaspoon chopped bacon pieces
2 cups bread crumbs	

Heat sauté pan with 2 teaspoons butter; add onions, mushrooms and sugar. Sauté until onions are clear. Remove from heat and add salt, pepper and bread crumbs. Set aside. Take pork tenderloin and slice down center (do not slice all the way through). Cover with plastic wrap and pound out until thin. Fill tenderloin with stuffing mixture and roll up. Truss tenderloin with butcher string and wrap each one with 4 strips of apple bacon. Bake in a 400° oven for 20 minutes until medium. Slice into medallions. To serve, place medallions atop Pepper Jack cheese grits; place wilted spinach on top of three pork medallions; put bacon pieces on top of spinach; and drizzle with Jack Daniels' Demi-Glace.

JACK DANIELS' DEMI-GLACE:

¼ cup balsamic vinegar	2 cups Jack Daniel's
2 quarts veal demi-glace	bourbon
¼ cup honey	¼ cup port wine

Mix all ingredients together in saucepan and cook until reduced by half. Store in refrigerator.

Mile High Mint Cookie

Whipped cream
2 chocolate cookies
2 scoops mint chocolate
   chip ice cream
Fresh mint sprig

Crème de menthe
Chocolate sauce
Chocolate shavings
1 mint chocolate stick

To assemble, place a thin line of whipped cream in center of large round plate. Place one cookie flat on top of whipped cream. Top with ice cream and place other cookie atop ice cream. Pipe whipped cream on front of ice cream in cookie. Use a generous amount. Put a whipped cream cloud off to side of cookie and place mint sprig in whipped cream cloud. Drizzle a little crème de menthe with spoon around cookie on plate. Drizzle a little chocolate sauce on plate as well. Sprinkle chocolate shavings around entire plate, and finally place mint stick in whipped cream on cookie. Serve immediately. Yields one serving.

Chocolate Cookie

2 cups shortening
4 eggs
2 cups sugar
12 tablespoons milk
1 quart chocolate chips,
   melted

6 cups flour
4 teaspoons salt
2 teaspoons baking
   powder

Mix shortening, eggs and sugar in small mixer. Blend thoroughly. Then blend in milk and melted chocolate. Thoroughly blend in flour, salt and baking powder until there are no lumps, and dry items are well blended. Mold in a 6-inch roll and wrap in parchment paper; refrigerate overnight.

Slice and place on cookie sheet. Leave room between cookies. Bake at 350° for 10 to 12 minutes.

TWO ZERO EIGHT SOUTH LAMAR

208 South Lamar Avenue
Oxford, MS 38655
662-234-0005

Two Zero Eight South Lamar opened October 5, 2002. The building had housed a few other restaurants before owners, Russell and Sari French took over. It was remembered best as Smitty's, a restaurant that served cafeteria-style home cooking for years.

The French family moved to Oxford from Charleston, SC, in hopes of offering Oxford an innovative and eclectic style of dining by opening the "Old Smitty's" and making it a new uptown sort of place with the same diner idea. Chef John Myrick also moved to Oxford from Charleston and has developed a menu that consists of low country food with an Asian flare. The restaurant is open Monday through Saturday 11 a.m. – 2 p.m. and 5 p.m. until.

Seared Duck Breast
Over Creamy Polenta, Sautéed Baby Bok Choy with a Red Miso Broth

Salt	4 duck breasts (skin on)
Pepper	1 tablespoon olive oil

Salt and pepper duck breasts. Heat olive oil in sauté pan. Place duck skin-side-down for 1 minute. Flip and cook to desired temperature, medium rare to medium.

CREAMY POLENTA:

1 cup milk	1/2 cup butter
2 quarts chicken stock	1/2 cup Parmesan cheese
16 ounces polenta	Salt and pepper

Bring milk and chicken stock to a boil. With a wire whisk, add polenta and cook on medium heat until it pulls away from side of pan. With a rubber spatula, fold in butter and cheese. Simmer until melted. Season to taste.

MISO BROTH:

4 tablespoons red miso paste	2 minced garlic cloves
	2 minced shallots

Combine red miso paste, garlic and shallots in pan. Bring to a low simmer for 5 minutes, then strain.

BOK CHOY:

1 tablespoon oyster sauce	2 bunches baby bok choy

Add oyster sauce to sauté pan on medium heat; add bok choy and sauté until tender.

To serve, place 1 cup of Polenta on plate; lay 1 duck breast on top of Polenta. Place 4 to 5 pieces of Bok Choy around duck breast and drizzle with 1 table-spoon of Miso Broth. Serves 4.

Grilled Salmon Fillet
Over Peruvian Blue Potatoes and Sautéed Spinach with a Saffron Cream Sauce

Salt and pepper to taste	4 (8-ounce) salmon fillets

Salt and pepper salmon fillets and grill or sear to desired temperature (medium rare to medium).

PERUVIAN BLUE POTATOES:

2 pounds Peruvian blue potatoes	4 tablespoons butter
	Salt and pepper to taste
1 1/2 cups heavy whipping cream	

Boil potatoes until soft, then drain. In a mixer, whip potatoes with butter and cream. Season to taste.

SAUTÉED SPINACH:

2 tablespoons olive oil	Salt and pepper to taste
1 teaspoon minced garlic	4 cups baby spinach

Heat olive oil in sauté pan; add garlic, salt and pepper. Fold in spinach and cook until slightly wilted.

SAFFRON CREAM SAUCE:

2 cups cream	1 pinch saffron
1 tablespoon lobster base	

Slowly reduce cream in saucepan; add lobster base and saffron and cook until thickened.

To serve, lay 1 cup Peruvian Blue Potatoes on plate; place salmon fillet on top of potatoes, then top with Sautéed Spinach. Drizzle 1 to 2 tablespoons Saffron Cream Sauce over dish. Serves 4.

Tomato-Basil Bisque

2½ sticks butter
1½ cups flour
2 tablespoons garlic minced
2 tablespoons shallots minced
2 cups chicken stock
2 cups heavy cream

2 (32-ounce) cans chopped tomatoes
2 cans tomato paste
½ cup sugar
½ cup basil chiffonnade (basil cut in small ribbons)
Salt and pepper

In a large saucepan, melt butter. Stir in flour and cook for a few minutes. Add garlic and shallots and stir until soft. Add chicken stock, heavy cream, chopped tomatoes, tomato paste and sugar. Slowly simmer until slightly thickened. Purée in a blender or food processor until smooth. Add basil, salt and pepper to taste. Serves 12.

YOCONA RIVER INN

842 Highway 334
Oxford, MS 38655
662-234-2464

Paige Osborn
Owner

Balsamic Vinaigrette

½ cup vegetable oil
½ cup balsamic vinegar
1 tablespoon sherry vinegar
1 tablespoon honey

1 teaspoon black pepper
½ teaspoon celery seed
¼ teaspoon salt
½–¾ cup vegetable oil

Place the first 7 ingredients into a blender and blend well for 2 minutes. Stop blender and taste for balance. Different brands of vinegar can differ greatly, so you must rely on your palate rather than exact measurements. At this point you may add more honey and/or sherry vinegar, to adjust the sweet and sour ratio. You may also add more salt, a pinch at a time, and more black pepper, ½ teaspoon at a time. The final addition of vegetable oil will tone down the flavors a little.

After adjusting for balance, blend for 2 minutes more. With blender running, slowly pour in ½ cup of the additional vegetable oil. If necessary, add more oil until you are left with a small hole across the surface, a whirlpool about one inch in diameter. More oil will make a dressing thicker, less will make it thinner. It is not crucial, merely your preference. Yields about 2 cups.

Note: Balsamic vinegars frequently don't have the clear, acid edge of other vinegars. That is why we add a small amount of sherry vinegar. You could substitute other unflavored vinegars such as white, white wine or cider. Don't be surprised if you need to add extra honey and vinegar. Add the vinegar first, and then adjust the sweetness. Any flavorless vegetable oil is fine; we use corn oil. Olive oil tends to mask the flavors, but it will work fine if you prefer the taste.

Corn Bisque

½ cup (4 ounces, one stick) butter, unsalted
2 cups chopped yellow onions
⅔ cup flour
1 teaspoon salt
1 teaspoon dried thyme
1 quart vegetable or chicken stock, heated
2 cups shaved corn kernels
2 cups heavy cream
½ teaspoon white pepper
Green onions, sliced (optional)

In large pot, melt butter. Sauté onions in butter, stirring occasionally, until they are translucent, but don't brown. Remove pot from heat. Sprinkle onions with flour, salt and thyme. Stir or whisk well, making sure to scrape the bottom and sides of the pan. Return pot to heat, and sauté roux for about 5 minutes, long enough to cook the raw taste out of the flour. Make sure to stir/whisk frequently, scraping bottom often.

Remove pan from heat, and slowly add hot stock. Stir as you do this. Once all stock is incorporated, scrape bottom and whisk to blend. Return to heat and bring to a simmer, stirring occasionally. Continue to scrape bottom of pot to keep flour from settling and scorching. Once soup is simmering, stir in corn. Allow soup to simmer, stirring occasionally, until corn is cooked tender, about 20 minutes. Stir in heavy cream and white pepper. Bring soup back to a simmer, continuing to stir faithfully.

At this point, you can purée some of the corn to give the soup added texture. Pull out most of the corn and enough liquid to purée roughly in a blender, or use an immersion blender in the pot itself. Return purée to soup pot. Taste soup for salt, white pepper and thyme. If you don't want to purée, skip the step and taste to adjust the seasonings. It's soup. Garnish with green onions, if desired. Yields about 2 quarts.

Pan-Roasted Salmon with Maple Glaze

1 cup maple syrup
¼ cup lemon juice
¼ cup water
2 tablespoons soy sauce
1 tablespoon minced gingerroot
1 tablespoon chopped garlic
1 teaspoon crushed red pepper
Salmon, filleted and individually portioned
Flavorless oil for sautéing (peanut, corn, safflower, canola, et al)

Combine all ingredients except salmon in a small saucepan. Bring to a boil, then lower to a gentle simmer. Reduce glaze by ⅓, or about 1 cup in volume. Position an oven rack in top third of oven. Preheat oven to 450°. While glaze reduces, prep salmon.

Rinse salmon in cold water and pat dry. Season with salt and pepper and refrigerate until glaze is finished. Once glaze is reduced, spoon a little on each piece of fish. Use a brush or your hands to rub entire fillet with glaze. Let fish rest at room temperature for 5 to 10 minutes.

Have ready an oven-proof sauté pan or a sturdy baking pan or dish of any material. Add enough oil to cover bottom of pan. In a nonstick sauté pan, add enough oil to cover bottom. Heat to a moderately high heat. (Do not let the oil smoke.) Gently lay salmon fillets into pan, pretty-side-down. Sauté for about 2 minutes, or until glaze has browned on the fish. Remove pan from heat, and flip salmon. Brush tops of fillets liberally with glaze. Transfer fillets to oven-proof pan. Place in top of oven and roast until just done. Depending on your oven and size of your fillets, this may take 4 to 6 minutes. (Fish flakes easily when it is thoroughly cooked.)

Place fish on serving plates, and brush again with remaining glaze. This should make enough glaze for 6 to 8 servings. Glaze will keep indefinitely in the refrigerator; just make sure that you don't contaminate it with the utensils you use on the salmon.

All recipes © 2000 by Paige Osborn

GLOSTER 205

205 North Gloster
Tupelo, MS 38804
662-842-7205

**Guy and Martha Jenkins
Owners**

Gloster 205 restaurant has been featured on PBS's "Southern Expressions," *Mississippi Magazine* and the travel magazine, *Ford Times*.

Coconut and Macadamia Fried Shrimp

Approximately 80 jumbo shrimp, peeled, deveined and butterflied	1 cup macadamia nuts, finely chopped or 2 (3¼-ounce) jars
12 egg whites*	2 cups flour
2 cups unsweetened, long-shredded coconut	

Place shrimp in bowl of ice water to cover; set aside. Beat egg whites until foamy. Combine coconut and nuts in small bowl. Drain shrimp (do not pat dry) and dredge in flour. Quickly dip in egg whites, then toss with nuts and coconut until completely covered. Fry approximately 2 minutes or until brown. Serves 16 (5 shrimp per serving).

  *May need to beat only 2 to 4 egg whites at a time in order for them to hold up better.

Maple Glazed Cedar Planked Salmon

MAPLE GLAZE:

4 cups pure maple syrup	2 tablespoons minced garlic
½ cup fresh lemon juice	
½ cup plus 2 tablespoons soy sauce	Salt and pepper to taste

Combine ingredients in saucepan and cook down (approximately 30 to 45 minutes) till reduced to approximately 4 cups (may be done up to 2 days in advance and refrigerated). Bring to room temperature prior to serving with fish.

TO COOK SALMON ON PLANK:

Soak a 12x12-inch plank in water for at least 3 hours. Preheat grill. Remove plank from water and place on grill until hot. Have a 6x16-inch piece of aluminum foil ready. Remove plank from grill with tongs, and place plank in center of foil. Brush salmon on both sides with Maple Glaze. Wrap foil around salmon and place in convection oven for 10 minutes or until done. May baste with additional Maple Glaze, if so desired.

*Elvis Presley's Boyhood Home
Tupelo, Mississippi*

The Delta Region

$\mathcal{A}$ trip through the Delta Region reveals a landscape dotted with casinos and cotton fields. Tunica boasts twelve Las Vegas-style casinos alone. However, the Delta is best known as the birthplace of the Blues and more specifically, B.B. King who was born in Indianola. To get a real feel for the music, visit Clarksdale's Delta Blues Museum and any of the Blues cafes found there. Learn about life in the Delta first-hand through the works of playright Tennessee Williams who was born here and created many of his characters and locations after real people and places. Another beloved southern writer Willie Morris immortalized his hometown of Yazoo City in the book *My Dog Skip*. And who could forget Jim Henson of Leland, creator of the Muppets? Whether it's the Blues you seek or a hot slot machine, the Delta has something for everyone.

The Delta Region Menu

(continued)

The Delta Region Menu

MADIDI

164 Delta Avenue
Clarksdale, MS 38614
662-622-7724

What began as two friends longing to enjoy fine dining without having to drive and hour or more has since blossomed into Madidi, one of the Mid-South's premiere restaurants located in Clarksdale.

Bill Luckett, a lifelong Mississippi Delta resident and attorney, and friend and business associate, actor Morgan Freeman, became partners in a restaurant venture. The resulting fine dining facility features a downstairs dining and bar area that seats approximately 70 patrons, along with an upstairs banquet room and three private dining rooms. The eclectic menu is southern-inspired, but with classical twists.

Madidi is open for dinner Tuesday through Saturday, and reservations are recommended.

Pecan-Fried Oysters with Red Cabbage Slaw

½ pound pecans, finely chopped (reserve some for garnish)	Kosher salt and white pepper to taste
¼ pound white cornmeal	16 fresh oysters
Chili powder to taste	32 ounces canola oil, heated to 350°

Combine pecans, cornmeal, chili powder, salt and pepper in a large bowl. Dredge oysters in dry mixture to coat well, shaking off excess. Deep-fry oysters in hot oil in batches, approximately 2 minutes. Drain on clean towels.

SLAW:

1 pound red cabbage, shredded	1 tablespoon whole-grain mustard
⅓ cup mayonnaise	Kosher salt and white pepper to taste
1 teaspoon rice vinegar	

Combine the first four ingredients in large bowl. Add Kosher salt and white pepper to taste. Place mound of Slaw in center of appetizer plate; arrange oysters over top and garnish with a dusting of finely chopped pecans. Serves 4.

Grilled Jumbo Shrimp with Blue Corn Polenta

1 teaspoon chopped garlic	3 tablespoons olive oil
Fresh parsley, roughly chopped, to taste (reserve some for garnish)	Kosher salt and white pepper to taste
	20 pounds (U-10) shrimp, peeled and deveined

Preheat grill. Combine garlic, parsley, oil, salt and pepper in a large bowl. Toss shrimp in the mixture to coat. Place shrimp on grill, cooking 2 minutes per side.

POLENTA:

2 quarts chicken stock	½ cup heavy cream
½ pound blue corn polenta	¼ pound smoked Gouda cheese, shredded

In a heavy-bottom saucepan, bring stock to a boil. Rain in the polenta, stirring constantly. Lower heat and continue to stir until completely soft. Add cream and cheese and stir to incorporate. Spoon polenta into serving bowls; arrange shrimp over top and garnish with chopped fresh parsley. Serve very hot! Serves 4.

Banana Bread Pudding with Warm Caramel Sauce

BREAD PUDDING:

1 quart heavy cream
8 whole eggs
Nutmeg to taste
Cinnamon to taste
1 cup sugar

Day old baguette, torn into 2-inch pieces
1 bunch ripe bananas, sliced ¼ inch

Combine the first five ingredients. Fold in bread and bananas. Let soak for 10 minutes; pour mixture in a suitable greased baking dish. Place in a 350° oven for 30 to 45 minutes. Let cool for 20 minutes, then cut or scoop into serving dish.

WARM CARAMEL SAUCE:

1 cup granulated sugar
⅓ cup water

10 ounces heavy cream

In a heavy-bottom saucepan, combine sugar and water. Let boil until liquid turns a dark amber color. Turn off burner and slowly add cream, stirring constantly. Drizzle Warm Caramel Sauce over Bread Pudding and garnish with fresh banana slices and/or fresh berries.

The Chapel at Delta State University
Cleveland, Mississippi

KC's

Highway 61 at First Street
Cleveland, MS 38732
662-843-5301

Wally C. Joe and Don Joe
Co-owners

Wally and Don were born in Hong Kong and came to this country when they were four and two years old, respectively. Their father, K.C. Joe, opened a small grocery store in Cleveland when the family first came to this country. In 1974, K.C. bought a small restaurant on the property where KC's now stands. His boys grew up in the business, washing dishes, waiting tables and helping their parents cook.

Wally and Don graduated from the University of Mississippi in business and finance. After graduation, the brothers returned to Cleveland to work in their father's restaurant. Wally's interest is primarily in cooking which he describes as "New American." Don had a wine cellar built onto the restaurant to house what has been described as the finest wine collection in the state.

In 1994, Wally became the first chef in the state of Mississippi to be invited to cook at the James Beard House in New York City, home of the Beard Foundation, where chefs from all over the country are invited to showcase their talent. In 1997, Wally appeared on the "Great Chefs of the South" series on The Discovery Channel. In 1998, KC's received a 4-star rating (the top award) from Memphis' *The Commercial Appeal* newspaper. They also received a 4-star rating from the Jackson, Mississippi *Clarion Ledger's* "Epicurius."

Grilled Muscovy Duck Breast
With Chinese Spices, Pecan Whipped Sweet Potatoes and Blood Orange-Ginger Sauce

SWEET POTATO PURÉE:

2 large sweet potatoes	¹⁄₂ teaspoon ground
¹⁄₂ cup chopped pecans	nutmeg
¹⁄₂ teaspoon ground	¹⁄₂ teaspoon ground
cinnamon	cloves
¹⁄₂ teaspoon ground	2 tablespoons butter
ginger	Maple syrup to taste

Bake sweet potatoes in a 500° oven until done. Purée sweet potatoes with remaining ingredients, except syrup, in a food processor until smooth. Adjust taste with syrup.

SAUCE:

1 cup red wine	1 cup duck stock (or
2 cups blood orange juice	substitute chicken stock)
1 tablespoon chopped	Sugar to taste
fresh ginger	
2 tablespoons red wine	
vinegar	

Reduce red wine, juice, ginger and vinegar in a saucepan to 1 cup. Add stock and reduce again to 1 cup. Adjust taste with sugar.

DUCK:

4 (8-ounce) Muscovy duck	1 tablespoon Chinese
breasts	five-spice powder
Salt and pepper	1 teaspoon sesame oil
3 tablespoons hoisin sauce	

Season duck breasts with salt and pepper. Add hoisin sauce, five-spice powder, and sesame oil to coat duck completely. Marinate for 1 hour.

Grill duck breasts until medium rare or to desired doneness. Mound Sweet Potato Purée on plate. Slice duck breasts and arrange on top of potatoes. Drizzle with sauce. Serves 4.

JIM'S CAFÉ

314 Washington Avenue
Greenville, MS 38701
662-332-5951

Gus Johnson
Chef Owner

Jim's Café is the oldest restaurant in Washington County. It dates back to the 1920s and was founded by Gus's father. Gus has been the proprietor since he graduated from the University of Mississippi and returned to Greenville to run the family business in 1959.

Gus's Chicken and Dumplings

1 hen	Onion
Celery	

First wash a whole hen; cut up and place into a stockpot with water, celery and a little onion. Boil until tender. Strip chicken from bone and put to one side, saving the stock.

DUMPLINGS:

1 cup plain flour	3 eggs, beaten
¹⁄₂ teaspoon salt	1 cup warm water
1 tablespoon shortening	

Mix flour, salt and shortening well. Add beaten eggs and 1 cup of warm water. Mix well. Batter must be stiff. Knead on a floured table until dough is smooth. Flour dough lightly and roll flat. Cut into strips or squares and drop into boiling prepared broth until done. Place into a shallow pan and add chicken. Let sit 30 minutes and serve. Serves 6 to 8.

Rosemary Roasted Russet Potatoes

6 large potatoes   Rosemary to taste
Nonstick spray   Paprika to taste
Butter to taste

Peel and boil potatoes until done. Remove from pot and slice in halves. In an open pan, spray with nonstick spray. Place potatoes in pan, then butter and sprinkle with rosemary. Cook at 350° until brown. Add a sprinkle of paprika and serve. Yields 6 to 8 servings.

Boneless Cajun Barbeque Ribs

Shrimp and crab boil mix   Red pepper
2 lemon halves   10 to 12 pounds ribs
2 bay leaves

Fill a large stockpot with water and shrimp and crab boil mix, lemons and bay leaves. Add red pepper to taste. Let mixture boil for 30 minutes before adding meat. Add meat to boiling water. Cook until done. Remove from water and pull bone from ribs. Put ribs on a barbecue rack and brush on barbecue sauce; serve when brown. Serve with baked beans and fresh cole slaw. Serves 6 to 8.

LUSCO'S

722 Carrollton Avenue
Greenwood, MS 38930
662-453-5365

Andy and Karen Pinkston, Proprietors

The Pinkstons are fourth-generation owners of this nationally known restaurant. It has been at this location since 1933. Lusco's has been featured in *Condé Nast Travelers, Vogue, Southern Living, Gourmet* and *G.Q.* magazines. It has also been featured in *USA Today*.

Please note: Special cooking sauces and seasonings are available at Lusco's. These items may be ordered by calling 662-453-5365.

Marie's Sweet Basil Gravy

This is an Italian family recipe that is easy and quick to make. Children love it served over seashell pasta and topped with grated Parmesan or Romano cheese.

2 cans tomato purée   Lots of fresh basil (roll up
2 tablespoons olive oil   and chiffonnade), or 2+
3 garlic cloves, minced   tablespoons dried basil
  finely   Salt and pepper to taste
3 tablespoons sugar
(may want to add more,
depending on your taste)

Pour tomato purée in large boiler and add 1 can of water. Stir well and add remaining ingredients. Allow to simmer and cook slowly so flavors can marry. (This pasta gravy should be slightly sweet, not bitter, so the amount of sugar and fresh basil may vary.) Simmering time is usually about 30 to 40 minutes or until it thickens up. Spoon over cooked pasta and top with cheese. This is a great, easy side dish.

Flan

4 cups whole milk	1 teaspoon vanilla
8 eggs	$^1/_4$ teaspoon salt
3 cups sugar, divided	$1^1/_2$ tablespoons water

Place 4 cups of whole milk in boiler and place over medium high heat. Allow to heat until bubbles appear around edge and beginning of film forms on top of milk. Remove from heat. Place eggs, $1^1/_2$ cups sugar, vanilla, and salt in large mixing bowl. Stir and mix all ingredients well. Slowly add milk to egg mixture so as to temper eggs. Do not add all at once. Set aside. Place remaining $1^1/_2$ cups sugar in skillet with water. Cook over high heat until sugar starts to brown. Start stirring constantly until all sugar is dissolved and light brown caramel sauce is made. Pour caramel sauce in bottom of ramekins that are placed in larger pan filled with warm water. Spoon custard mixture in ramekins after caramel sauce. Bake in warm bath at 375° for 40 minutes+. Flans are ready when toothpick inserted comes out clean. When ready, remove from oven and allow to cool. Remove from water and drain larger pan. Place back in large pan; cover with foil and refrigerate to serve cold. May serve warm or cold, but to serve, take a knife and loosen from sides of ramekin; invert on plate allowing caramel sauce to run over top of custard. Top with whipped cream and fresh fruit.

Chocolate Sheet Cake

Easy . . . and great for a large group.

2 cups all-purpose flour	3 tablespoons cocoa
2 cups sugar	$^1/_2$ cup buttermilk
1 cup water	1 teaspoon baking soda
1 stick margarine	2 eggs, slightly beaten
$^1/_2$ cup shortening	1 tablespoon vanilla

Combine flour and sugar in a mixing bowl. In a saucepan, bring to a boil the water, margarine, shortening and cocoa. Pour saucepan mixture over flour and sugar. Add buttermilk, soda, eggs and vanilla. Mix well. Pour into greased and floured 9x13-inch baking pan. Bake at 350° for 35 minutes or until toothpick inserted comes out clean.

ICING:

1 stick margarine	1 cup chopped pecans
3 tablespoons cocoa	1 teaspoon vanilla
6 tablespoons milk	
1 box powdered sugar (or more to suit your own taste)	

Mix well the margarine, cocoa and milk. Bring to a boil and remove from heat. Add powdered sugar, pecans and vanilla. Allow cake to cool, then spread Icing over cake.

THE RIVER'S INN
Bed & Breakfast

1109 River Road
Greenwood, MS 38930
662-453-5432

"A Unique Setting for a Special Occasion"

Greenwood's first bed and breakfast is owned and operated by Rose Marie Kennedy. It was established in 1991 and is located on historic River Road which was once referred to as "Silk Stocking Avenue." Built in the early 1900s, the compound-style inn is framed in antique New Orleans ironwork and overlooks the Yazoo River. The River's Inn is listed in "The Insiders Guide to Mississippi." Make yourself comfortable in the glassed-in Garden Room with cable television and refreshments. Enjoy the pampering that only true southern hospitality affords.

Each of the five bedrooms offers a different style décor and cable television. Wake to the aroma of a full southern breakfast, prepared for you by the resident owner/caterer and served in the light-drenched sunroom. After spending an afternoon visiting Cottonlandia Museum, Florewood Living Plantation, the blues museum, and strolling through antique shops, return to the inn for a refreshing dip in the pool.

South Seas Sauce for Chicken or Catfish

3 cloves garlic, minced
3 tablespoons olive oil
1 large onion, chopped
1 green bell pepper, chopped
1 (28-ounce) can stewed tomatoes (with liquid)
3 tablespoons chili sauce
3 tablespoons Worcestershire sauce
Salt and pepper to taste
¼ cup sliced mushrooms
1 small jar capers, drained
⅓ cup green salad olives

Sauté garlic in olive oil. Add onion and bell pepper and cook until onion is transparent. Add tomatoes and liquid, chili sauce, Worcestershire sauce and salt and pepper to taste. Add mushrooms, capers and olives. When heated through, spoon over cooked boneless chicken breasts or baked catfish fillets. Yields 6 servings.

Salmon with Cucumber-Caper Sauce

SAUCE:
1 egg yolk
⅔ cup olive oil, divided
1 tablespoon lemon juice
2 teaspoons Dijon mustard
1 teaspoon fresh parsley, minced
2 teaspoons dill weed
Salt and pepper to taste
1 teaspoon chopped chives
1 large cucumber, peeled, seeded, grated and drained
1 tablespoon drained capers
½ cup heavy cream, whipped

In food processor, combine egg yolk, 2 tablespoons of the oil, lemon juice, mustard, parsley, chives, dill weed, and salt and pepper. Process 10 seconds. While running, add rest of oil in thin, steady stream. Pour into bowl and stir in drained cucumber and capers. Fold in whipped cream. Chill for two hours.

4 salmon fillets   Salt and pepper to taste

Rinse salmon and pat dry. Season with salt and pepper. Place in lightly oiled baking pan and bake for approximately 10 to 12 minutes or until done. Plate the salmon and spoon some Sauce over. Garnish with fresh parsley and lemon slices. Serves 4.

Balsamic Vegetables

2 small yellow squash
2 small zucchini squash
½ green bell pepper
½ red bell pepper
2 small carrots, scraped,
   halved lengthwise, and
   cut into 3-inch spears
2 ribs of celery, cut into
   3-inch pieces

1 small red onion, cut
   into wedges
1 tablespoon olive oil
3 tablespoons balsamic
   vinegar (good quality)
Salt and pepper to taste

Cut ends off squashes and cut them in half cross-wise, then cut into spears. Clean bell peppers, cut in half cross-wise, then cut into strips. Place carrots in boiling water and cook until carrots begin to soften slightly. Place all vegetables in 9x13-inch baking dish. Sprinkle with olive oil and balsamic vinegar. Add salt and pepper to taste and roast in 350° oven until all vegetables are crisp-tender. Do not overcook. Serve immediately. Serves 4.

YIANNI'S

506 Yalobusha
Greenwood, MS 38930
662-455-6789

Ryan and Candice Holloway
Owners

Yianni's specializes in French Creole Cuisine including fresh fish, steaks, homemade casseroles, desserts, and yeast rolls. The beautiful restaurant has banquet facilities that accommodate 20 to 50 people for business meetings, rehearsal dinners, and other special occasions. Ryan is a native of Indianola. He attended culinary school in New Orleans and trained under several five-star chefs. He and his wife Candice bought Yianni's in March 2001.

New Orleans-Style BBQ Shrimp with Blackened Beer Sauce

2 ounces real butter
2 tablespoons minced
   onion
1 teaspoon minced garlic
1 teaspoon chopped
   rosemary (fresh)

6 jumbo shrimp
2 tablespoon blackened
   seasoning
4 ounces of your favorite
   beer
4 ounces heavy cream

Sauté butter, onion, garlic, rosemary and shrimp until garlic is light golden brown. Add blackened seasoning and deglaze with beer. Simmer 1 minute, then add heavy cream and simmer 2 to 3 minutes or until consistency will coat spoon. If sauce is overcooked, it will separate. Yields 1 serving.

White Chocolate Bread Pudding

1 pound white chocolate
1 quart heavy cream
10 egg yolks
2 cups sugar

2 tablespoons vanilla
Old, stale French bread,
    crumbled

Melt white chocolate in a double boiler. Heat cream in another boiler to approximately 190°. Put yolks in a mixing bowl and slowly pour ¼ of the hot cream into eggs, whipping continuously. (Pour the cream slowly or your yolks will scramble.) Pour egg-cream mixture back into boiler of remaining cream. (You're looking for custard-like consistency). Add melted white chocolate and pour onto 9x9-inch pan of stale bread. Bake in a 350° oven for 15 to 20 minutes or until golden brown.

Typical Cotton Plant

ANTIQUE MALL and CROWN RESTAURANT

110 Front Street
Indianola, MS 38751
662-887-4522

Evelyn and Tony Roughton
Chef Owners

The Antique Mall & Crown Restaurant has been featured in *Southern Living Magazine, USA Today, The Washington Post,* and *The New York Times* to name a few! The following recipes are just a sampling of some of the wonderful recipes that can be found in the Roughtons' *Classic Catfish Cookbook.*

Delta Bisque

2 large catfish fillets
1 tablespoon butter
3 green onions, chopped
2 stalks celery, finely
    chopped
⅓ cup butter
⅓ cup flour
4 cups milk

1 cup cream
1 teaspoon Tabasco sauce
1 tablespoon chopped
    parsley
1 bay leaf
1 tablespoon chopped
    chives
1 teaspoon salt

Wash catfish fillets and cut into ½-inch pieces. Place in a large heavy boiler with 1 tablespoon butter, onions and celery. Simmer slowly 3–4 minutes; do not brown. Remove fish and vegetables. In the same pan, melt ⅓ cup of butter. Add flour and stir 2–3 minutes to cook the flour. Slowly add milk and cream, continuing to stir while the bisque thickens. Add catfish mixture and remaining ingredients. Simmer very slowly for 15 minutes. Serve immediately or may be refrigerated for up to 3 days. This lovely thick bisque is excellent served with pasta. Serves 6 to 8.

Fried Catfish and Hushpuppies

Serve with coleslaw and ketchup for a perfect Delta fish fry!

4–6 catfish fillets	**White cornmeal**
Buttermilk	**Peanut or vegetable oil**
Salt & pepper	**to fry**

Wash the catfish fillets and pat dry. Place the fillets in a shallow pan and pour about 2 tablespoons of buttermilk over each. Rub the milk into the fish, then turn the fillet over in the pan to coat the other side with the milk. Lightly salt the fish, but sprinkle the pepper generously! Pour approximately 2 cups of cornmeal into a bag or a deep bowl. Place the fillets, one at a time, into the cornmeal and shake the bag or bowl, covering the fish thoroughly with meal. Heat the oil to approximately 375° and fry the fish until lightly browned. Do not crowd the fish. To hold the cooked fish while the rest are frying, place the cooked fillets in a brown paper bag and close tightly. Serve immediately with Hushpuppies and fried potatoes cooked in the same hot oil. Serves 4.

HUSHPUPPIES:

1 cup white self-rising cornmeal	**1 teaspoon black pepper**
4 green onions, chopped	**1/2 cup milk**

Mix the corn meal, onions and pepper in a small bowl. Add the milk and mix thoroughly. Make sure that the oil is hot and ready. Using a teaspoon, scoop out a rounded spoonful of Hushpuppy batter. Lightly roll and mash it against the side of the bowl on one side and then the other. This will compress the mixture slightly and prevent the Hushpuppy from falling apart in the hot oil. Using another teaspoon, push the Hushpuppy off the spoon into the hot oil. Work quickly to fry 6 to 8 at a time, but do not crowd them. Fry until they are browned and serve immediately. Serves 4.

THE CATFISH INSTITUTE

1100 Highway 82 E
Indianola, MS 38751
662-887-2988

"Catfish: The Cultured Fish"
No longer seafood's poor country cousin, farm-raised catfish has become one of the country's most popular and versatile foods. 140,000 acres of farm-raised catfish ponds have made Mississippi, Louisiana, Alabama and Arkansas the largest catfish producing states in the Unites States.

The Real Beauty is in the Taste
One of the main differences between farm-raised and wild catfish is their living conditions. Farm-raised catfish are raised in a quality-controlled environment of clay-based ponds filled with pure fresh water pumped from underground wells. Another notable distinction between farm-raised and wild catfish is what and how they eat. Farm-raised catfish are fed a "gourmet diet" of puffed, high-protein pellets (a mixture of soybeans, corn, wheat, vitamins and minerals) that give them a mild, almost sweet taste.

Catfish Fillets with Spring Herbs and Vegetables in Parchment

6 U.S. farm-raised catfish fillets
1 zucchini, cut into julienne strips
1 carrot, cut into julienne strips
3 scallions, cut into julienne strips
3 tablespoons chopped fresh herbs, such as parsley, basil and chives, or 1 tablespoon dried herbs
1 clove garlic, minced
2 tablespoons butter, cut into cubes
6 tablespoons white wine
Salt and freshly ground black pepper

Preheat oven to 400°. Cut parchment paper or aluminum foil into 6 (12-inch) squares. Fold each in half to make a crease down center, then open up. Place a catfish fillet on one side of each square of parchment or foil. Divide the vegetables among the packets of fish. Sprinkle each packet evenly with herbs and garlic. Dot each packet with butter, then drizzle each with 1 tablespoon of wine. Season each packet with salt and pepper. Fold parchment or foil in half to cover fillet, then tightly fold in edges, crimping around each of the sides to seal packets completely. Place sealed packets on a baking sheet and bake for 8 to 10 minutes or until fish flakes easily when tested with a fork; carefully unfold one side of one of packets to check fish for doneness. To serve, tear or cut open packets carefully at table, taking care not to get burned by the steam.

Catfish Al Forno

4 U.S. farm-raised catfish fillets
2 tablespoons olive oil, divided
1 garlic clove, cut in half
1 egg, lightly beaten (2 egg whites may be substituted to reduce cholesterol)
1/4 cup milk
1/4 cup fresh bread crumbs
1/4 cup fresh grated Parmesan cheese
1 tablespoon chopped fresh oregano or 1 teaspoon dried
1/2 teaspoon salt
1/4 teaspoon freshly ground black pepper

Preheat oven to 400°. Lightly oil a baking pan large enough to hold the 4 catfish fillets in a single layer. Rub cut side of garlic into pan. Combine egg and milk in shallow dish. Combine bread crumbs, Parmesan cheese and seasonings in another shallow dish. Dip each fillet first into the egg mixture, then roll in Parmesan mixture to coat completely. Arrange fillets on baking pan and drizzle remaining oil on top. Bake for 20 minutes or until fish is flaky. Serve with risotto or rice with peas and prosciutto. Yields 4 servings.

Ranchero Catfish

4 U.S. farm-raised catfish fillets
1 cup finely crushed tortilla chips
1/2 teaspoon chili powder
3 tablespoons lime juice
1 tablespoon vegetable oil
1 cup prepared salsa
1 tablespoon chopped fresh cilantro (optional garnish)

Preheat the oven to 450°. Lightly grease baking sheet. Cut each catfish fillet in half. Rinse in cold water and pat dry with paper towels. Combine crushed tortilla chips and chili powder in shallow dish. Mix well. Combine lime juice and vegetable oil in another shallow dish. Dip each fillet piece into lime-oil mixture, then immediately into seasoned tortilla crumbs to coat. Place on prepared baking sheet. Sprinkle fillets with any remaining crumbs and bake in preheated oven until crisp and golden, about 8 to 10 minutes or until catfish flakes when tested with a fork. Gently warm salsa. Spoon salsa across center of catfish fillets. Sprinkle with fresh cilantro, if desired, and serve. Yields 4 servings.

Oven Fried Catfish with Pineapple Chutney

1 pound U.S. farm-raised catfish fillets	2/3 cup cornflake crumbs
2 tablespoons lemon juice	2 teaspoons cooking oil
1/4 cup evaporated skim milk	

Heat oven to 450°. Spray baking pan with nonstick coating; set aside. Sprinkle catfish with lemon juice. Dip fillets in milk, then roll in crumbs. Arrange fillets in prepared pan; drizzle with oil. Bake about 20 minutes or until fish flakes easily. Garnish with Pineapple Chutney.

PINEAPPLE CHUTNEY:

1 (8-ounce) can crushed pineapple (or 1 cup fresh diced pineapple)	2 tablespoons cider vinegar
1/2 cup chopped green apple	2 tablespoons instant minced onion
1/2 cup chopped red pepper	3/4 teaspoon curry powder
3 tablespoons sugar	3/4 teaspoon mustard seeds

In small saucepan, combine all the ingredients; simmer, stirring 5 minutes. Yields 4 servings.

Cheesy Catfish

2 tablespoons margarine	1/2 teaspoon pepper
1/2 cup grated Parmesan cheese	1 teaspoon Spanish paprika
1/4 cup yellow cornmeal	2 pounds U.S. farm-raised catfish fillets
1/4 cup all-purpose flour	

Preheat the oven to 400°. Place margarine in a 9x13-inch baking pan and put in the oven to melt while oven is heating. Remove pan from oven. Mix Parmesan cheese, cornmeal, flour, pepper and paprika in a plastic bag. Add catfish fillets, one at a time, and shake to coat with Parmesan mixture. Arrange fillets in a single layer in prepared pan, turning once to coat with margarine. Sprinkle remaining cheese mixture over fish. Bake for 10 to 15 minutes or until golden brown and fish flakes easily when tested with a fork. Serves 4–6.

Catfish Saté

2 tablespoons vegetable oil	1 teaspoon sugar
3 cloves garlic, minced	1 teaspoon soy sauce
1 teaspoon grated lime zest	1/2 teaspoon cayenne pepper
2 tablespoons lime juice	1 pound U.S. farm-raised catfish fillets, cut into bite-size pieces
1 tablespoon curry powder	Cooked rice

Mix oil, garlic, lime zest, lime juice, curry powder, sugar, soy sauce and cayenne pepper in a shallow dish. Add catfish fillet pieces, stirring and tossing until well coated. Cover with plastic wrap, and refrigerate for 1 hour to marinate.

Preheat the oven to 350°. Place catfish pieces on a baking sheet. Bake for about 20 minutes or until fish flakes easily when tested with a fork. Serve with Spicy Peanut Sauce and rice.

SPICY PEANUT SAUCE:

2 tablespoons vegetable oil	1 tablespoon brown sugar
1 medium onion, chopped	2 teaspoons soy sauce
1/2 teaspoon cayenne pepper	1/2 teaspoon curry powder
1 cup cream of coconut	1/2 teaspoon ground cinnamon
1 cup peanut butter	
1/2 cup milk	
1 teaspoon grated lime zest	

Heat oil in a large skillet over medium heat. Add onion and sauté until tender. Stir in the remaining ingredients. Reduce the heat to low and cook for 5 minutes or until thickened to desired consistency. Yields 3 cups.

Grilled Lemon Grass Catfish with Hoisin-Ginger Sauce

4 U.S. farm-raised catfish fillets
2 tablespoons vegetable oil
1 tablespoon minced fresh lemon grass or grated lemon zest to taste

Place catfish in a shallow pan; sprinkle with oil and lemon grass or lemon zest. Set aside.

HOISIN-GINGER SAUCE:

1 tablespoon vegetable oil
2 tablespoons finely minced yellow onion
1 clove garlic, finely minced
1 cup hoisin sauce
1 cup water
$\frac{1}{3}$ cup rice wine vinegar or white vinegar
$\frac{1}{4}$ teaspoon ground chili paste (optional)
Sliced green onions and roasted peanuts for garnish

Heat oil in a small saucepan over medium heat. Add onion and garlic and sauté for about 1 minute. Add hoisin sauce, water, vinegar and, if desired, chili paste. Reduce heat and simmer for about 10 minutes or until a creamy consistency. If sauce is too thick, add more water. Set aside.

Prepare a grill or preheat the broiler. Place fillets on an oiled grill rack or broiler pan rack. Grill or broil fillets about 4 inches from the heat source for 2 or 3 minutes on each side, or until fish flakes easily when tested with a fork. Place fillets on serving plates and spoon a little of the sauce on top. Sprinkle with green onions and peanuts and serve. Serves 4.

Note: Hoisin sauce and chili paste are available at Asian markets.

Moroccan Catfish Couscous

$\frac{1}{4}$ cup slivered almonds
2 tablespoons olive oil
1 medium onion, chopped
2 cloves garlic, minced
2 medium carrots, sliced on the diagonal
1 small red bell pepper, cut into strips
1 teaspoon ground coriander
$\frac{1}{2}$ teaspoon cayenne pepper
2 cups water
$1\frac{3}{4}$ cups chicken stock or canned broth
4 U.S. farm-raised catfish fillets, cut into 2-inch strips
1 cup canned chickpeas, drained
1 medium zucchini, cut in half lengthwise, then into 1-inch strips
1 cup uncooked couscous or rice

Preheat oven to 350°. Place almonds on a baking sheet and toast in oven for 8 to 10 minutes or until golden brown. Set aside. Heat olive oil in a large skillet over medium heat. Add onion and sauté about 5 minutes or until softened. Add garlic, carrots, bell pepper, coriander, cayenne pepper, water and chicken stock. Bring to a boil and cook for 5 minutes. Add catfish fillet strips, chickpeas and zucchini and simmer for 12 to 15 minutes or until fish flakes easily when tested with a fork.

Prepare couscous or rice according to package directions. Mound prepared couscous or rice on a large serving platter, making a well in center. Fill well with catfish and vegetables, reserving some of the cooking broth for serving. Sprinkle toasted almonds over top. Serve with remaining cooking broth spooned over individual servings.

BALLY'S

1450 Bally's Boulevard
Robinsonville, MS 38664
800-38-BALLY

*Delta Steakhouse
is located on the grounds of
Bally's Casino.*

Barry Rhodes, Executive Chef

After graduating from Hotel Management School in Liverpool, England, Barry joined the Intercontinental Group of Hotels and worked in London, Switzerland, Moscow, Jakarta, Los Angeles, New Orleans, and Miami before joining Bally's Casino in Tunica.

Crab Stuffed Oysters with Remoulade Sauce

CRAB DRESSING:

1 tablespoon mayonnaise	$1/4$ pound jumbo lump crab
1 tablespoon sour cream	1 tablespoon bread crumbs, white
$1/16$ ounce bell pepper, finely chopped	
1 whole egg, beaten	
$1/2$ teaspoon Creole mustard	

Combine first five ingredients. Add crab and bread crumbs. Squeeze out excess liquid. Refrigerate until needed. Yields $1/2$ pound. Serves 4.

WHITE REMOULADE SAUCE:

$5/8$ cup mayonnaise	1 ounce finely chopped onion
4 teaspoons Creole mustard	Salt and pepper to taste
$1/2$ teaspoon finely minced celery	2 dashes Tabasco sauce
$1/8$ bunch finely chopped parsley	$1 1/2$ tablespoons prepared horseradish

Mix ingredients in a blender. Refrigerate until needed. Yields 8 ounces.

16 whole oysters, shucked	Rock salt
Shortening	4 lemon halves

Divide Crab Dressing between oysters, keeping them in shell; cover and pat down mixture on top to seal in the oyster. Heat shortening in a deep fryer to 360°. When temperature has been reached, place oysters on base of basket (do not stack) and deep-fry for about 1 to $1 1/2$ minutes. Remove from heat and place rock salt on a plate; top with oysters, lemon wrap and ramekins of Remoulade Sauce. Serves 4.

*Recipe by Chef Barry Rhodes,
Delta Steakhouse at Bally's*

Maine Lobster Bisque

½ pound lobster, stiffs
  or culls, chopped
1 tablespoon olive oil
½ ounce brandy
  (optional)
3 ounces white wine
1½ ounces chopped
  onion
1½ ounces chopped
  celery

1½ ounces chopped
  carrot
⅛ head garlic, chopped
⅛ whole bay leaf
⅛ tablespoon parsley
2 ounces tomato paste
4¼ cups chicken stock
⅔ cup heavy cream
Cornstarch, to thicken
Salt and pepper to taste

Sauté lobster in olive oil until bright orange, and excess liquid is reduced to a dark brown coat on the base of sauté pan. Add brandy and flame. When flames have died down, add white wine and reduce until almost dry. Add vegetables and tomato paste and sauté for several minutes. Add chicken stock and bring to a boil; simmer for approximately 45 minutes. Reduce liquid by ⅛, then add cream and bring back to a boil. Thicken with some cornstarch, if needed; season with salt and pepper, then pass through a strainer. Yields 1⅝ pints. Serves 4.

MAIN LOBSTER BISQUE (SERVICE):

12 ounces cooked lobster
  meat, diced
1 tablespoon chopped
  chives

4 teaspoons whipped
  cream

Place the lobster meat and the chopped chives in the base of a soup plate; add lobster bisque and top with whipped cream. Serves 4.

Recipe by Chef Barry Rhodes,
Delta Steakhouse at Bally's

Grilled Salmon Fillets with Saffron Risotto and Lobster Cream

4 (7-ounce) salmon fillets
1 tablespoon olive oil
Salt and pepper
1 recipe Saffron Risotto
  (recipe follows)

20 each baby carrots,
  peeled and cooked
8 ounces Maine Lobster
  Bisque (see opposite
  page for recipe)

Brush salmon fillets with olive oil and season with salt and pepper. Place on a preheated hot grill and mark criss-cross style on serving side. Place on a greased sheet tray in a 350° to 375° oven for about 10 minutes or until a knife inserted comes out clean. Heat risotto and place in center of plate; top with grilled salmon and insert carrots in rice to make a crown. Finally, top with the lobster bisque. Serves 4.

SAFFRON RISOTTO:

⅛ teaspoon saffron
  threads
2 cups clam broth
1 tablespoon olive oil
4 ounces finely chopped
  onion

¾ cup arborio rice
2 ounces white wine
2 ounces heavy cream
1 ounce Pecorino Romano
  cheese, freshly grated

Add saffron to clam broth and bring to a boil, then simmer. Meanwhile, add olive oil to a heavy-bottom casserole over moderate heat. Add onions and sauté for 2 minutes until onions begin to soften. Do not brown onions. Add rice into onions and stir for one minute using a wooden spoon, making sure all the rice is well coated. Add wine and stir until absorbed completely. Begin adding simmering broth, ¼ cup at a time, stirring frequently. When broth is almost completely absorbed, add next ¼ cup broth and continue until all broth is used up. Stir often to prevent sticking. After approximately 20 minutes, when rice is tender but firm, add heavy cream and cheese. Stir quickly to combine all ingredients with rice. Remove from heat and serve immediately. Serves 4.

Recipe by Chef Barry Rhodes,
Delta Steakhouse at Bally's

Veal and Crawfish Monica

3 ounces olive oil, divided
8 (2-ounce) veal cutlets, slightly pounded
2 ounces seasoned flour
4 ounces crawfish tails
1 tablespoon butter
8 ounces fettuccine, cooked
4 whole crawfish, for garnish

Heat $\frac{1}{2}$ the olive oil in a sauté pan. Lightly flour cutlets. Cook cutlets on both sides with the minimum of color. The cutlets should be a delicate light brown. Place cutlets on serving plate and keep warm. Sauté crawfish tails in a little butter. Sauté fettuccine in remaining olive oil. Heat Monica Sauce. Place crawfish on top of veal cutlets and top with Monica Sauce. Take a carving fork and turn pasta over; place on serving plate behind the veal. Garnish with whole crawfish. Serves 4.

MONICA SAUCE:
$\frac{1}{8}$ cup unsalted butter
$\frac{1}{8}$ cup chopped green onions
Salt and black pepper
$\frac{1}{2}$ tablespoon minced garlic
$\frac{3}{4}$ teaspoon dried basil
$\frac{3}{4}$ teaspoon dried thyme
$\frac{1}{2}$ teaspoon dried oregano
1 cup white gravy
1 tablespoon tomato paste
4 tablespoons chopped fresh parsley

In skillet, melt butter over medium heat. When almost melted, add green onions, salt, pepper, garlic, basil, thyme and oregano. Stir well. Add country gravy and tomato paste; cook for about 30 minutes. Finish sauce with chopped parsley. Yields $\frac{3}{4}$ pound. Serves 4.

Recipe by Chef Barry Rhodes, Delta Steakhouse at Bally's

FITZGERALD'S CASINO

711 Lucky Lane
Robinsonville, MS 38664
662-363-5825

**Moulay Elabdellaoui
Executive Chef**

Chef Moulay is a native of Morocco. He graduated from culinary schools in Morocco and France. He was employed as a chef at the Oak Hurst Country Club in Greensboro, NC. He was a banquet chef and executive sous chef at Fitzgerald's prior to becoming Executive Chef.

Trout Stuffed with Couscous, Almonds and Herbs

4 tablespoons olive oil, divided
1 small onion, finely chopped
2 garlic cloves, crushed
1 tablespoon chopped sun-dried tomatoes
1 tablespoon chopped kalamata olives
$\frac{1}{2}$ cup couscous
$1\frac{1}{2}$ cups fish stock
1 tablespoon chopped parsley
2 tablespoons chopped basil
4 whole trout
Salt and pepper to taste
$\frac{1}{2}$ cup slivered toasted almonds
Lemon juice

Heat 2 tablespoons of olive oil in the sauté pan; add onion and sauté until softened. Add garlic, sun-dried tomatoes and kalamata olives. Stir in couscous, fish stock, parsley and basil. Bring to a boil. Remove from heat and leave for 8 minutes.

Season trout with salt and pepper and fill with $\frac{1}{4}$ of the couscous mixture. Spoon the almonds over the trout and cook in the oven on medium heat for 10 to 12 minutes. Squeeze the lemon juice over the fish. Yields 4 servings.

Recipe by Chef Moulay Elabdellaoui

Grouper with Almond Chermoula

3 (8-ounce) pieces of grouper	4 garlic cloves
2 cups cilantro	1 teaspoon red pepper flakes
Large handful of mint, roughly chopped	1 cup virgin olive oil
3 tablespoons slivered almonds	Juice of 2 lemons
	Salt and pepper to taste

Put all ingredients, except grouper, in a food processor to make chermoula. Make 2 cuts, deep slashes on both sides of grouper. Spread chermoula over grouper, working it well into the slashes. Cover and leave in a cool place for 1 hour. Cook to your liking. Serves 4.

Recipe by Chef Moulay Elabdellaoui

Chicken with Preserved Lemon

MOROCCAN PRESERVED LEMONS:

16 small ripe, thin-skinned lemons	4 sprigs of fresh bay leaves
Coarse salt	12 cloves of garlic

Soak lemons for three days. Change water daily. Cut lemons lengthwise as if about to quarter it. Do not cut quite through. Leave pieces joined. Pack one teaspoon of salt into cuts. Pack them in a jar with their own juice, bay leaves and garlic.

1 whole chicken, cut in pieces	$\frac{1}{2}$ teaspoon turmeric
6 tablespoons olive oil	1 teaspoon crushed red peppers
2 large onions, grated	3 cups water
3 cloves garlic, grated	$1\frac{1}{2}$ Casablanca olives
1 teaspoon saffron	2 tablespoons lemon juice
$\frac{1}{2}$ teaspoon ground ginger	3 tablespoons cilantro

Brown chicken in oil in hot sauté pan. Transfer chicken and its juices to stock pot. Add onions, garlic, spices and water. Cover and cook over a low heat, turning chicken in sauce from time to time until chicken is done. Add peel of 2 Moroccan Preserved Lemons and olives. Test the sauce and adjust the seasoning. Add lemon juice and chopped cilantro. Yields 4 servings.

Recipe by Chef Moulay Elabdellaoui

Stuffed Baked Lamb

STUFFING:

$\frac{1}{2}$ cup couscous	$\frac{1}{2}$ cup pine nuts
1 cup boiling water	1 cup sliced almonds
2 tablespoons coriander seeds	1 cup chopped diced onions
2 tablespoons cumin seeds	4 garlic cloves, crushed
1 teaspoon ground cinnamon	6 tablespoons chopped cilantro
3 tablespoons olive oil, divided	1 cup chopped dates

Put couscous into a bowl. Pour boiling water over couscous. Cover and let sit until water has been absorbed. Put coriander and cumin seeds in hot sauté pan for 1 minute, then grind to a powder and mix with cinnamon. Heat 1 tablespoon of oil in sauté pan and toast pine nuts and almonds until browned. Remove from heat and dry. Add more oil to sauté pan. Add onions, spices and garlic and cook for 5 minutes, then add pine nuts, almonds and cilantro and cook for 2 minutes. Season to taste.

1 boned leg of lamb	4 tablespoons olive oil
Salt and pepper to taste	4 tablespoons fresh lemon juice
1 onion, cut into big wedges	

Open the lamb, skin-side-down, and season inside with salt and pepper. Fill with Stuffing. Roll the lamb into a neat sausage, then tie with a string. Preheat the oven to its highest setting. Sear the lamb in a roasting pan. Put the lamb over the onions and pour over oil and lemon juice. Cook for 35 minutes at 425° until the lamb is done. Yields 8 servings.

Recipe by Chef Moulay Elabdellaoui

SHERATON
Casino and Hotel

1107 Casino Center Drive
Robinsonville, MS 38664
662-363-4900

Tony Harrington
Executive Chef

Executive Chef Tony Harrington has been a chef for thirty years, working in the United States as well as the United Kingdom, Bermuda, and the Netherlands.

Reno's Roasted Chicken with Herbs

HERB RUB:

¼ pint of salad oil	Crushed bay leaves or
¼ pint olive oil	dried bay leaves
1 cup finely minced onion	2 tablespoons
1 tablespoon finely	Worcestershire sauce
minced garlic	1 tablespoon Coleman's
2 tablespoons paprika	mustard powder
powder	1 teaspoon crushed
½ teaspoon cayenne	rosemary leaves
pepper	Juice of 1 lemon

Blend all ingredients together and reserve for use.

4 halves of two whole chickens,
approximately 1½ pounds each

Partially de-bone the half chickens by removing rib cage and pelvic bone. Trim wing and leg bone by chopping through cleanly with heel of a French cook's knife. Trim any excess fat and skin to ensure chicken has a nice shape. Plunge each chicken half into Herb Rub; rub each piece to ensure that they are coated well. Place on a roasting pan and cook at 375° for approximately 20 to 25 minutes.

Thai Style Scallop Salad

THAI DRESSING:

¼ cup rice wine vinegar	¼ cup toasted and
2½ tablespoons	chopped cashew nuts
granulated sugar	1 teaspoon minced ginger
⅓ cup soy sauce	½ cup peanut oil
2 tablespoons diced	2 tablespoons sesame oil
green onions	Salt and pepper to taste
1 teaspoon toasted sesame	
seeds	

Place the first seven ingredients into a bowl and whisk in the peanut and sesame oils. Add salt and pepper as necessary.

10 ounces scallops (large)	**¼ cup sesame oil**
Salt and pepper to taste	

Dry the scallops and season with salt and pepper; lightly dredge in sesame oil and drain off any excess. Heat a nonstick skillet to very hot and sear the scallops at high heat, allowing them to become golden brown on both sides, turning only once when scallops are just cooked; remove and plunge into a little Thai Dressing, then allow to cool and reserve for use.

SALAD:

8 ounces napa cabbage	⅓ cup carrot
1½ cups bean sprouts	1 teaspoon cilantro
½ cup red pepper,	leaves
julienned	½ cup Thai Dressing
½ cup Mandarin orange	4 tablespoons fried
segments, drained	rice noodles
¼ cup toasted sliced	
almonds	

Prepare the Salad and place in a salad bowl; add the Thai Dressing and toss. Arrange chilled scallops over top and finish with fried rice noodles. Yields 4 salads.

Blondie Brownies

4 cups Crisco vegetable shortening	8 cups all-purpose flour
$\frac{1}{2}$ cup milk	4 teaspoons baking powder
8 cups firmly packed brown sugar	1 teaspoon salt
8 eggs	1 teaspoon vanilla
	4 cups chopped walnuts

Preheat oven to 350° and grease a sheet pan with Crisco; set aside. Combine Crisco and milk in a suitable size saucepan and place on low heat until Crisco melts. Remove from heat and stir in the brown sugar and eggs. Stir until well blended. Combine flour, baking powder and salt. Stir into sugar mixture. Stir in vanilla and nuts. Spread evenly into baking pan. Bake at 350° for 27 to 30 minutes or until a wooden cocktail pick inserted in the center comes out clean. Cool and use as needed. Serve with vanilla ice cream.

GRAND CASINO
Tunica

13615 Old Highway 61 North
Tunica, MS 38664
(662) 363-2788

Restaurants located on the grounds of Grand Casino:
Grand Buffet
Grand Replay's
LB's Steakhouse
Murano's

Beef Brisket

1 (12$\frac{1}{2}$-pound) beef brisket	11 ounces rib rub seasoning

Rub brisket with rib rub. Place in 275° preheated smoker and cook for 4 hours; check for internal temperature of 180°. Continue to smoke until an internal temperature of 180° is reached.

Recipe by Chef Benjamin Turk,
Grand Buffet at Grand Casino

BBQ Sauce

4 ounces concentrated orange juice	1$\frac{1}{2}$ ounces lemon juice
1 pound sugar	1 teaspoon dry mustard
12 ounces brown sugar	1 teaspoon rib rub seasoning
3$\frac{1}{2}$ ounces Worcestershire sauce	1$\frac{1}{2}$ teaspoons celery salt
7$\frac{1}{2}$ ounces white vinegar	1 teaspoon liquid smoke
1 pinch black pepper	5 cups ketchup

Combine all ingredients until well incorporated. Yields 1 quart.

Recipe by Chef Benjamin Turk,
Grand Buffet at Grand Casino Tunica

Southern Fried Shrimp Salad

12 ounces (71–90 count) shrimp	6 ounces diced tomatoes
4 ounces buttermilk	2 ounces red onion
4 ounces seasoned flour	8 ounces honey mustard dressing
8 ounces mesclun spring mix	4 ounces romaine lettuce
3 ounces Cheddar cheese	1 ounce chopped scallions
3 ounces jalapeño Jack cheese	4 sprigs Italian parsley
	8 wedges cornbread

Dip shrimp in buttermilk, then seasoned four. Shake off excess and deep-fry to golden brown. Toss all ingredients and place in 12-inch bowl. Garnish with Italian parsley and serve with cornbread. Yields 4 servings.

Recipe by Chef Richard Lyons,
Grand Replay's at Grand Casino Tunica

Portobello Mushroom Strips

RED PEPPER RANCH DIP:

7 ounces Bellagio red peppers, roasted	1 quart ranch dressing

Purée peppers. Mix ingredients until well blended. Yields 1 quart.

24 ounces portobello mushrooms	1 tablespoon minced garlic
2 ounces balsamic vinegar	8 ounces seasoned flour
2 ounces olive oil	4 sprigs Italian parsley

Clean and slice portobello mushrooms into 1/2-inch-thick strips. Marinate in balsamic vinegar, olive oil and garlic. Drain marinade.

Dredge in seasoned flour and shake off excess. Fry to a deep golden brown. Drain grease. Place 12 ounces Red Pepper Ranch Dip in ramekin on the side. Garnish with Italian parsley. Yields 4 servings.

Recipe by Chef Richard Lyons,
Grand Replay's at Grand Casino Tunica

Halibut with Tomato Relish and Jalapeño Vinaigrette

JALAPEÑO VINAIGRETTE:
(Should be made 24 hours in advance.)

1 cup cider vinegar	1/4 yellow onion, minced
1 tablespoon honey	1 tablespoon minced scallion
2 1/2 cups sunflower oil	
1/2 cup light sesame oil	2 teaspoons chopped cilantro
1/4 cup puréed red bell pepper	2 teaspoons Kosher salt
2 jalapeño peppers, minced	1 teaspoon ground black pepper
1 clove garlic, minced	

Combine vinegar and honey. Combine the two oils. Slowly add oils to vinegar while steadily mixing. Once all oils are incorporated, add remaining ingredients and stir well. Makes 1 quart.

TOMATO RELISH:

12 fresh tomatoes, quartered	1 cup cider vinegar
1/2 yellow onion, minced	1/4 cinnamon stick
1 teaspoon minced garlic	1 tablespoon sugar
1/2 jalapeño pepper, minced	1 teaspoon Kosher salt
	2 teaspoons fresh ginger, minced

In a stockpot, combine tomatoes, onion, garlic, pepper and vinegar. Bring to a boil.

Add remaining ingredients and simmer until thickened to a jam consistency. Refrigerate until cooled. Yields 1 quart.

1 cup chestnut flour	8 ounces Tomato Relish
1 teaspoon salt	6 ounces Jalapeño Vinaigrette
1/2 teaspoon black pepper	
4 (8-ounce) portions halibut, fresh block cut	4 sprigs fresh cilantro
	4 jalapeños, fried
3 ounces clarified butter	

Season flour with salt and pepper. Dust halibut in flour. Heat clarified butter in a 12-inch sauté pan. Add halibut, skin-side-up, and sear to a light gold color. Turn each fillet over and roast in a 375° oven for 12 minutes. Place each halibut in center of a 12-inch bowl and spoon 2 ounces of Tomato Relish over one corner of fillet. Stir Jalapeño Vinaigrette well, and spoon 1 1/2 ounces around halibut. Garnish with fresh cilantro and fried jalapeños. Yields 4 servings.

Recipe by Chef Allan Rupert,
LB's Steakhouse at Grand Casino Tunica

Smoked Salmon

8 ounces romaine hearts, shredded	4 lemon wraps
1 pound smoked salmon	2 extra large eggs, boiled, separated, diced
2 teaspoons dill	4 teaspoons capers
4 teaspoons chopped parsley	4 sprigs dill
4 tablespoons diced jumbo red onions	8 slices white bread, toasted

Place shredded lettuce in a bed on bottom of chilled pewter plate. Lay salmon pieces over lettuce overlapping each other on bottom of plate. Sprinkle chopped dill over salmon. Place parsley at 11:00 on plate, then red onions at 11:30, then egg whites at 12:00, then egg yolks at 12:30, and then capers at 1:00. Lay sprig of dill on top and middle of salmon.

Toast and butter bread; trim edges. Cut diagonally and serve overlapping each other. Place lemon wrap in front of bread. Yield: 4 servings.

Recipe by Chef Allan Rupert,
LB's Steakhouse at Grand Casino Tunica

Bruschetta Pomodoro

8 (⅓-inch) slices Ciabatta bread	2 teaspoons chopped Italian parsley
8 ounces olive oil, divided	4 sprigs Italian parsley
8 Roma tomatoes	4 slices Pecorino Romano, shaved paper thin
4 teaspoons garlic	2 ounces basil oil
1 pinch salt	1 ounce balsamic vinegar
1 pinch pepper	
2 teaspoons basil	

Lightly coat Ciabata in olive oil. Grill on charboiler to mark. Dice Roma tomatoes and toss with remaining olive oil, garlic, salt, pepper, basil and chopped Italian parsley. Cut Ciabatta in half on the bias. Evenly distribute tomatoes over top of Ciabatta. Arrange 4 pieces Bruschetta in pinwheel on 10-inch plate. Garnish with Italian parsley sprigs and shaved Pecorino Romano. Drizzle with olive oil, basil oil and balsamic vinegar. Serves 4.

Recipe by Chef Steven Pairolero,
Murano's at Grand Casino Tunica

Eggplant Rollantine

FILLING:

1 cup ricotta cheese	1 tablespoon chopped fresh basil
¼ cup shredded mozzarella	½ teaspoon chopped fresh parsley
¼ cup Parmesan cheese	
1 egg	

Combine all ingredients until well blended

1 eggplant	2 ounces shredded Parmesan
3 eggs, beaten	4 basil leaves
1 cup flour	
1 cup olive oil	
1 cup Pomodoro Sauce (see recipe page 56)	

Peel eggplant and slice ⅛ inch thick, lengthwise, then place in beaten eggs. Take eggplant out of eggs and let excess run off. Dust with flour. Place in heated olive oil and fry until golden on either side, about 3 minutes. Cool eggplant, then place 2 tablespoons Filling on one end and roll. Bake in oven with Pomodoro Sauce at 375° for 15 minutes or until Filling starts to run. Garnish with fresh basil leaf and shaved Parmesan cheese. Yields 8 servings.

Recipe by Chef Abraham Martinez,
Murano's at Grand Casino Tunica

Frutte De Mare

3 ounces olive oil, divided
12 shrimp, U-12
6 ounces sea bass
2 teaspoons chopped
  garlic
4 teaspoons chopped
  shallots
8 ounces chicken stock
8 ounces white wine
12 fresh mussels
12 clams
8 ounces lobster
  knuckle meat
3 ounces Pomodoro
  Sauce

8 ounces diced tomato
4 teaspoons Italian
  parsley, divided
1 pinch salt
1 pinch pepper
3 ounces whole butter
12 ounces dry fettuccine
2 teaspoons basil
4 sprigs Italian parsley
3 ounces Pecorino
  Romano, divided
Salt and pepper to taste

In hot sauce pan, add ½ olive oil, shrimp, sea bass, garlic and shallots. Quickly sauté. Deglaze the chicken stock with white wine. Add mussels and clams. Simmer covered until shellfish open. Add lobster, Pomodoro Sauce, tomatoes and 2 teaspoons Italian parsley. Season to taste with salt and pepper, and melt in whole butter.

Cook fettuccine until al dente, then toss in remaining olive oil, remaining 2 teaspoons Italian parsley, 2 ounces Romano, salt and pepper to taste. Nest fettuccine in center of pasta plate. Arrange seafood around pasta. Garnish with parsley and remaining Romano. 4 servings.

POMODORO SAUCE:

¼ cup olive oil
¼ cup finely chopped
  onions
5 garlic cloves, pressed
4½ pounds Italian
  tomatoes, peeled
¼ cup chopped basil

1 pinch salt
1 pinch white pepper
1 tablespoons chopped
  fresh oregano
¼ bunch parsley,
  chopped
1 pinch sugar

Heat olive oil in a stockpot and add onions and garlic. Cook for about 5 minutes. Do not let onions change color. Add tomatoes, basil, salt, pepper, oregano, parsley and sugar. Simmer for about 1½ hours, stirring constantly. Purée until smooth. Adjust seasoning to taste. Yields 2 quarts.

Recipe by Chef Steven Pairolero,
Murano's at Grand Casino Tunica

HOLLYWOOD
Casino and Hotel

1150 Casino Strip
Tunica, MS 38664
662-357-7700

Fairbanks Steak House is located on the grounds of Hollywood Casino.

Fairbanks Steakhouse serves Certified Angus Beef, and is currently the only restaurant in the state to offer "Kobe" rib eye steak. This is the celebrated beef from Japan that is hand massaged and fed beer. Fairbanks has received the prestigious DiRoNa Award (Distinguished Restaurants of North America) for the past six years.

Fairbanks' wine list has received the Platinum Award from the International Restaurant and Hospitality Rating Bureau (IRHRB). We have been awarded Best Steakhouse/Best Gourmet Room in Tunica five consecutive years. Fairbanks was also selected in 2001 as one of the ten best steakhouses in the United States by the IRHRB.

Marc Silverberg, C.E.C
Vice President, Food and Beverage

Chef Marc is a native of Philadelphia, PA. He is a graduate of the Culinary Institute of America in Hyde Park, NY, and the Philadelphia Restaurant School in Philadelphia, PA. Chef Marc has received the Certified Executive Culinary Federation and the Certified Food and Beverage Executive designation for the American Hotel and Motel Association. His team was invited to cook at the James Beard Foundation in New York City two years ago.

Fried Mozzarella with a Plum Tomato Sauce

2 ounces fresh mozzarella, packed in water*
2 slices fresh white bread, crusts trimmed
6 tablespoons high quality olive oil, divided
½ cup finely chopped onion
1 (14-ounce) can peeled plum tomatoes in purée
1 teaspoon dried basil
1 teaspoon dried thyme
1 teaspoon dried oregano
1 teaspoon salt
1 teaspoon fresh-ground black pepper
1 bay leaf
½ cup chopped Italian parsley (may substitute domestic parsley)
2 cloves garlic, finely chopped

Slice cheese thinly and cover one side of bread with cheese. Cover cheese with other slice of bread, so cheese is in middle (like making a grilled cheese sandwich). Sauté in a skillet with 2 tablespoons olive oil until brown.

Heat oil in a 10- or 12-inch skillet and turn heat to medium. Sauté onion until translucent, stirring often. Add tomatoes, basil, thyme, oregano, salt, pepper and bay leaf. Reduce heat to a simmer, stirring frequently as to avoid burning the bottom. Let simmer for 30 minutes. Remove bay leaf. Either transfer to a food processor or insert immersion blender and purée sauce. Return sauce to pot and set pot over medium heat. Add parsley and garlic and cook for 10 minutes. Stir frequently. Taste and adjust for seasoning, adding salt and pepper. To serve, ladle sauce on bottom of plate. Place sautéed cheese on top of sauce. Sprinkle with grated Parmesan cheese and chopped parsley.

Options: You can add balsamic vinegar if the sauce lacks intensity. You can add a touch of sugar if the sauce is very acidic.

*Examples are Polly-O brand or the more expensive Di'Buffalo brand from Italy.

Recipe by Chef Marc Silverberg, Fairbanks Steakhouse at Hollywood Casino

Crispy Salmon with Rosemary Cream Sauce

2 (8-ounce) salmon fillets, skin off
4 ounces all-purpose flour, seasoned with salt and pepper
4 tablespoons honey
6 ounces Dijon mustard
2 cups plain bread crumbs

Dredge salmon in flour. Dip salmon into mixture of honey and mustard. Cover completely with bread crumbs. Sauté until golden brown with olive oil. Cook for 10 minutes in a 325° oven.

ROSEMARY CREAM SAUCE:

4 tablespoons unsalted butter
¼ cup finely diced onion
6 tablespoon all-purpose flour
1 cup milk
1 cup half-and-half
1 teaspoon lemon juice
Salt and white pepper to taste
¼ teaspoon nutmeg
2 teaspoons rosemary

Melt butter in a heavy saucepan. Sauté onions until translucent. Sprinkle in flour and stir constantly until there are no lumps. Cook about 5 minutes over low heat. Do not let butter or flour brown at all. Bring milk and half-and-half to a simmer in a separate pot (do not boil). Add it all at once to flour and butter mixture. As mixture boils, beat it vigorously with a wire whisk. When bubbling stops, return pan to medium heat and bring back to a boil, stirring constantly for 5 minutes. Season to taste with salt, pepper, nutmeg, and fresh rosemary. To serve, add sauce to bottom of plate and place salmon on top (if you put the sauce on top of the salmon, the bread crust will get soggy). Serves 2.

Options: You can add Chardonnay wine, or for a thinner sauce, use 3 tablespoons butter and 4 tablespoons flour, while using the same amount of milk.

Recipe by Chef Marc Silverberg, Fairbanks Steakhouse at Hollywood Casino

The Capital/River Region

$\mathscr{F}$rom Jackson to the historic towns of Vicksburg and Natchez along the Mississippi River, and on to Brookhaven, the Capital/River Region is a great place to discover Mississippi's past and present. Jackson is the hub of state government, and home to a world-renowned medical center. Civil War battlefields are carefully preserved in Vicksburg, as is the building where Coca-Cola was first bottled in 1894. The oldest settlement on the Mississippi River, Natchez hosts pilgrimages in the spring and fall that attract thousands of tourists from all over the world to its many elegant antebellum homes. In Brookhaven, visitors will marvel at the largest concentration of historic structures found in the state. Modern Mississippi with the perfect blend of the past—the Capital/River Region has it all.

The Capital / River Region Menu

The Capital / River Region Menu

CHRISTINE'S BACK PORCH

123 Depot Drive
Canton, MS 39046
601-855-2484

Christine's Back Porch is owned and operated by Christine Vanburen. She serves a home-cooked breakfast and a southern lunch Monday through Saturday. Christine has many years of experience in cooking and can't number the people that have stopped by to satisfy their hunger!

Barbecue Meat Loaf

2 pounds ground beef
1 cup barbecue sauce
1 cup ketchup
1 cup chopped onions
2 eggs, beaten

2 cups crushed bread
  crumbs
4 tablespoons steak
  seasoning

Mix all ingredients together. Shape into a loaf. Place in 11x13-inch baking dish. Cook at 350° for 1¼ hours. Serves 8 to 10.

Baked Sweet Potatoes

2 medium sweet potatoes
½ cup brown sugar
½ cup granulated sugar

¼ cup margarine
2 teaspoons vanilla

Peel and slice sweet potatoes. Place in small greased baking pan. Add brown sugar, granulated sugar, margarine and vanilla. Cover and place in oven. Bake at 350° for 30 to 35 minutes. Serves 4 to 6.

DAVIDSON'S

108 West Center Street
Canton, MS 39046
601-855-2268

**Debbie Davidson
Owner**

Davidson's opened in October of 1999 on the northeast corner of the historic downtown square in Canton. We offer catering from the finest full service receptions to small casual parties. The mid-1800s building with its brick walls and large windows that look out onto the square offer a relaxed and enjoyable atmosphere while dining. Executive Chef Edward Nash is constantly creating mouth-watering dinner specials while manager Sheaford Davidson is making sure your service is second to none. Our goal is to create a dining experience unlike any other. We invite you to come enjoy an evening of delicious food, great service and all around fun.

Kahlúa Pecan Pie

3 eggs, beaten
1 cup sugar
¾ cup light corn syrup
1 stick butter
1 teaspoon vanilla extract
2 tablespoons Kahlúa

⅔ cup chopped pecans
½ cup semisweet
  chocolate chips
1 (9-inch) pie shell,
  uncooked

Combine all ingredients except chocolate chips. Pour into pie shell. Sprinkle chocolate chips on top. Bake at 350° for 1 hour.

Garlic Cheese Grits

4 cups water
2 teaspoons salt
1 cup quick cooking grits
1 stick butter
1 roll garlic cheese
2 eggs
1 cup milk

Bring salted water to boil, then add grits and butter. Stir until thickened. Add cheese and stir until melted. Beat eggs with milk. Add to grits mixture. Place in a greased casserole. Bake at 350° for 40 to 45 minutes.

Stuffed Free-Range Chicken Breast
with Roasted Potatoes and
Roasted Red Bell Pepper Butter Sauce

6 free-range boneless
  chicken breasts
1 cup feta cheese
1 red bell pepper, diced
1/4 cup chopped parsley
Salt and pepper to taste
New potatoes
Onions, quartered
Green bell peppers,
  cut in strips
Diced garlic

Prep chicken by cutting the top bone off. Stuff with a mixture of feta cheese, diced red bell peppers, parsley, salt and pepper. Season chicken with salt and pepper. Spray chicken with nonstick spray and place on grill until skin browns. Remove from grill and finish roasting in oven for 20 to 30 minutes.

Wash new potatoes and cut them in half. Cover with water and bring to a boil. Drain and place on a sheet pan with onions, peppers and garlic. Roast until golden brown. Season with salt and pepper.

ROASTED BELL PEPPER BUTTER SAUCE:

1 cup white wine
1/2 cup lemon juice
2 red bell peppers,
  roasted and puréed
1/2 teaspoon garlic
1 cup whipping cream
1 pound butter, softened

In a sauce pot, combine white wine and lemon juice. Heat. Add puréed red bell peppers, garlic and whipping cream. Reduce by half. Over low heat, add butter to mixture, stirring constantly until melted.

Artichoke and Crab Dip

2 (14-ounce) cans
  artichoke hearts,
  drained and chopped
1 cup mayonnaise
2 cups grated Parmesan
  cheese
1/4 teaspoon garlic salt
12 ounces crabmeat

Mix and place in a greased 1 1/2-quart casserole. Bake at 325° for 15 to 20 minutes. Serve with Wheat Thins.

Corn Bread Salad

1 (9-ounce) package
  corn bread mix
1 (1-ounce) envelope
  Ranch dressing mix
1 (8-ounce) carton
  sour cream
1 cup mayonnaise
3 large tomatoes, chopped
1/2 cup chopped red bell
  pepper
1/2 cup chopped green
  bell pepper
1/2 cup chopped green
  onions
2 (16-ounce) cans pinto
  beans
2 cups shredded Cheddar
  cheese
12 slices bacon, cooked
  crisp and crumbled
1 (15-ounce) can whole-
  kernel corn, drained

Prepare corn bread mix according to directions and cool. Stir together salad dressing mix, sour cream and mayonnaise until blended. Combine tomatoes, red pepper, green pepper and onions. Crumble 1/2 of the corn bread into large salad bowl. Top with 1/2 of the beans, tomato mixture, cheese, bacon, corn and dressing mixture. Repeat layers. Cover and chill at least 4 hours.

Note: Can be made a day ahead. One 8-inch square pan of your own corn bread can be substituted.

Coffee Punch

1 quart strong coffee
1/2 gallon chocolate milk
3 teaspoons almond
  extract
1 quart Cool Whip
  topping
1/2 gallon premium
  vanilla ice cream

The day before serving, mix all together except the ice cream; chill. If using a punch bowl, pour punch over ice cream 15 minutes before serving. If serving individual cups, pour punch over a spoon of ice cream.

Spinach Madeline

2 (10-ounce) packages
frozen spinach
½ cup vegetable liquor
(from cooked spinach)
4 tablespoons butter
2 tablespoons flour
2 tablespoons chopped
onion
½ cup evaporated milk
Red pepper or Tabasco
sauce to taste

½ teaspoon black pepper
¾ teaspoon celery salt
¾ teaspoon garlic salt
1 teaspoon Worcestershire
sauce
1 (6-ounce) roll of
jalapeño cheese
(Pepper Jack cheese
can be substituted)
Buttered bread crumbs

Cook spinach according to directions on package. Drain, reserving liquor. Melt butter in a saucepan. Add flour and stir until blended, but not browned. Add onion and cook until tender. Add evaporated milk and vegetable liquor slowly, stirring constantly. Cook until smooth and thick, stirring constantly. Add seasonings and cheese. Stir until cheese melts. Add to cooked spinach. Put in greased casserole and top with buttered bread crumbs. Bake at 350° for 20 to 30 minutes.

Caramel Cake

3 cups flour
2¼ cups sugar
¾ cup shortening
1½ teaspoons salt
1 cup milk
3 eggs

1½ tablespoons baking
powder
¾ cup milk
1½ teaspoons vanilla
extract

Combine the first 5 ingredients and mix for 2 minutes. Stir in baking powder. Add the last 3 ingredients and mix for 2 more minutes. Pour into 3 greased and floured 9-inch cake pans. Bake at 350° for 25 to 30 minutes. Cool and ice with Caramel Icing.

CARAMEL ICING:
3¾ cups sugar
1½ sticks butter
2 eggs, beaten

1⅛ cups milk
1½ teaspoons vanilla

Brown ¾ cup sugar in black skillet over medium heat stirring constantly. Heat remaining sugar, butter, eggs and milk in saucepan at the same time. When all of the sugar in skillet has melted and turned a golden brown, pour it into milk mixture. Cook until it reaches soft-ball stage. Strain into mixing bowl and add vanilla. Beat until it thickens, but has not hardened. (It loses its shine when ready.) Ice cake quickly.

AMERIGO
An Italian Restaurant

6592 Old Canton Road
Jackson, MS 39157
601-977-0563

**Al Roberts and Bill Latham
Proprietors**

The original—opened in Jackson in 1987. The traditional and distinctively Italian menu features veal, chicken and pasta dishes along with a heavy emphasis on fresh fish and seafood. Amerigo has sister restaurants in Nashville and Memphis.

Artichoke Cheese Dip

Sounds too simple, but it's great. One of the best sellers in the restaurant!

2½ pounds canned
quartered artichokes,
chopped
2½ pounds mayonnaise
1 pound Grana Padonna
Parmesan cheese, grated

1½ pounds Swiss cheese,
grated
Diced fresh tomato and
scallion for garnish

In a mixing bowl, electric or other, place all ingredients except garnish and blend or stir well. Store in refrigerator.

When ready to serve, place in microwave-safe dish and microwave on HIGH until hot. (Be sure to remove from microwave occasionally and stir to prevent mayonnaise from separating.) When hot, place in oven on broil and brown the top well. (Stay close and watch or it will burn.) Top with diced fresh tomato and scallion. Serve with favorite crackers or chips. (Amerigo uses chips they make from focaccia bread. It's similar to Melba toast.) Serves 12.

Tuscan Crab Cakes
with White Bean Salsa and Basil Olive Oil

WHITE BEAN SALSA MIX:

4 cups drained and rinsed canned white beans
½ cup finely diced red onion
2 cups white corn, drained
¼ cup finely diced each: red, green and yellow bell peppers
Dash diced fresh basil and cilantro
¼ cup olive oil
4 Roma tomatoes, diced
Dash salt and pepper
Dash Teriyaki soy sauce

Mix all ingredients together and hold in refrigerator.

BASIL OIL:
Blend ½ cup fresh basil with 1 cup olive oil and purée in blender. Hold in refrigerator.

CRAB MIX:

1 pound fresh lump crabmeat
¼ cup mayonnaise
1 egg
1 tablespoon Worcestershire sauce
¼ cup each: red, green and yellow bell peppers, diced fine
1 teaspoon Tabasco sauce
1 teaspoon fresh lime juice
¼ cup chopped scallion
1 tablespoon Old Bay Seasoning
1 hoagie roll, finely ground
½ teaspoon salt
1 cup saltine cracker crumbs
½ tablespoon dry mustard

In a large bowl, place all ingredients. Gently toss all together to prevent lumps of crab from breaking up. Store in refrigerator at least 4 hours prior to cooking.

When ready to cook, form into 3-ounce patties. (Amerigo uses a 3-inch metal ring to form the cakes giving them a much better look than hand-formed.) This recipe should yield 8 to 10 (3-ounce) cakes.

In a sauté skillet or flat griddle utilizing olive oil, sauté crab cakes until well browned on each side and hot through. Lightly sauté or microwave White Bean Salsa until hot. Place bean salsa in center of plate and lay crab cake on either side of bean salsa. Drizzle Basil Oil around and over. Garnish with lemon wedges. Serve 2 cakes per person.

BRAVO!
Italian Restaurant and Bar

244 Highland Village
Jackson, MS 39211
601-982-8111

Chef Dan Blumenthal and Jeff Good Proprietors

Bravo! is a seven-time recipient of the Wine Spectator "Award of Excellence" and one of only a handful of restaurants in the state to be recognized for this prestigious award. Bravo! was also named "Restaurant of the Year" five times by the Jackson Convention and Visitors Bureau. This nouveau Italian restaurant features a wood-burning oven for its pizzas, pasta, seafood, steaks, etc.

Baked Chicken with Artichokes, Sweet Peppers and Fresh Herbs

1 red bell pepper, sliced
1 green bell pepper, sliced
1 yellow bell pepper, sliced
1 (6- to 8-ounce) jar artichoke hearts
4 garlic cloves, sliced
4 chicken breasts, bone-in and skin on
5 sprigs fresh Italian parsley
5 sprigs fresh rosemary
5 sprigs fresh oregano
1 cup white wine
⅓ cup lemon juice
2 tablespoons extra virgin olive oil
1 cup chicken broth
2 teaspoons chile flakes
Salt and pepper to taste

Line the bottom of an oven-proof casserole dish with bell peppers, artichoke hearts, garlic and fresh herbs. Place chicken breasts on top. Pour in wine, lemon juice, olive oil and chicken broth. Top with chile flakes, and season with salt and pepper. Cover and bake in a 375° oven for 25 minutes. Uncover and bake another 10 minutes or until the skin on the breasts starts to brown. Yields 4 servings.

Asian Tuna Tartare Appetizer

12 ounces fresh tuna loin	1 tablespoon mirin
2 stalks green onion, finely sliced	1 teaspoon rice wine vinegar
1 teaspoon minced fresh ginger	2 teaspoons Sambal chili paste
1 teaspoon minced garlic	1 teaspoon sugar
2 teaspoons soy sauce	1 tablespoon sesame oil

Cut tuna loin into thin slices (about $\frac{1}{8}$ inch) against the grain of flesh using a sharp knife. Cut slices into thin pieces, about match-stick size. Finally, cut match-stick-sized pieces of tuna into small dice. Place diced tuna into a bowl and add remaining ingredients. With spoon, combine all of the ingredients well, and chill until ready to serve. The tartare is best made about an hour prior to serving, but can be made up to a day in advance and held in the refrigerator prior to serving. Serves 6 as an appetizer.

Creamy Oyster and Fennel Soup

5 bundles fennel	$\frac{1}{3}$ cup heavy cream
$\frac{1}{4}$ cup extra virgin olive oil, divided	3 teaspoons lemon juice
1 medium onion, diced	3 teaspoons Pernod (anise-flavored liqueur)
3 cups clam juice	Salt and pepper to taste
3 cups water	
1 cup oysters in their liqueur	

Clean fennel bulbs by cutting off base and any outside leaves that are damaged. Reserve green tops for garnish. Finely chop 4 bulbs. Reserve the remaining bulb for garnish.

Heat half the olive oil in a soup pot; add the onion and chopped fennel and sauté until soft. Add clam juice, water and oyster liqueur and simmer about half an hour. Allow to cool slightly.

Purée soup in batches in a blender. Slice remaining fennel bulb into fine julienne. Heat remaining olive oil in a skillet and sauté fennel, covered, over low heat until soft, but still crispy. Place soup back in soup pot and add the oysters, cream, lemon juice and Pernod; season with salt and pepper. Bring soup back up to heat on the stove and serve garnished with the green fennel tops. Serves 6.

Cuban Grilled Pork

2 pounds pork tenderloin or loin	1 teaspoon ground cumin
$\frac{1}{2}$ cup extra virgin olive oil	2 teaspoons sugar
	4 bay leaves, crumbled
$\frac{1}{2}$ cup freshly squeezed lemon juice	1 tablespoon minced garlic
$\frac{1}{2}$ tablespoon freshly ground black pepper	$\frac{1}{2}$ tablespoon minced shallots
$\frac{1}{2}$ tablespoon Kosher salt	2 teaspoons Tabasco or other hot sauce
1 tablespoon dried oregano leaves	

If using pork tenderloin, slice into $\frac{1}{2}$-inch medallions, or loin into $\frac{1}{4}$-inch medallions. Place the medallions between sheets of plastic wrap and pound very thin using a meat tenderizing mallet. Combine remaining marinade ingredients in a bowl; add the pounded pork and marinate at room temperature for 1 hour, or in the refrigerator for up to three hours. Place the pork on a hot grill, cooking until just barely done through–about a minute on each side. Serve with black beans and rice or on your favorite bread as a sandwich with dressings of your choice. Serves approximately 4–6.

Buttermilk Pound Cake

3 cups all-purpose flour, sifted	8 ounces unsalted butter
1 tablespoon hot water	1 teaspoon baking soda
5 eggs, separated	1 cup buttermilk
3 cups sugar	1 teaspoon vanilla extract

In a mixer with paddle attachment, cream butter and sugar together. Dissolve baking powder in water and add to butter-sugar mixture. Slowly incorporate egg yolks. Add flour and buttermilk. Beat egg whites to stiff peaks and fold into batter. Pour into a greased loaf or Bundt pan and bake at 325° for approximately 1 hour.

Crab Crusted Fish

7 ounces lump crabmeat
2 ounces mayonnaise
1$\frac{1}{2}$ ounces Creole
  mustard
1 tablespoon chopped
  parsley
1 tablespoon minced
  chives

1$\frac{1}{2}$ teaspoons Creole
  seasoning
1$\frac{3}{4}$ pounds meaty fish
  such as escolar, grouper
  or swordfish, cut into
  6- to 7-ounce fillets
$\frac{1}{2}$ cup all-purpose flour
$\frac{1}{3}$ cup corn or canola oil

To prepare crab crust, mix crabmeat, mayonnaise, mustard, parsley, chives and Creole seasoning together by hand in a bowl. Coat the top of each fish fillet with an even $\frac{1}{2}$-inch layer of crust mixture. Heat an appropriately-sized skillet over high heat and add oil. Dip the top of each piece of crusted fish in flour. When the oil in the pan begins to smoke, place fish in pan, crust-side-down. When crust is browned (about 1 minute), flip fish over. Since the fillets are thick, they will need to be finished in a 450° oven. Pour off excess oil and place the whole skillet in oven. The oven cooking time will vary with the oven, and type and thickness of the fish used. To be safe, take a knife and pierce the middle of one of the fillets to make sure it is cooked through before serving it. Serves 4.

Chocolate Mascarpone Pudding

6 egg yolks
$\frac{3}{4}$ cup sugar
1$\frac{1}{2}$ teaspoons vanilla
  extract
3 ounces unsweetened
  cocoa

$\frac{3}{4}$ pound mascarpone
  cheese
3 ounces Marsala wine

In a large metal bowl, beat yolks and sugar with a whisk until light and fluffy. Place the bowl over a saucepan half-filled with simmering water and whip until "ribbons" form. Continue whipping while adding the vanilla, cocoa and mascarpone. Whip until smooth and homogenous. Add the Marsala wine and whip constantly until the custard thickens. Pour the custard into serving container(s). Makes approximately 7 to 8 (5-ounce) portions.

Cappellini with Roman Style Shrimp and Asparagus

$\frac{1}{2}$ bunch asparagus
  spears
$\frac{1}{2}$ pound dried capellini
  or angel hair pasta
$\frac{3}{4}$ pound shrimp, peeled
  and deveined, tail on
$\frac{1}{4}$ cup extra virgin
  olive oil
4 ounces unsalted butter
$\frac{1}{2}$ tablespoon garlic,
  minced
1 tablespoon shallots,
  minced

Pinch red pepper flakes
Pinch dried Italian
  seasoning
$\frac{1}{3}$ cup dry white wine
$\frac{1}{2}$ tablespoon julienne-
  cut fresh mint
1 tablespoon julienne-
  cut fresh basil
Salt and pepper to taste
1 ounce Parmesan cheese,
  grated

Cut off tough, bottom ends of asparagus spears and discard. Drop asparagus in salted, boiling water and cook for 30 seconds. Quickly remove asparagus to a bowl filled with ice water so that asparagus cools rapidly. Remove from water; cut into $\frac{1}{2}$-inch pieces, and reserve. Cook pasta according to directions on the manufacturer's package. Drain in a colander and coat with olive oil to prevent clumping.

Heat a skillet over high flame. Add olive oil and butter. When the butter is melted, add the shrimp to the pan, making sure to space them so that each shrimp touches the bottom of the pan. Sauté for thirty seconds, then turn the shrimp over. Add garlic, shallots, red pepper flakes, Italian seasoning and asparagus. Move the ingredients around in the pan so they cook evenly. Cook another 30 seconds, then pour in the wine and flame away the alcohol by tipping the pan towards the flame. (Be careful!) Allow wine to reduce by $\frac{1}{2}$. Add mint and basil, and season to taste with salt and pepper. Add the pasta to pan and toss well so as to combine all the ingredients. Serve topped with freshly grated Parmesan cheese. Serves 2 to 3.

Caribbean Shrimp

4 tablespoons unsalted
  butter
1½ pounds shrimp,
  heads removed, peeled,
  and deveined
1 tablespoon minced
  garlic
½ tablespoon minced
  ginger
⅓ cup diced red onion
1 red bell pepper, diced
2 jalapeño peppers, diced
⅓ cup white rum

⅓ cup pineapple juice
¼ cup lime juice
¼ cup clam juice
1 can coconut milk
3 stalks green onions,
  sliced
1 bunch cilantro, roughly
  chopped
¼ cup brown sugar
1 teaspoon ground cumin
1 teaspoon ground
  coriander
Salt and pepper to taste

Place a skillet over medium-high heat. Add the butter. When the butter melts, add shrimp, garlic, ginger and red onion. Sauté for a minute, turning shrimp while doing so. Add red bells, yellow bells and jalapeños. Deglaze with rum. If using a gas stove, tilt the skillet towards the flame to ignite the liquor; if using electric, use a match. (Be careful, as the liquor will then flame.) After the flame subsides, add pineapple, lime and clam juice. Reduce by ½. Remove cooked shrimp to a plate and set in a warm oven (200°). Add coconut milk, green onions, cilantro and brown sugar. Reduce until the sauce thickens. Season with cumin, coriander, salt and pepper. Place shrimp back in the sauce and toss to coat. Serve over white rice. Serves 4.

Observatory at Millsaps College
Jackson, Mississippi

Campanelle with White Bolognese

½ cup extra virgin
  olive oil
½ yellow onion, finely
  diced
2 carrots, peeled and
  finely diced
1 tablespoon minced
  garlic
1 stalk celery, finely
  diced
1 pound sweet Italian
  sausage meat, removed
  from casings
1 pound ground beef
  (not too lean)

2 teaspoon dried oregano
1½ cups dry white wine
1 (14-ounce) can chicken
  broth
1½ ounces dried porcini
  mushrooms, rehydrat-
  ed in 3 cups hot water
⅔ cup heavy cream
1 pound campanelle,
  conchigle, or penne
  pasta
Salt and freshly ground
  pepper to taste
¾ cup grated Parmesan
  cheese

Heat a large, deep sauté pan over medium-high heat and add olive oil. When the oil simmers, add onion, carrots, garlic and celery and sauté until soft–about 5 minutes. Add sausage, beef and oregano to pan and break up meat as it cooks. Once meat is all the way cooked, add wine and keep at a rapid simmer until the pan is almost dry. Add chicken broth and lower heat to medium. Simmer gently until broth is almost fully absorbed.

Meanwhile, strain porcinis from the rehydrating liquid and chop into small pieces. Reserve liquid. Add the porcini, about 1 cup of its liquid, and cream to the sauce; continue simmering for about another 10 minutes. Season as needed with salt and pepper. Cook pasta; drain and return to pot. Pour sauce over pasta and mix thoroughly with a spoon. If pasta needs more liquid, pour in some reserved porcini juice. Top with Parmesan cheese and serve immediately. Serves 4.

BROAD STREET
Baking Company and Café

101 Banner Hall
Jackson, MS 39206
601-362-2900

**Chef Dan Blumenthal and Jeff Good
Proprietors**

D's Cold Broccoli Salad

1 head broccoli, cut into
   florets
5 cloves garlic, peeled
1 teaspoon Kosher salt
4 anchovy fillets
¼ cup "green" extra
   virgin olive oil
¼ cup balsamic vinegar
Freshly ground pepper
   to taste

Place broccoli florets in a bowl. Next, place the garlic cloves, salt and anchovy fillets in mortar and pestle and grind into a fine paste. Add the anchovy-garlic paste and the rest of the ingredients to the broccoli and toss well. The salad is best when it is made about 15 minutes prior to serving and chilled just a bit. Serves 4.

Cane Syrup Vinaigrette

1 cup Steen's cane syrup
¼ cup cane vinegar
1 teaspoon minced shallots
2 teaspoons minced garlic
½ teaspoon ground black
   pepper
½ teaspoon salt
1 teaspoon Tabasco hot
   sauce
2 teaspoons Cajun spice
   blend
1 tablespoon Creole
   mustard
1 cup olive oil

Place all ingredients except for olive oil in a blender or food processor. Turn on machine and slowly drizzle in oil until it is all incorporated and dressing is "emulsified." This dressing can be served cold or warmed on the stovetop and poured over greens or spinach just prior to serving. Makes approximately 2½ cups.

Broad Street Seafood Salad

DRESSING:
½ cup mayonnaise
½ cup sour cream
¼ cup Creole mustard
2 tablespoons lemon juice
2 teaspoons Creole
   seasoning
Salt and pepper to taste

GARNISH:
2 stalks celery, thinly
   sliced
2 stalks green onions,
   thinly sliced
1 tablespoon lemon zest
1 small red bell pepper,
   small dice
¼ cup fresh dill,
   chopped

SEAFOOD:
¼ pound lump crabmeat
½ pound small shrimp,
   cooked
½ pound crawfish tails,
   cooked and rinsed

In a large bowl, mix Dressing ingredients together with a spatula. Fold in Garnish ingredients, then Seafood. To serve, make a bed of lettuce greens of your choice tossed in your favorite dressing. Place a large tomato slice on top of the greens and scoop a generous portion of seafood salad on top of tomato slice. Serves approximately 5 to 6.

Cheddar Cheese Cake

⅓ pound graham cracker
   crumbs
1¾ cups sugar, divided
⅓ cup butter, melted
4 (8-ounce) packages
   cream cheese, room
   temperature
6 ounces sharp Cheddar
   cheese, finely grated
6 eggs
¼ cup sour cream,
   room temperature
3 tablespoons cornstarch
¼ cup beer

Position oven rack in center of oven and preheat to 325°. Combine graham cracker crumbs, ¼ cup sugar and butter in bottom of a 9-inch springform pan. Blend remaining 1½ cups sugar, cream cheese, Cheddar cheese, eggs, sour cream, beer and cornstarch in food processor and pour into springform pan. Bake for 1 hour; turn off the oven, open door and let cake cool in oven. Makes 1 (9-inch) cake.

BRUNO'S

1855 Lakeland Drive
Jackson, MS 39216
601-362-7779

**Luis Bruno
Chef/Owner**

Chef Luis Bruno is a native New Yorker and worked in Florida and New York before moving to Jackson, his wife's hometown. Kathleen Bruno is the culinary chef instructor at the Jackson campus of Hinds Community College. Chef Bruno received a diploma in Culinary Arts from Pinellas Technical Education Center in Clearwater, FL, and studied at the Culinary Institute of America at Hyde Park, NY. Prior to opening his own restaurant and catering company in Jackson, Chef Bruno was the Chef de Maison at the Mississippi Governor's Mansion.

Roasted Garlic Vinaigrette

12 garlic cloves, roasted and peeled
1/4 cup red wine vinegar
1 tablespoon honey
Juice of one fresh lime
1/2 cup olive oil
1 teaspoon Kosher salt
1/2 teaspoon freshly ground black pepper

Combine the garlic, vinegar, honey and lime juice in a blender and purée until smooth. With the motor running, slowly add the oil until emulsified. Season with salt and pepper.

Note: To roast garlic, heat oven to 350°. Remove top 1/3 of whole garlic cloves without peeling. Drizzle a tiny bit of olive oil over garlic cloves and wrap in aluminum foil. Place on a cookie sheet and bake 1 hour, or until soft throughout. If garlic has not browned, remove foil and allow to cook, uncovered, for another 5 to 10 minutes. Set aside to cool, then squeeze pulp out of bulbs. Yields 6 to 8 servings.

Spanish Red Bean and Yuca Soup

1 pound dried kidney beans
1 gallon chicken broth
1 medium onion, chopped
3 cloves garlic, minced
2 large green bell peppers, seeded and chopped
1 medium yuca, peeled and chopped
1/8 cup cilantro, chopped, divided
2 tablespoons olive oil
1 (16-ounce) can tomato sauce
Tabasco sauce to taste
Salt and pepper to taste

Soak beans overnight.

Simmer beans in water over medium high heat until tender. Water will reduce by approximately 1/2. While beans are cooking, sauté in olive oil the onion, garlic, peppers, yuca and 1/2 the cilantro until soft and translucent. When beans are tender, add all sautéed items and tomato sauce to the soup. Add Tabasco sauce and salt and pepper to taste. Soup should be thick and hearty and is delicious served with rice. Garnish with remaining cilantro. Yields 3 to 4 quarts.

Note: Yuca is Spanish for Yucca.

Chick Pea and Chorizo Soup

1 pound dried chickpeas
1 gallon chicken broth
1 medium onion, chopped
3 cloves garlic, minced
2 tablespoons olive oil
1/2 medium green bell pepper, chopped
1 cup chopped chorizo sausage
1/8 cup chopped parsley, divided
1 (16-ounce) can tomato sauce
Tabasco sauce to taste
Salt and pepper to taste

Soak chickpeas overnight.

Simmer chickpeas in chicken broth on medium-high heat until tender. Broth will reduce by approximately 1/2. While chickpeas are cooking, sauté onion, garlic, peppers, chorizo sausage and 1/2 the parsley until soft and translucent. When chickpeas are tender, add all sautéed items and tomato sauce to the soup. Add Tabasco sauce and salt and pepper to taste. Soup should be thick and hearty and is delicious served with rice. Garnish with remaining parsley. Yields 3 to 4 quarts.

CHAR

4500 I-55 North
142 Highland Village
Jackson, MS 39211
601-956-9562

Pecan Pie

This is the most popular dessert at CHAR. The secret is in the white chocolate and the Mexican vanilla.

1¼ cups granulated sugar
6 tablespoons whole lightly salted butter
1 cup light corn syrup
3 eggs, lightly beaten
1 cup chopped pecans
1½ teaspoons Mexican vanilla extract or regular
1 pinch salt
½ cup white chocolate chips
1 (9-inch) pie crust, unbaked

Place sugar, butter and corn syrup in small pot and cook on medium high for 3 minutes. Set aside to cool. In a bowl, mix eggs, pecans, vanilla and salt and blend with a whisk. When the syrup mixture has cooled, mix with other ingredients and pour into prepared pie crust. (At CHAR we use a torte pan with a removable bottom which makes for a nicer presentation and is easier to cut.)

Bake in convection oven at 275° for 30 to 40 minutes. (This may take longer in a conventional home oven.) When cooked, remove from stove and allow to cool at room temperature. Wrap pie with plastic film and place in freezer until frozen or you are ready to serve. Remove from freezer and allow pie to stand at room temperature 1 hour before cutting. (At CHAR we heat each portion of pie and top with French vanilla ice cream. We garnish each plate with confectioners' sugar sprinkled around the plate.)

Crab, Shrimp and Andouille Gumbo

SEASONING MIX:
5 each bay leaves
2½ tablespoons salt
2½ teaspoons white pepper
2½ teaspoons cayenne pepper
2½ teaspoons ground black pepper
2½ teaspoons thyme, dried
2½ teaspoons oregano, dried
5 tablespoons gumbo filé
5 tablespoons chopped fresh garlic

Place bay leaves, salt, white pepper, cayenne pepper, black pepper, thyme, oregano, gumbo filé and fresh garlic in food processor and blend well.

ROUX:
4 cups clarified margarine
5 cups all-purpose flour
2½ pounds yellow onions
2½ pounds diced green bell pepper
2½ pounds fresh diced celery

In a large sauté skillet, place clarified margarine over high heat until margarine begins to smoke lightly. Gradually add flour, whisking constantly with a long-handled, metal whisk. Continue cooking, whisking constantly until the Roux is a dark reddish brown. Cooking time should be about 8 to 10 minutes. (Make sure that the Roux mixture does not scorch or splash on your skin.) Remove from heat; at this point add the chopped onions, green bell peppers, and celery to the hot Roux mixture, stirring well. Add the Seasoning Mix to the Roux and vegetables, stirring well.

SOUP:
10 quarts shrimp stock
2 ounces chicken base
5 cups diced canned tomatoes, drained
5 pounds (90-110 count) frozen shrimp
5 pounds cubed andouille sausage
3 pounds lump crabmeat

In a medium stock pot or soup pot, place shrimp stock and chicken base over high heat and bring to a full boil. As stock is boiling, add the roux-veggie mixture by large spoonfuls, stirring well into the boiling stock. Add tomatoes. Cook on medium heat at a slow boil approximately 15 minutes. Turn heat to low; add shrimp and sausage. Remove from heat and add crabmeat to Soup at end. Stir gently trying to keep lumps of crabmeat intact. Yields approximately 5 gallons—can be cut in half. This gumbo freezes well.

THE GOVERNOR'S MANSION

300 East Capitol
Jackson, MS 39201
601-359-3175

Walter Smith, CCC
Chef de Maison

Sun-Dried Tomato Risotto

1 ounce vegetable oil	1 quart chicken stock,
½ yellow onion, sliced	heated
julienne	8 ounces riso
2 to 3 ounces sun-dried	2 ounces shredded
tomatoes, chopped	Parmesan cheese
1 tablespoon chopped	
garlic	

In vegetable oil, sauté onion, tomatoes and garlic until onions start to clear. Add raw risotto and cook for a few minutes to break down the husks. Then start adding stock 4 ounces at a time, allowing risotto to absorb stock before adding more. Continue to add stock until all is absorbed and risotto is tender. Then remove from heat and fold in shredded Parmesan.

Tomato Fennel Broth

Extra virgin olive oil	Kosher salt to taste
1 onion, diced	4 ounces fresh fennel
4 to 5 tomatoes, chopped	1 quart chicken stock
2 tablespoons chopped	
garlic	

In olive oil, sauté onion until clear. Add tomatoes, garlic, salt and fresh fennel. Add stock and bring to a boil. Remove from heat and purée. Place back into pot and reduce by ¼ to concentrate flavors.

Crawfish Andouille and Potato Soup

BLONDE ROUX:

1 pound butter	1 pound flour

Combine butter and flour in sauté pan and cook over medium heat for about 5 minutes, stirring constantly. Remove from heat and allow to cool. This can and should be done in advance because roux is very hot and dangerous to handle at that temperature.

Note: Once the roux is cool, place in a mixing bowl and add enough soup to liquefy the roux and allow incorporation into the soup without lumps forming. Add to the soup while stirring constantly.

1 pound unsalted butter	2 quarts heavy cream
2 medium onions, diced	3 pounds new potatoes,
1 bunch celery, diced	diced
2 pounds andouille	2 pounds crawfish tails
sausage	1 pound Blonde Roux
2 tablespoons chopped	1 teaspoon Tabasco sauce
garlic	1 tablespoon
2 tablespoons Creole	Worcestershire sauce
seasoning	Kosher salt, Tony's Creole
2 tablespoons dried thyme	Seasoning and black
1 tablespoon black pepper	pepper to taste
2 quarts chicken stock	

In butter, sauté onions and celery until they start to clear. Roast sausage in oven until well browned. Add garlic, seafood seasoning, thyme and black pepper to vegetables and continue cooking until vegetables start to caramelize. Add sausage and cook an additional 5 minutes. Then add stock and heavy cream; bring to a simmer and add new potatoes. Allow to cook an additional 15 minutes, then add crawfish tails. Bring to a boil and thicken with Blonde Roux. Add Tabasco sauce and Worcestershire sauce and allow to cook an additional 15-20 minutes. Season to taste with salt, Tony's seasoning and black pepper.

Seared Duck Breast

1 duck breast	Extra virgin olive oil
Fresh spinach	Fresh shredded Parmesan
Fresh basil	cheese
Chopped garlic	Applewood smoked bacon
Tony's Creole Seasoning	

Remove and reserve fat from duck breast. Split breast in half, lengthwise, and pound out slightly. Sauté spinach, basil and chopped garlic in olive oil, seasoning lightly with Tony's Creole Seasoning. Place mixture on duck breast and top with shredded Parmesan cheese. Roll up from the bottom of the breast. Wrap in a bacon strip and secure with a toothpick; set aside.

Dice reserved duck fat, then place in a hot sauté pan. Render fat until well cooked; strain and reserve both the fat and the cracklings. Season cracklings with Tony's Creole Seasoning. Keep warm and use for garnish on finished dish.

In sauté pan, heat duck breast in reserved duck fat; sear off bacon. Drain fat and place pan in a 350° oven to finish cooking (about 5 minutes). Allow to rest for a few minutes before slicing. Slice into 4 medallions to serve.

French Toast

PRALINE SAUCE:

½ pound whole butter	½ cup praline liquor
1 pound brown sugar	1 cup pecan pieces
3 tablespoons vanilla extract	1 cup heavy cream

In a small sauce pot, melt butter and add brown sugar, then cook until sugar melts and makes a sauce. Add vanilla, praline liquor, pecans and heavy cream and cook until all is combined.

FRENCH TOAST BATTER:

12 eggs	1 cup sugar
1 tablespoon cinnamon	1 cup heavy cream
1 tablespoon vanilla	

Mix well. Coat bread in French Toast Batter and fry in vegetable oil until well browned. Serve topped with Praline Sauce.

Seared Duck Breast with a Saffron Pear and Cranberry Reduction

MARINADE:

8 ounces salad oil	2 tablespoons Tony's
4 ounces molasses	Creole Seasoning
1 pound brown sugar	1 tablespoon cumin
2 tablespoons black	1 tablespoon cinnamon
pepper	½ cup juniper berries
3 sprigs fresh rosemary	

In a heavy-bottom pan, heat all above ingredients until brown sugar melts. Allow to cool, but not completely.

8 ounces duck breast

Score the duck breast in a diamond pattern and add duck to Marinade while it is still warm; allow to cool in cooler. It is best to marinate the duck breast for 1 to 2 hours before serving, or overnight if you have time.

When ready to serve, sear breast skin-side-down in a skillet and finish in a 350° oven to medium rare.

SAUCE:

1 quart chicken stock	1 cup red wine
½ pound whole butter	½ cup demi-glace
8 pears, peeled and cored	2 tablespoons Creole
1 tablespoon saffron	Seasoning
½ pound dried cranberries	Kosher salt

In a heavy-bottom saucepan, heat chicken stock and butter to a simmer. Add remaining ingredients and allow pears to poach until soft. Drain liquid and reserve. Purée solid ingredients. Put both the liquid and purée back into skillet; cook on low heat until sauce is thick enough to coat the back of a spoon. Strain through a fine sieve or chinois before serving.

Whether it be traditional cooking or exotic international cuisine, you're sure to find something to satisfy your taste at one of the many fine dining establishments scattered throughout Mississippi.

The magnolia is Mississippi's official state tree and its blossom the official state flower. The tree's stately beauty is honored in Mississippi's best-known nickname—"The Magnolia State."

The Birthplace of Elvis Presley is a modest, two-room house built by Elvis's father, Vernon Presley, with $180 borrowed for materials. From this humble beginning on January 8, 1935, Elvis began his musical journey to become the King of Rock & Roll. (Elvis Presley Center, Tupelo)

Mississippi's beautiful highways and country roads lead to many antique shops offering an eclectic range of discoveries.

MISSISSIPPI DEVELOPMENT AUTHORITY, DIVISION OF TOURISM

Mississippi is the undisputed birthplace of a music form that is known worldwide simply as the Blues. As the sun sets in the beautiful Mississippi Delta, listen closely and hear the "Bentonia Blues" echo across the cotton fields from the Blue Front Café. (Bentonia)

MISSISSIPPI DEVELOPMENT AUTHORITY, DIVISION OF TOURISM

Fishing is one of the most popular outdoor activities in Mississippi. From the Gulf of Mexico to the many rivers and streams, from man-made reservoirs to countless lakes, ponds, bayous and marshes, anglers can find an endless supply of places to get hooked on fishing.

Jackson (then known as LeFleur's Bluff) was originally designed by Thomas Jefferson. City blocks were to be alternated with parks and other open spaces, giving the appearance of a checkerboard. Today, as Mississippi's capital and largest city, Jackson is the state's center for business, economic development and cultural experiences.

One of the most decisive battles of the American Civil War was the campaign, siege and defense of Vicksburg, a fortress city that controlled the middle stretch of the Mississippi River. Here, a lone cannon oversees the Mississippi River which so long ago was the turning point of a war between the states.

Built in 1927 and listed on the National Register of Historic Places, the Natchez Eola Hotel is one example of the many fine hotels that can be found throughout Mississippi. Ann Bailey, pictured here, enjoys the ambiance of the hotel's New Orleans-style Courtyard.

The Natchez Trace Parkway, a 444-mile engineered road connecting Natchez, Mississippi, to Nashville, Tennessee, commemorates an ancient trail traveled by traders, soldiers, boatmen, mail riders, Native Americans and outlaws. Today, this All-American road provides a great opportunity for hiking, biking, horseback riding and camping.

PHOTO BY JOHN M. BAILEY

D'Evereux, an example of pure Greek Revival architecture, is one of many beautiful antebellum homes open for the Natchez Pilgrimage. Twice each year, Spring Pilgrimage and Fall Pilgrimage, guided tours are conducted daily by hoop-skirted hostesses who interpret the rooms, furnishings and history of approximately 30 homes.

MISSISSIPPI DEVELOPMENT AUTHORITY, DIVISION OF TOURISM

Meridian's historic Dentzel Carousel was built in 1896 by German immigrant Gustav Dentzel for the 1904 St. Louis Exposition and later sold to the city of Meridian. The gaily ornate merry-go-round is one of the country's oldest, and has been placed on the National Register of Historic Places.

Harness racing at Mississippi's only licensed horse track is a big attraction at the Neshoba County Fair. Called Mississippi's Giant House Party, the fair fosters political, agricultural and social exchanges of knowledge and ideas when Neshoba County families gather every summer for a week-long family reunion.

It's no surprise that Mississippi was named the 2003 Best Up-and-Coming Domestic Golf Destination by *The Golf Insider* magazine. With 140 courses across the state, some by the best designers in the business, golf is quickly becoming a favored Mississippi pastime.

MISSISSIPPI DEVELOPMENT AUTHORITY, DIVISION OF TOURISM

John C. Stennis Space Center, the primary center for testing and flight certifying rocket propulsion systems for the Space Shuttle and future generations of space vehicles, is one of ten NASA field centers in the United States.

MISSISSIPPI DEVELOPMENT AUTHORITY, DIVISION OF TOURISM

Whether you're looking for the quiet beauty of a peaceful walk or a day of frolicking in the hot, summer sun, fun is aways waiting along the shore of the Mississippi Gulf Coast, the world's longest man-made beach.

JACKSON YACHT CLUB

700 Yacht Club Drive
Jackson, MS 39236-2386
601-856-8844

Ken Crotwell
Club Manager/Executive Chef

The Jackson Yacht Club is located on the 33,000-acre Ross Barnett Reservoir. The members-only club offers a wide array of activities such as dining, swimming, rowing, sailing, power boating and lots of adult and youth social events.

Crawfish Katherine

This is a fun dish that can top your favorite pasta or New Orleans French bread, or you can add bread crumbs and make a great party dip.

2 tablespoons olive oil	Dried oregano, black
3 tablespoons butter	pepper and salt to taste
4 cloves garlic	Juice of 1 lemon
1 cup sliced mushrooms	$\frac{1}{2}$ cup chopped green
4 ounces evaporated milk	onions
1 ounce white wine	1 pound crawfish tails
$\frac{1}{2}$ teaspoon parsley	(rinsed)

Place olive oil and butter in French skillet and heat. Add garlic and mushrooms and sauté for 5 minutes. Add evaporated milk, white wine, parsley and seasonings and allow to cook on medium heat for 10 minutes. Add remaining ingredients and adjust seasoning, if needed.

Chocolate and Crème Brûlée with Bananas

1 cup brown sugar	13 ounces milk chocolate
$4\frac{1}{4}$ cups milk	20 egg yolks
6 cups heavy whipping	$1\frac{1}{2}$ cups raw sugar
cream	8 ripe bananas

Sift the brown sugar on a half sheet pan and allow to dry overnight.

Preheat the oven to 300°. In a heavy saucepan, bring the milk and cream to a simmer. Remove from the heat and pour over the chocolate, stirring until smooth. In a large mixing bowl with the whip attachment, whip the egg yolks and granulated sugar on medium speed until they form ribbons. Reduce the speed to low and fold the chocolate mixture. Pour into 9-ounce bowls, about $\frac{1}{2}$ inch from the top. Place the bowls on a level sheet pan and place in the oven. Pour hot water into the sheet pan until it is $\frac{2}{3}$ of the way up the side of the sheet pan. Bake at 300° for 40 minutes or until set around the edges. Remove from the oven and cool at room temperature. Refrigerate overnight.

Slice bananas on the bias, and arrange over the top of each bowl. Once the bowls are covered with bananas, sprinkle with brown sugar. At this point grab your butane torch and caramelize the sugar.

Preston Hall at Belhaven College
Jackson, Mississippi

Ratatouille

In the South we are always blessed by having an abundant supply of fresh vegetables. One of my favorite things to do is to go down to the Farmer's Market and buy fresh vegetables...and this is one of my favorite recipes. —Ken Crotwell

3 tablespoons oil	2 medium zucchini, cubed
1/4 cup tasso	2 yellow crookneck
2 cups diced yellow onion	squash, cubed
1 cup chopped green	3 cups chopped, seeded
bell peppers	and peeled tomatoes
1 cup minced celery	4 tablespoons fresh
2 teaspoons salt	minced garlic
1 teaspoon black pepper	1 teaspoon chopped
1 teaspoon cayenne	fresh basil
1 large eggplant, cubed	1/2 teaspoon dried thyme
(1-inch cubes)	

Heat oil in a French skillet and sauté tasso for about 2 minutes; add onions, bell peppers, celery, salt, black pepper and cayenne. Stir constantly while cooking for another 2 minutes or until vegetables are slightly wilted. Add eggplant and cook for 3 minutes. Then add all remaining ingredients and reduce heat to medium; allow to simmer for 10 minutes. (The vegetables should have some crunch [al dente]. Ken thinks that it is best if it is cooked the day before so the mixture can marry all those wonderful flavors...and it goes great with any dish.)

*White House, Reformed Theological Seminary
Jackson, Mississippi*

JULEP
Restaurant and Bar

105 Highland Village
Jackson, MS 39211
601-362-1411

**Patrick and Mary Kelly
Owners**

Meatloaf Stuffed Tomato

3 teaspoons minced garlic	1 cup shredded Parmesan
1/2 cup diced red onions	cheese, divided
1/2 cup diced white onions	Salt and pepper to taste
2 tablespoons oil	6 large tomatoes (cored
2 1/2 pounds ground beef	and insides removed)
tenderloin	1/2 cup Maytag blue
3/4 cup toasted bread	cheese (crumbled)
crumbs	

Sauté vegetables in oil. Add meat and bread crumbs and brown to medium. Once cooked, add 1/2 the Parmesan cheese and blend until melted. Season with salt and pepper. Cool in large container covered with perforated plastic wrap to allow steam to escape.

When cool, add blue cheese. Place 3-ounce portion into tomato. Bake at 350° for 10 minutes. Garnish with remaining Parmesan and top with Brown Gravy. Yields 6 servings.

BROWN GRAVY:

3/4 cup ketchup	4 teaspoons
1/2 cup red wine	Worcestershire sauce

Combine ingredients in saucepan and heat over medium heat. Serve over baked tomatoes.

Fried Green Tomatoes

1 large green tomato	2 tablespoons white wine
3 eggs, beaten	Salt and pepper to taste
1 cup cornmeal	2 ounces Alabama goat
3 ounces jumbo lump	cheese
crabmeat	1 small Roma tomato,
½ teaspoon shallots	diced
½ tablespoon minced	1 cup mixed greens
garlic	2 tablespoons Julep's
½ tablespoon butter	Pepper-Jelly
⅓ cup heavy whipping	Vinaigrette
cream	

Slice tomato into 6 thin slices. Dip in egg wash and cornmeal. Fry until golden brown and floating. Sauté crabmeat, shallots and garlic in butter. Add heavy cream and white wine. Reduce to desired consistency. Season to taste. Top tomatoes with goat cheese and crab topping. Garnish with diced Roma tomatoes. Place around bed of fresh mixed greens tossed in Julep's Pepper-Jelly Vinaigrette. Yields 6 slices.

Catfish Taco

1 whole onion, chopped	2 cups cornmeal
½ cup Pepper Jack	(seasoned to taste)
cheese	2 jalapeño-Cheddar
2 (8-ounce) catfish fillets	tortillas
1 cup flour	2 tablespoons remoulade
4 eggs, beaten	sauce

In hot skillet with small amount of olive oil (enough to coat bottom of pan), add onions and immediately reduce heat to simmer. Cook for about 20 minutes (or until dark brown). Once finished cooking, fold in cheese until melted. Remove from heat and set aside.

Dust catfish with flour, dip in egg wash, then dip in cornmeal. Pan-fry catfish fillets until golden brown and cooked. Put caramelized onion mixture in middle of tortilla. Place 1 tablespoon remoulade sauce on each tortilla; spread evenly. Place catfish fillet on tortilla. Tuck sides of tortilla and roll. (Add remoulade sauce to edges to help edges stick). Yields 2 tacos.

NICK'S

1501 Lakeland Drive
Jackson, MS 39216
601-981-8017

Nick Apostle
Chef/Owner

Nick Apostle graduated with a degree in business from the University of Mississippi. He then attended the Culinary Institute of America in Hyde Park, NY, for a six-week Continuing Education Program offered by the CIA. He started working in his father's restaurant while in high school and college. After graduation he went to work full time. He worked for Paul's Restaurant from 1974 until he became the owner of Nick's in Jackson from 1983 to the present.

Nick has served as the president of the Jackson Chapter of the Mississippi Restaurant Association, president of the Mississippi Restaurant Association, and chairman of the board of the Mississippi Restaurant Association. He has participated in "A Salute to Southern Chefs" for the Share Our Strength Program sponsored by American Express and has been featured on the Great Chef's program, shown on public broadcast stations around the country, specifically "The Great Chefs of the South." Nick won the title of Wine Spectator "Award of Excellence" wine list for 2002, and for many years preceding. Nick serves on the board of the National Restaurant Association.

Panéed Soft-Shell Crab
Served with Shrimp and Crabmeat Butter Cream Sauce

SHRIMP AND CRABMEAT BUTTER CREAM SAUCE:

8 ounces unsalted butter, divided	$1/4$–$1/2$ teaspoon cayenne pepper (to taste)
$1/4$ cup finely chopped onion	2 dozen (about $3/4$ pound) medium shrimp, peeled
3 tablespoons all-purpose flour	1 cup (about $1/2$ pound) packed, lump crabmeat, picked over
$1^1/2$ cups shrimp stock	
1 cup heavy cream	
$1/2$ teaspoon salt	

In heavy 4-quart saucepan, melt 4 ounces butter with onion over medium heat; sauté about 1 minute. Add flour and blend with metal whisk until smooth. Reduce heat to low and continue cooking and whisking constantly for 1 minute. Meanwhile, bring shrimp stock to a boil in a 2-quart saucepan. Add butter-flour mixture and remaining 4 ounces of butter. Cook over medium-high heat until butter melts, whisking constantly. Gradually add cream, whisking constantly, then mix in salt and cayenne pepper. Lower heat to medium low and stir in shrimp; when they turn pink and are just done, add crabmeat. Continue to cook for 2 minutes, stirring occasionally and remove from heat. Hold in double boiler arrangement on stove top at lowest possible setting, stirring occasionally. Yields 5 cups.

SEASONING MIX:

1 tablespoon salt	$1/2$ teaspoon black pepper
1 teaspoon onion powder	$1/4$ teaspoon dry mustard
1 teaspoon sweet paprika	$1/4$ teaspoon dried oregano leaves
$1/4$ teaspoon cayenne pepper	$1/4$ teaspoon dried thyme leaves
$1/2$ teaspoon white pepper	
$1/2$ teaspoon garlic powder	

In a small bowl, thoroughly combine seasonings.

$1/2$ cup milk	Corn oil for pan frying
1 egg, beaten	6 large soft-shell crabs, cleaned
1 cup all-purpose flour	

Combine the milk and egg in a pan until well blended. In a small bowl, thoroughly combine the seasonings. In a separate pan, add 2 tablespoons of Seasoning Mix to flour and mix well. Heat about $1/4$ inch of oil in a

(continued)

(Panéed Soft-Shell Crab continued)

very large, heavy skillet to about 350°. Meanwhile, dredge each crab in seasoned flour, shaking off excess. Then soak crab in egg mixture. Just before frying, drain off egg mixture and dredge crabs once more in flour, and again shake off excess. (Make sure that the features [i.e., legs and claws] of crab are not stuck together, but loose, as to have a natural appearance.) Fry crabs shell down, first in hot oil for 1 minute, then turn over for about 30 seconds to a minute. Drain on paper towel, then place on your plates (which have been warmed in a 250° oven). Spoon 4 ounces of Shrimp and Crabmeat Butter Cream Sauce over crabs, then serve. Yields 6 servings.

Brie and Crabmeat Soup

12 ounces unsalted butter	1 pound brie (white, mold removed)
2 medium yellow onions, freshly chopped	Salt and white pepper to taste
6 large (outside) stalks celery, finely chopped	$1/4$ teaspoon red cayenne pepper
12 ounces flour	2 pounds picked jumbo lump crabmeat (fresh, not frozen)
$3/4$ gallon milk (hot)	
2 cups heavy cream (hot)	
2 cups clam broth (bottled)	
6 to 8 ounces dry vermouth (to taste)	

In a heavy-bottom stockpot, melt 12 ounces of butter over medium heat, then sauté onions and celery until onions are soft, not browned. Add flour and reduce heat to low; stir constantly to incorporate flour into mixture, and cook, stirring, for 8 to 10 minutes.

Add milk (hot), heavy cream (hot), clam broth, and dry vermouth. Turn heat to medium and stir constantly until thickened. Be careful to stir the bottom well so all the roux-vegetable mixture is incorporated and soup thickens without lumps. (At this point it would be best to put the stockpot that you are cooking your soup in into another larger stockpot with water, so in effect you have a double boiler arrangement.)

Add the brie; season with salt, white pepper and cayenne and stir until cheese is melted completely into soup. Add crabmeat and don't over stir, because the crabmeat will shred. Check seasoning and adjust, if necessary. If soup is too thick, thin with milk and check seasoning again. Yields $1^1/4$ gallons.

Mustard Seed Crusted Salmon with Mustard Cream Sauce

MUSTARD CREAM SAUCE:

1 tablespoons unsalted butter
$\frac{1}{4}$ cup shallots, chopped finely
1 tablespoons yellow mustard seeds
$\frac{1}{2}$ cup dry white wine
$\frac{3}{4}$ cup heavy cream (whipping cream)
2$\frac{1}{2}$ tablespoons whole-grain Dijon mustard
1 tablespoon chopped fresh tarragon
Salt and ground white pepper to taste

In heavy-bottom saucepan, melt butter and soften shallots with mustard seeds over low heat. Add wine, turning heat to high, and reduce by half, about 2 to 3 minutes. Whisk in heavy cream, whole-grain Dijon mustard and tarragon. Reduce until thickened to sauce-like consistency, about 3 minutes. Season with salt and ground white pepper. Remove from heat; cover and hold.

4 to 6 ounces skinless salmon fillets
2$\frac{1}{2}$ tablespoons whole-grain Dijon mustard
1 tablespoons yellow mustard seeds
Salt and ground white pepper to taste
2 tablespoons unsalted butter

Brush salmon on both sides with whole-grain Dijon mustard. Sprinkle mustard seeds, salt and white pepper onto both sides of the salmon. Melt butter in large skillet over medium-high heat. Add salmon and cook until opaque in center, anywhere from 2 to 4 minutes per side depending on thickness of fish (maybe less depending on the grain of the flesh). Transfer to plate and spoon Mustard Cream Sauce over salmon. Yields 4 servings.

Chocolate Marble Cheesecake with Ginger Snap Crust

GINGERSNAP COOKIES:

2 cups flour
1 tablespoon baking powder
1 teaspoon ground cloves
1 teaspoon ground cinnamon
1 teaspoon ground ginger
$\frac{1}{4}$ teaspoon salt
6 ounces unsalted butter, room temperature
1$\frac{1}{3}$ cups sugar, divided
$\frac{1}{4}$ cup light molasses
1 egg, beaten

Preheat oven to 350°. Sift first 6 ingredients into bowl. In a separate bowl, using electric mixer, cream butter with 1 cup sugar until light and fluffy. Mix in molasses and egg. Add sifted dry ingredients and mix until just combined. Cover and refrigerate dough at least one hour (can be prepared a day ahead).

Using one tablespoon per cookie, form into rounds. Roll rounds into $\frac{1}{3}$ cup sugar. Arrange on ungreased cookie sheets, 2 inches apart. Bake until brown on bottom, about 12 minutes. Transfer to rack and cool completely. Cookies will crisp as they cool. Store in air-tight container at room temperature. Yields 4 dozen.

16 Gingersnap Cookies
3 tablespoons melted butter
5 (8-ounce) packages cream cheese, softened
1$\frac{3}{4}$ cups sugar
3 tablespoons flour
1$\frac{1}{2}$ tablespoons vanilla
1 tablespoon grated orange peel
5 eggs plus 3 egg yolks, room temperature
3 ounces bittersweet or semisweet chocolate, melted

Grind cookies in processor to form crumbs. Toss 2 cups of crumbs and butter in 9$\frac{1}{2}$-inch springform pan; press mixture into bottom of pan. Refrigerate crust until ready to use. Position rack in center of oven and preheat to 400°. Using electric mixer, beat cream cheese with next 4 ingredients until smooth. Add eggs and yolks, one at a time, and blend just to combine. Transfer 2 cups batter to another bowl. Stir melted chocolate into 2 cups batter. Pour plain batter into crust. Pour chocolate batter over, spreading evenly. Using spatula, swirl chocolate into plain batter. Bake 10 minutes. Reduce oven temperature to 200° and bake until center of cake is almost set, about 1$\frac{1}{2}$ hours. Turn oven off. Let cheesecake remain in oven with door closed until firm and completely cool, about 1$\frac{1}{2}$ hours. Refrigerate covered overnight. Make at least one day before serving. (Can be made 3 days ahead). Yields 12 to 14 servings.

SCHIMMEL'S
Fine Dining and Cocktails

2615 North State Street
Jackson, MS 39216
601-981-7077

Jay Shimmel, Owner
Mike Carle, Executive Chef

Sautéed Rainbow Trout

1 (7-ounce) trout fillet,
    skin on and full boneless
Salt and pepper to taste
1 ounce vegetable oil
1 ounce white wine
2 ounces butter
¼ cup lemon juice
½ ounce capers, drained
1 teaspoon freshly
    chopped dill

Preheat sauté pan over medium flame. Season both sides of trout with salt and pepper. Pour oil into pan and raise to full flame; very gently place trout into pan, skin side down. (Careful not to splash hot oil!) When edges of fillet start to brown, less than one minute, lightly shake pan to loosen fillet and turn with spatula. Allow second side to sear and lightly brown, then pull pan to edge of range and add wine. (If pan is near flame, wine will "flame-up" as it's heated. This can be prevented by removing pan from range while adding wine and returning it to fire only after it has had a chance to boil-off for a second.) Add butter and lemon juice and allow butter to brown lightly. Finish with capers and freshly chopped dill. Yields 1 portion.

Turkey Scaloppini

12 ounces boneless,
    skinless turkey breast
1 cup seasoned flour
2 ounces light vegetable
    oil
1 teaspoon minced garlic
½ tablespoon minced
    shallot
½ tablespoon freshly
    chopped parsley
1 ounce whole butter
2 ounces white wine
½ ounce lemon juice
Salt and pepper to taste
½ tablespoon capers,
    drained

Place sliced turkey on cutting board and cover with plastic wrap. Pound with meat mallet till ¼ inch thick. Preheat sauté pan over medium flame. Check that all ingredients are measured and ready for quick use. Place seasoned flour in bowl. Dust turkey with flour and gently shake off any excess. Pour oil into hot sauté pan, coating entire bottom of pan. Gently place dusted turkey into pan, taking care not to splash oil. Turn flame up to high. Cook until edges of turkey start to brown. Turn turkey over gently. Quickly add garlic, shallot, parsley and butter. Shake pan to stir. Prepare for small flames. Add wine and lemon juice. Shake pan well to blend flavors. Taste sauce and season as desired. Place turkey on preheated plate and top with the sauce remaining in pan. Enjoy! Yields 1 portion.

Mississippi State Capitol
Jackson, Mississippi

STEAM ROOM GRILLE

5402 I-55 North
Jackson, MS 39211
601-899-8588

Steam Room Grille has something for everyone. Steam Room Grille offers only the finest aged hand-cut, prime beef, prepared blackened or grilled and served on sizzling platters. For those desiring lighter fare, Steam Room Grille has a wide array of salads and appetizers and a large selection of fresh grilled fish. As the name implies, the steamed seafood available includes live Maine lobster, Alaskan king crab, Dungeness crab or jumbo Gulf shrimp. Stone crabs, snow crabs, oysters, clams and mussels round out the steam offerings.

Marinated Shrimp

3 package zesty Italian
  dressing
3 cups vegetable oil
1 cup balsamic vinegar
1 cup water
4 tablespoons lemon juice
1 tablespoon oregano
1 tablespoon basil
6 tablespoons garlic
$\frac{1}{2}$ cup Worcestershire
  sauce

1 cup chopped parsley
4 tablespoons white wine
4 tablespoons Tiger sauce
2 teaspoons black pepper
1 red onion, sliced into
  rings
5 pounds (26-30 count)
  shrimp, tail on, cooked,
  peeled, deveined

Add all ingredients except onion and shrimp into small bowl and mix thoroughly. Add onion and shrimp to mixture. Cover tightly and refrigerate. Shrimp should be stirred or turned several times while marinating to make sure all shrimp are marinated.

Note: This recipe should be made at least 8 hours prior to serving, but no more than 2 days, as the shrimp will become tough. Place in crystal bowl or deep glass tray to serve. Pour marinade over shrimp after arranging. Garnish with lemon crowns and parsley. Have cracker basket nearby, but not necessary to serve with crackers. Yields 5 pounds.

Crabmeat and Brie Soup

8 celery stalks
2 gallons chicken stock
1 pound butter
8 cups diced onions
$2\frac{1}{2}$ cups flour
2 teaspoons cayenne
  pepper
2 teaspoons salt

2 tablespoons Tabasco
  sauce
8 pints half-and-half
$\frac{1}{2}$ gallon milk
5 pounds brie cheese
2 pounds jumbo lump
  crabmeat

Add celery stalks to chicken stock, and cook it down at least 30 minutes. Melt butter in braiser pot; add onions and cook them until they become tender. Mix in flour and stir constantly. Cook for 7 minutes. Flour should become a smooth white roux. Add all the seasonings and stir to eliminate any clumps. Gradually add $\frac{1}{3}$ hot chicken-celery broth while stirring. **Do not add the celery to the soup** – strain it out. Bring this to a boil. Add $\frac{1}{3}$ more of the broth and stir until it boils. Add remaining $\frac{1}{3}$ broth and stir it until it boils. Slowly add half-and-half and milk while stirring. Reduce heat and cook sauce until it becomes creamy and thickens. Do not allow to boil once milk is added. (It is important that the chicken broth and milk products are added slowly and mixed well to prevent the sauce from breaking up.) Add brie cheese to soup and allow it to melt and mix into soup. Simmer on a low flame for 5 minutes. **Do not boil!** Add crabmeat and cool soup in an ice bath immediately! If this yield is too large, cut in half.

THE DINNER BELL

229 Fifth Avenue
McComb, MS 39648
601-684-4883

Celebrating over 50 years as one of the South's most unique dining experiences, The Dinner Bell in McComb draws visitors from around the country and around the world. Located in the historic depot district in a beautifully restored mansion, this boarding house-style eatery serves its specialties on enormous Lazy Susan tables.

Featuring fried chicken, fabulous famous fried eggplant, chicken and dumplings, and sweet potato casserole along with a host of fresh vegetables, salads and desserts. The Dinner Bell has been featured in *Redbook, Country Living, Southern Living* and *Mississippi Magazine,* as well as numerous literary features including raves in *Roadfood/Goodfood* by Jane and Michael Stern. *Chicago Tribune* said, "The best southern cooking in the country."

John's Italian Eggplant Casserole

3 medium eggplants
1 pound lean ground beef (can use shrimp, ham or sausage, etc.)
1 cup chopped onion
1 cup chopped green onions
1 cup chopped celery
6 small cloves garlic, chopped fine
1 stick margarine, divided
1½ cups Italian-flavored bread crumbs, divided
4 large eggs
½ teaspoon basil
¼ teaspoon oregano

Peel, dice, and boil eggplants in salted water till tender; drain some of the water off and place in large mixing bowl. Brown meat lightly (till red's gone), then add to eggplants; sauté onions, celery and garlic in ½ stick margarine. Add to eggplant mixture. Add 1 cup bread crumbs and remaining ingredients to taste. Mix well and pour into a lightly buttered casserole dish. Bake 30 minutes in 350° oven.

Mix remaining ½ cup crumbs in remaining ½ stick melted margarine until crumbs are moistened. Spread evenly and lightly over casserole mixture and bake till crumbs are lightly browned. Serves 8 to 10.

Sweet Potato Casserole with Marshmallows

8 average-size sweet potatoes
1 tablespoon vanilla
3 to 5 tablespoons sugar to taste
½ stick margarine
¼ teaspoon cinnamon to taste (optional)
¼–1 teaspoon orange juice to taste
¼–1 teaspoon nutmeg to taste
Marshmallows (large or miniature)
Cinnamon-sugar (optional)

Boil (or bake) sweet potatoes till done. Remove peeling from hot potatoes and in a large bowl, mash well, removing all strings. Add all ingredients except marshmallows and cinnamon-sugar; mix well. Lightly spray or grease a 9x13-inch casserole dish. Put a layer of potatoes, then a layer of marshmallows till filled. Sprinkle with cinnamon sugar for added flavor. Bake at 350° until hot. Remove from oven and put marshmallows on top. Place again in oven to brown lightly. Serves 10 to 12.

Pistachio Nut Cake

3 tablespoons rum extract
1 package yellow cake mix
¾ cup vegetable oil
3 large eggs
1 cup 7-Up (diet or regular)
1 (3-ounce) box pistachio instant pudding
1 cup chopped unsalted walnuts or pecans
½ cup flaked coconut

Mix all ingredients well. Pour into greased and floured 9x13-inch pan or casserole dish. Bake 45 minutes at 350°. Test to make certain cake is done.

ICING:

2 tablespoons rum extract (optional)
3 envelopes Dream Whip dry topping mix
1½ cups milk
1 (3-ounce) box pistachio instant pudding
½ cup flaked coconut
¾ cup chopped unsalted walnuts or pecans

Beat all ingredients until thick, except coconut and nuts. Spread on cooled cake and sprinkle with coconuts and nuts.

Note: Can also be made as a layer cake. Try melting 2 teaspoons margarine in a skillet, then add coconut and stir constantly until lightly browned. Drain and cool on paper towel. This gives a nice taste to the above Icing.

Spinach Casserole

1 can artichoke hearts, packed in water (drained)
4 packages chopped (frozen) spinach, cooked by directions, drained
1 (8-ounce) package Philadelphia Cream Cheese, softened
1 stick margarine, melted
2 tablespoons Worcestershire sauce
2 tablespoons crumbled dry onions

In large lightly greased casserole dish, slice drained artichoke hearts and line bottom of dish. Mix spinach with all other ingredients and pour over artichoke lined dish. Cover with butter-flavored bread crumbs. Bake in 350° oven till lightly browned. Serves 8 to 10.

AUNT COZY'S CAFÉ
Canal Street Depot

200 State Street
Natchez, MS 39120
601-304-0200

Aunt Cozy's Café is located in an old train station built in 1910. Karen Lewis, owner, and Sara Blough, caterer, put their heads together and created Aunt Cozy's. Breakfast muffins and Canal Street coffee start the day. Lunches consist of a variety of soups, sandwiches, salads, lunch specials and homemade desserts. You can dine in or enjoy your food on the covered loading dock. Aunt Cozy provides the entertainment with knee-slapping antics. Sara's outstanding fare and Karen's desire to meet the needs of tourists and local diners have succeeded in the birth of a delightful café with old southern charm!

Aunt Cozy's Turnip or Mustard Green Soup

Easy to make and delicious – our best selling soup!

1 (16-ounce) package frozen chopped turnip or mustard greens
1 onion, chopped
1 bell pepper, chopped
1 teaspoon minced garlic
8 ounces tasso sausage, diced
8 ounces ham, diced
3 potatoes, peeled and diced
3 cans white navy beans, drained
2 cans chicken broth
1 tablespoon sugar
Salt, pepper, and red pepper to taste

Place all ingredients in large, heavy-bottom pot. Simmer for 2 hours until potatoes are tender and vegetables are soft.

Serve topped with crumbled or cubed cornbread, if desired. Serves 12.

Mississippi Mud Puddin' Pie

10 ounces semisweet chocolate chips	1 teaspoon rum extract
1 cup unsalted butter	1 cup flour
4 cups sugar	1 teaspoon salt
8 large eggs, slightly beaten	2½ cups chopped toasted pecans
1 teaspoon vanilla extract	

Preheat oven to 350°. In large, heavy-bottom saucepan over medium heat, stir chocolate chips and butter until smooth. Remove from heat and cool.

Stir sugar into chocolate mixture. Whisk eggs into mixture, one at a time. Add extracts, flour and salt. Stir in nuts. Bake in buttered 10x15-inch baking dish for 50 minutes until top is crisp. This dessert has been known to make grown men cry (honestly!). Serves 12.

Tipsy Roasted Pork

1 (3-pound) pork loin, well trimmed	¼ cup of Worcestershire sauce
¼ cup extra virgin olive oil	1 cup soy sauce
2 tablespoons Greek seasoning	¼ cup Pickapeppa sauce
	1 (12-ounce) beer

Preheat oven to 400°. Rub loin with olive oil, and sprinkle with Greek seasoning, making sure the meat is well coated. Place meat in a baking dish. Drizzle with the sauces. Place in hot oven for 30 minutes, then add beer to the pan and reduce heat to 350°. Continue to bake 50 minutes until pork juices run clear. The pan drippings make a wonderful sauce. Serves 12 to 15.

DUNLEITH PLANTATION

84 Homochitto Street
Natchez, MS 39120
601-446-8500

Dunleith is a stately, white colonnade, Greek Revival mansion standing on a terraced rise in the heart of Natchez. Dunleith is surrounded by forty acres of landscaped gardens and wooded bayous, and is sometimes referred to as the most photographed house in America. It was cited by the Southern Heritage Society for the beauty and grace of its architecture and appeared in Southern Accents' *Historic Houses of the South*.

Beautiful Dunleith is listed on the National Register of Historic Places and is a National Historic Landmark. The majestic mansion has been the backdrop for such films as *Huckleberry Finn* and *Showboat*. Dunleith has eleven bed and breakfast rooms in the courtyard wing, and eight rooms in the main house.

Hays Vaughan, Executive Chef

Chef Vaughan is a native of Yazoo City, MS, and a graduate of Johnson & Wales Culinary School in Vail, CO. Chef Vaughan has worked at Commander's Palace and Mike's on the Avenue in New Orleans, Mansurs in Baton Rouge, and Nick's in Jackson.

Roasted Corn and Crawfish Bisque

2 medium yellow onions,
   diced
4 to 5 stalks celery, diced
2 tablespoons oil
1 (1½-cup) bottle white
   wine
2 quarts heavy cream
Crawfish base (or you
   can sub a shrimp
   base or stock)

1 teaspoon dried thyme
1 teaspoon dried basil
½ teaspoon dried
   oregano
Salt and pepper to taste
1 teaspoon of paprika
1 pound corn
White roux (flour and oil)
1 pound crawfish tails

Sauté onions and celery in hot oil. Then add about ¾ bottle of white wine; let this reduce by ½, then add your heavy cream. When it comes back to a boil, add crawfish base and all of your dry ingredients. Fill the pot ¾ of the way with water. Put your corn on a coated sheet pan and place in the oven; bake until cooked. Make a white roux and add to your soup. Turn heat down and let soup thicken. Pull out your roasted corn; cut and add to bisque. Now add crawfish tails. Cook until crawfish tails are done. Do not overcook.

Roasted Mushrooms

1 cup portobello
   mushrooms
1 cup shiitake mushrooms
1 cup cremini mushrooms
½ cup sliced onion
2 cloves garlic

1 sprig thyme
1 sprig rosemary
2 tablespoons olive oil
¼ cup chicken stock
Salt and pepper

In an oven-proof pan, place mushrooms with rest of ingredients and toss to coat well. Season with salt and pepper. Cover loosely with foil and bake at 325° for 30 minutes. Remove from oven; uncover, stir and cool in cooking juices.

Dunleith
Natchez, Mississippi

OAK SQUARE
Bed and Breakfast

1207 Church Street
Port Gibson, MS 39150
800-729-0240

Oak Square Plantation is located in Port Gibson. Port Gibson is located on U.S. Highway 61 between Natchez and Vicksburg. Oak Square Plantation is the largest mansion in Port Gibson and has grand accommodations for overnight guests. The circa 1850 Greek Revival manor is named for the massive oaks that surround the plantation.

Chicken Tetrazzini

1 whole chicken, boiled,
   deboned, torn or cut
   into pieces
½ cup chopped onions
   or scallions
½ cup chopped bell
   peppers
½ stick margarine
3 tablespoons flour
1 small jar pimento
1 cup milk

1 can cream of
   mushroom soup
1 can cream of chicken
   soup
½ cup chopped
   mushrooms
1 (7-ounce) package
   spaghetti
Chicken broth
3 or 4 cups grated
   Cheddar cheese

Boil and debone chicken; reserve broth and set aside. Cut chicken into bite-size pieces. Sauté onion and bell pepper in margarine until tender. Add flour, pimento, milk, mushroom and chicken soups, and mushrooms. Mix well. Then add chicken to mixture; stir and set aside. Boil spaghetti in reserved chicken broth; drain.

   Layer in baking dish half of each: spaghetti, chicken mixture, and cheese, then repeat ending with cheese. Bake at 350° about 40 minutes.

Surprise Meat Balls

½ pound ground beef
1 egg, beaten
¼ cup dry bread crumbs
¼ cup milk
⅛ teaspoon onion salt
⅛ teaspoon garlic salt
24 small pimiento-stuffed
    green olives

Combine all ingredients except olives. Place 1 tablespoon of meat mixture into palm of hand. Flatten. Place olive in center of meat and mold meat around olive. Broil until brown, about 8 minutes, turning once. Keep hot in chafing dish. Serve with food picks. Makes 2 dozen meat balls.

Harvest Loaf Cake

Award Winning Cake!

1¾ cups plain flour
1 teaspoon baking soda
½ teaspoon salt
½ teaspoon nutmeg
¼ teaspoon ginger
¼ teaspoon ground
    cloves
1 teaspoon cinnamon
½ cup margarine
1 cup sugar
2 eggs
¾ cup canned pumpkin
¾ cup semisweet
    chocolate morsels
¾ cup finely chopped
    pecans, divided

Grease bottom of 9x5x3-inch pan. Combine flour with soda, salt and spices and set aside. Cream butter in large bowl. Gradually add sugar and cream at high speed until light and fluffy. Blend in eggs and beat well. At low speed, add dry ingredients alternately with pumpkin; begin and end with dry ingredients. Blend well after each addition. Stir in chocolate morsels and ½ cup pecans. Pour into pan. Sprinkle with remaining ¼ cup pecans. Bake at 350° for 65 to 75 minutes, until cake springs back when touched lightly in center. Cool. Drizzle with Spice Glaze. Let stand 6 hours before slicing.

SPICE GLAZE:

½ cup sifted
    confectioners' sugar
⅛ teaspoon nutmeg
⅛ teaspoon cinnamon
1 to 2 tablespoons cream

Combine confectioners' sugar, nutmeg and cinnamon. Blend in cream until the desired consistency of glaze is reached.

KEEGAN'S

7049 Old Canton Road
Ridgeland MS 39157
601-898-4554

Lump Crab Cakes

3 tablespoons olive oil
⅓ cup minced onion
¼ cup minced green
    bell pepper
¼ cup minced red bell
    pepper
¼ cup minced green
    onion
1 tablespoon minced
    garlic
½ teaspoon salt
¼ teaspoon white pepper
1 teaspoon ground
    black pepper
2 teaspoons Creole
    seasoning, divided
2 eggs
2 teaspoons Creole
    mustard
6 tablespoons grated
    Parmesan cheese
1 pound lump crabmeat
1 cup bread crumbs,
    divided
1 egg, beaten
½ cup flour
Salt, pepper, and creole
    seasoning to taste

Heat oil in skillet, add all peppers and onions and sauté 1 minute. Add garlic, salt and peppers and 1 teaspoon Creole seasoning. Remove from heat. In a bowl, whisk the vegetables and eggs together; add mustard, cheese, crabmeat and ¼ cup crumbs. Gently fold together and form 8 crab cakes.

In 3 separate bowls, place remaining bread crumbs, egg wash, and flour; season all three. After dredging and breading all cakes, pan-fry until they are golden brown. Yields 8 servings.

Smoked Tomato Tartar Sauce

6 cups mayonnaise
½ cup chopped capers
½ cup minced red onion
2 cups smoked tomato
    purée
1 can chipolte peppers
1 to 2 teaspoons cayenne
    pepper
¼ cup fresh lemon juice

Mix all ingredients together thoroughly; refrigerate.

Lobster and Mushroom Cheesecake

1 cup grated Parmesan cheese	2 teaspoons salt
1 cup Japanese bread crumbs	1½ teaspoons ground black pepper
½ cup unsalted butter, melted	4 eggs
1 tablespoon olive oil	3½ (8-ounce) packages cream cheese, room temperature
1 cup chopped onion	½ cup heavy cream
½ cup chopped Anaheim peppers	1 cup grated, smoked gouda
½ cup chopped red bell pepper	2 cups medium-chopped lobster meat
4 cups chopped wild mushrooms	

For crust, combine first 3 ingredients and press into bottom of a 9-inch pan. Heat oil in heavy-duty skillet; add onions and peppers and sauté for 2 minutes. Add mushrooms. Sauté with salt and pepper for 3 minutes, then remove from heat. Beat eggs and cream cheese for 5 minutes; add cream, gouda, vegetables and lobster, and mix well. Pour filling over crust and bake at 350° for 1 hour; let cool before cutting. Yields 12 to 16 servings.

COULIS:

1 tablespoon chopped shallots	1 teaspoon salt
1 tablespoon chopped garlic	½ teaspoon ground black pepper
2 eggs	1½ cups olive oil

For green onions, add ¾ cup chopped onion and ½ cup chopped parsley. For sweet pepper, add 1 cup roasted and peeled sweet pepper. Place herbs and vegetables in blender and purée. Add eggs, salt, and pepper and continue blending. Slowly stream in oil until incorporated. Refrigerate. Yields 2 cups.

Using squirt bottles, swirl green onion Coulis on the bottom of a plate. Place cheesecake on center of plate, top with sweet pepper Coulis.

Shrimp and Artichoke Chimichanga with Goat Cheese Sauce

GOAT CHEESE SAUCE:

8 ounces soft goat cheese	2 cups heavy cream

Simmer cream over medium heat for 5 minutes. **Do not boil.** Stir in goat cheese until melted and smooth. Set aside and keep warm.

CHIMICHANGA:

3 tablespoons olive oil	1 pound shrimp, peeled, tails removed, chopped
1 can small artichoke hearts, drained and chopped	1 teaspoon dried oregano
2 Anaheim chilies, roasted and peeled, chopped	1 teaspoon dried basil
	6 large flour tortillas
	½ cup peanut oil

Heat olive oil in 10-inch sauté pan. Add artichokes and peppers; sauté for 2 minutes. Add shrimp and herbs and sauté until shrimp are pink. Pour into colander and drain; let cool. Place ¼ cup mixture in center of tortilla. Roll tortilla over mixture once, fold in outer flaps, then tightly roll. Secure end with a toothpick. Heat peanut oil in skillet until 350°. Brown on all sides. Place on cookie sheet. Cook at 350° for 5 minutes. Serve immediately. Serves 6.

To serve, place 2 ounces of Goat Cheese Sauce on plate, then place Chimichanga on top.

*Longwood
Natchez, Mississippi*

THE PARKER HOUSE

104 S.E. Madison Drive
Ridgeland, MS 39157
601-856-0043

Steve and Barbara Parker, both native Mississippians, opened their first restaurant "The Parker House Restaurant" on April 14, 1994. Steve's love of good food and cooking gave them the idea for their new business venture together. Having no formal training or restaurant experience did not deter the couple from bringing The Parker House into the forefront of fine dining in the Jackson Metropolitan area.

As co-owner/executive chef, Steve leads the kitchen in the preparation of traditional "continental-American" cuisine with a Southern flair. Barbara's attention to detail has helped to create an elegant atmosphere of home some have described "as romantic a setting to be found" in the Jackson-Ridgeland area. Barbara has worked to create a service staff that assures the guest a wonderful dining experience.

The Parker House received "The Restaurant of the Year Award" for 2001 from the Mississippi Restaurant Association, the "Wine Spectator Award of Excellence" for 2002 and 2003, and is a past recipient of the "Business of the Year" Award from the city of Ridgeland Chamber of Commerce.

Roasted Duck Jezebel

1 (2 to 3 pound) duckling	Salt and pepper
Canola oil	Worchestershire sauce
Garlic, minced	

Wash duck thoroughly. Remove excess fat around neck. Remove wings, except for large bone. Using an ice pick or other pointed object, puncture skin of duckling. (This is especially important in the fatty areas of the duck.) Rub the duck so that the entire duck is coated with canola oil. Rub the duck with freshly minced garlic, salt and pepper. Place duckling in deep-slotted roasting pan or rack. In bottom of pan, beneath the duck, place approximately 1 inch of a mixture of water and Worcestershire sauce. Cover with foil and roast at 375° for approximately 2 hours. Check for tenderness by twisting the leg bone. When tender, remove foil and place back in oven at 425° until golden brown. Serve with Cranberry Jezebel Sauce.

CRANBERRY JEZEBEL SAUCE:

1 (16-ounce) can whole cranberry sauce	½ cup brown sugar
½ cup white sugar	1 cup champagne
	Horseradish to taste

Place cranberry sauce in sauce pot. Add sugars. Slowly simmer until sugar is dissolved. Add champagne. (Use a good one and save the rest for dinner.) Simmer for another 5 minutes. Remove from heat and add horseradish to taste. This is wonderful with duck, beef, port, etc.

Crawfish Bisque

4 quarts heavy cream	Cayenne to taste
1 bunch chopped green onions	Salt to taste
	1 cup blond roux
1 cup sherry	2 pounds crawfish tails
3 tablespoons paprika	with fat, cooked

Bring all ingredients except roux and crawfish tails to a boil. Add half of roux to cream mixture and simmer. Slowly add remaining roux until desired thickness is reached. Add crawfish tails; simmer for 5 minutes and serve.

ROSSINI
Cucina Italiana

1060 E. County Line Road, Suite 22
Ridgeland, MS 39157
601-899-9111

**"A combination of new world class
with old world style"**

Owners Tony and Lori Spreafico opened
their Italian restorante in 1999. Nestled in
Centre Park, Rossini offers homemade
pasta dishes, seafood, fowl, lamb, filets,
and the widest variety of Italian veal dishes in the Metro area. A popular menu item
is the "FEED ME, TONY," a customized
special feast just for you! Tony and Lori
love what they do and their passion is not
only reflected in the dishes prepared by
Tony, but also by the romantic casual
ambiance. Everyone loves Rossini and . . .
That's Amore!

Osso Bucco

4 to 6 (2½-inch-thick) veal shanks	3 ounces peppercorns
1 (6-pack) Moretti Italian Beer	3 orange bell peppers, roasted
8 cups red wine, divided	8 ounces honey
2 ounces rosemary	32 ounces marinara sauce
	2 cups Parmesan

In a large deep pan, combine veal shanks, beer, 4 cups
wine, rosemary and peppercorns. Cover and marinate
in refrigerator for 12 hours. Bake at 275° for 11
hours. Bring bell peppers and honey to a boil and add
remaining 4 cups of wine and marinara sauce.
Simmer for 30 minutes and add Parmesan cheese.
Pour over veal shanks and serve. Serves 4 to 6.

Seafood Bisque
"Crema di Pesce"

2 quarts heavy cream	3 ounces marinara sauce
8 ounces unsalted butter	Cornstarch (mix with a little water to make a paste)
1 pound shrimp	
Meat of 1 large lobster	
Salt and pepper	1 pound crabmeat

Bring cream, butter, shrimp and lobster to a boil and
simmer for 20 minutes. Add salt and pepper to taste.
Add marinara sauce and simmer for another 15 minutes. Add cornstarch to desired thickness, then add
crabmeat and serve hot. Serves 14 to 16.

Tiramisu

3 cups coffee	16 ounces mascarpone cheese
1 cup amaretto	
2 quarts heavy cream	4 ounces Frangelico
1 (16-ounce) box powdered sugar	48 ladyfingers

Mix coffee with amaretto and chill. Whip cream,
sugar, mascarpone cheese and Frangelico. Place one
layer of ladyfingers in bottom of baking pan and soak
with coffee mixture, then top with cream mixture.
Repeat with another layer of ladyfingers and mixtures.
Chill for 2 hours before serving. Serves 8 to 12.

*Melrose
Natchez, Mississippi*

BALDWIN HOUSE

1022 Crawford Street
Vicksburg, Mississippi 39180
601-638-8130

**Bruce and Marion Baldwin
Proprietors**

This casual fine dining restaurant is located in a restored Victorian home (circa 1890) in the Historic District of Downtown Vicksburg at the corner of Adams and Crawford Street. Other sites on the block: Southern Cultural Heritage Center, Pemberton Headquarters, and the Balfour House.

The restaurant features espresso drinks, wine and spirits, homemade desserts and pastries as well as delicious entrées. Lunch is served Tuesday through Sunday 11 a.m. to 3 p.m. Sunday breakfast is served 9 a.m. to 11 a.m. Dinner is served Wednesday through Saturday from 6 p.m. to 9 p.m. (Reservations appreciated.)

Chicken Enchiladas

SAUCE:
$2/3$ cup of flour
1 full tablespoon of onion soup mix
$1\frac{1}{2}$ cups of milk
$\frac{1}{2}$ cup picante sauce

Mix the flour, milk and onion soup mix to thicken, then add picante sauce.

2 (8-ounce) packages cream cheese, softened
1 cup sour cream
2 cups shredded Jack cheese
1 bunch green onions, chopped
1 ($4\frac{1}{2}$-ounce) can chopped green chiles
4 cups cooked, cubed chicken
10 medium-size flour tortillas

Mix cream cheese and sour cream, then add the rest of the ingredients. Warm 10 flour tortillas in microwave or oven. In 10x14-inch pan that has been oiled, add a small amount of the Sauce. Fill tortillas with chicken mixture and line the pan. Pour some Sauce on the top of the prepared tortillas and sprinkle with more shredded cheese. Bake for 30 minutes at 350°. For garnish, put a little Sauce on the plate and place cooked tortilla on Sauce. Serve with green salad. Garnish with fresh cilantro.

Healthy Muffins

MIX:
1 cup All-Bran cereal
$1\frac{1}{2}$ cups milk
1 cup crushed pineapple
1 cup grated carrots
1 cup chopped walnuts
$\frac{3}{4}$ cup oil
3 eggs
$\frac{1}{2}$ cup honey
2 cups brown sugar
2 teaspoons grated orange rind

Mix all of the above ingredients in large bowl.

$3\frac{1}{2}$ cups flour
$\frac{3}{4}$ cup wheat flour
2 teaspoons baking powder
$1\frac{1}{2}$ teaspoons baking soda
$1\frac{1}{2}$ teaspoons salt
1 teaspoon cinnamon
$\frac{1}{4}$ teaspoon ground cloves

Sift ingredients. Gently stir in to Mix. Pour into large greased muffin pans. Bake for 25 to 30 minutes at 400°.

Baldwin House
Shrimp Stuffed Flounder

STUFFING:

2 cups Progresso crumbs
$\frac{1}{2}$ cup butter, melted
$\frac{1}{2}$ cup chopped red pepper
$\frac{1}{2}$ cup chopped green pepper

$\frac{1}{2}$ cup chopped yellow onion
$\frac{3}{4}$ cup white wine

Mix the Stuffing ingredients together.

Cooked shrimp ($\frac{1}{2}$ cup per person)
Flounder (2 pieces per person)

Melted butter

Butter a 9x13-inch baking pan. Cut up cooked shrimp. Using thawed flounder, put one piece on the bottom and fill with Stuffing; top with $\frac{1}{2}$ cup shrimp. Put another piece of flounder on top. If large flounder, cut in half and use one half on the bottom and one half on the top. Brush with butter and cook at 350° for 18 minutes.

SAUCE:

$\frac{2}{3}$ cup flour
1 cup milk

$\frac{1}{4}$ cup real butter
Salt and pepper to taste

Combine ingredients thoroughly and cook until thickened. When fish is done, serve Sauce over fillets, and sprinkle with bread crumbs. Serve with rice and vegetables.

Cedar Grove Mansion
Vicksburg, Mississippi

CEDAR GROVE MANSION
Inn and Restaurant

2200 Washington Street
Vicksburg, MS 39180
800-862-1300

Ted Mackey, Owner
Pamela Netterville, Public Relations
Elizabeth Browne, Chef

Cedar Grove Mansion, featured in numerous publications, consistently voted "Best Antebellum Home" in Vicksburg, "A Top Ten Most Romantic Place" assures guests of the exceptional quality in accommodations and service.

Cedar Grove Mansion (circa 1840) has been featured on The Travel & Discovery channel, and TLC's' "Great Country Inns." This 50-room mansion has 34 guest rooms and suites all nestled in five acres of gardens. Relax with a Mint Julep or cocktail in the mansion bar—the perfect prelude to a romantic gourmet dinner by candlelight and piano music in Andre's Restaurant.

Back Fin Crab Cakes in a Remoulade Cocktail Sauce

REMOULADE SAUCE:

1 clove garlic, finely minced	1 tablespoon anchovy paste
1 cup mayonnaise	3 tablespoons chopped fresh parsley
2 tablespoons mustard	2 tablespoons grated onion
1 tablespoon horseradish	
4 tablespoons lemon juice	
2 tablespoons Lea & Perrins sauce	

Mix all well and chill.

COCKTAIL SAUCE:

¾ cup ketchup	1 tablespoon Lea & Perrins sauce
¼ cup chili sauce	4 to 5 dashes Tabasco hot sauce
2 tablespoons fresh lemon juice	
3 tablespoons horseradish	

Mix all well and chill.

1 pound back fin crabmeat	2 tablespoons chopped parsley
½ cup toasted bread crumbs	1 tablespoon heavy cream
½ bunch green onions	4 tablespoons olive oil
	2 tablespoons butter

Mix first 5 ingredients together lightly and pat into 3-inch cakes. Heat olive oil and butter in a skillet and sauté cakes for 2 to 3 minutes on each side until golden brown. (Don't overcook!) Spoon 3-inch round serving of remoulade sauce with a 2-inch round size of cocktail sauce in center. Garnish with a sprig of thyme.

New Orleans Style Barbecue Shrimp

2 pounds shrimp, in shell, heads off	½ pound butter, cut in small pieces
6 lemons, cut in half and juiced	1 to 2 tablespoons Lea & Perrins sauce
1 tablespoon black pepper	Tabasco sauce to taste
1 tablespoon salt	1 bunch green onions, finely chopped
1 tablespoon paprika	½ cup white wine
2 teaspoons granulated garlic	

Wash and dry shrimp. Put everything in a large sauté pan and cook over low heat until butter melts, then raise heat to medium high and cook until shrimp are pink, stirring constantly. Serve with French bread, lots of napkins and finger bowls. Garnish each serving with a lemon slice.

Honey-Roasted Mashed Sweet Potatoes

6 sweet potatoes (about 6 pounds total)	¼ teaspoon grated nutmeg
8 tablespoons butter, cut in small pieces	1 cup honey
1 teaspoon ground cinnamon	Kosher salt and ground pepper to taste

Preheat oven to 350°. Peel and quarter sweet potatoes and place in roasting pan. Place the butter pieces evenly on top of the potatoes. Sprinkle the cinnamon and nutmeg on top; drizzle with honey and season with the salt and pepper. Gently pour about 2 cups of water into pan without washing anything off potatoes. Cover and bake for 1½ hours, or until tender.

Remove the cover; stir and cook for 30 minutes more. (The potatoes should have a dark brown color.) Remove potatoes with a slotted spoon; place them in a large bowl and mix with electric mixer until large lumps are gone. Drizzle liquid from pan and mix until desired consistency.

Honey-Glazed Nutmeg Carrots

3 pounds medium carrots, cut length-wise, half or ¼ of carrot
8 tablespoons butter, cut in pieces, divided
½ cup water

Kosher salt and ground pepper to taste
¾ cup honey
Juice of 1 lemon
2 tablespoons grated nutmeg

Preheat oven to 350°. Place carrots in a large casserole with cover. Add half the butter pieces plus water, salt and pepper. Stir lightly and bake, covered, for 20 minutes or until tender and carrots turn bright orange. Remove the cover and stir lightly. Bake for 30 minutes more until the carrots are done and most of the water has evaporated.

Remove the casserole from oven and place on stove. The carrots should be tender and sitting in a creamy, syrup sauce. Adjust the consistency of the liquid, if necessary, by removing the carrots and cooking a bit more to thicken or by adding a little water to thin. Return carrots to pan, add the remaining butter and honey over medium heat, then add the lemon juice and nutmeg. Stir and adjust seasoning. Serve hot.

Old Covered Bridge
Brookhaven, Mississippi

PORCHES
Traditional Southern Dining with an Imaginative Flair

1193 Highway 51
Wesson, MS 39191
601-643-9035

Al and Ceal McSweyn
Owners

The one aspect missing from most modern dining is a heritage that for generations has been a part of our way of life—hospitality. It is something that is hard to find in chain operations and other large establishments where the managers and employees do not have a personal stake in the operation. We invite you into our home to dine with us.

And the food is something special—from Grandmother's Corn Bread Dressing, Christopher's Bread Pudding, to Porches Hot Pineapple. It's not taking the shortcuts, but doing the hard things that make the meals special. It's recipes from family, aunts, and friends that are time-tested and true. We cook what we would like to eat.

Porches is located in one of Wesson's historic houses—an 1878 turn-of-the-century Victorian home just recently added to the National Register. We are two blocks south of the 4-way stop on U.S. 51—the big pink house with the white picket fence.

Cream of Turnip Green Soup with Essence of Ham Hock

We serve this as a starter for our annual Christmas Eve Luncheon and everyone just loves it!

3 large meaty ham hocks
3 pounds chopped turnip
  greens with roots
  (frozen or fresh)
2 quarts heavy cream,
  divided

1 tablespoon Tabasco
  sauce
Salt to taste

In a large pot, boil ham hocks in about 4 quarts of water for 2 hours or until fork-tender. Remove ham hocks from water and set aside to cool. Add turnip greens and salt to water and cook for 30 to 45 minutes or until done. Adjust water as needed. You don't want too much liquid (pot liquor) left, about 4 to 6 cups, as you will be adding the cream later.

After ham hocks have cooled, remove all bone and cartilage; coarsely chop. Place chopped ham hocks in food processor and process 3 to 5 minutes until smooth and creamy. Add 1 quart of heavy cream, half of the puréed ham hock, Tabasco sauce, and salt to the turnip greens. Bring back to a low boil and simmer about 5 to 10 minutes. Adjust flavor and texture with remaining ham hock purée and heavy cream.

The Natchez

Best Ever New York Strip with Onion Frits

ONION FRITS:
2 cups buttermilk
1 tablespoon Tabasco
  sauce
1 large onion, thinly
  sliced

2 cups corn flour
2 tablespoons Creole
  seasoning
Oil for deep frying

In a bowl, combine buttermilk, Tabasco sauce and sliced onion. Let marinate while prepping steaks.

2 New York Strip Steaks,
  about 12 to 14 ounces
  each, 1 inch thick
Salt to taste

Freshly cracked black
  pepper to taste
2 tablespoons butter

Preheat oven to 550° (or as high as it will go). Place a cast-iron skillet on burner on high heat. If there is a thin membrane on upper outer edge of steak, carefully remove with a good sharp knife. (This makes all the difference later as this membrane is extremely tough.) Liberally season each side of steaks with salt and black pepper. (The salt gives the steak a nice brown crispy flavor, so do not go lightly on the salt.)

When skillet starts to smoke, test for readiness by lightly dragging the tail of one steak across skillet. If tail sticks, skillet is not hot enough. Place both steaks in skillet; reduce heat to medium high. DO NOT TOUCH OR MOVE STEAKS FOR NEXT 3 MINUTES. After 3 minutes, turn steaks over and immediately place in center rack of oven. Leave in oven 4 minutes for medium rare, 6 minutes for medium, or 8 minutes for well done.

While steaks are in oven, mix corn flour and Creole seasoning. Toss Onion Frits in flour; shake off excess flour, then deep-fry 3 to 4 minutes or until golden brown. Remove Onion Frits and drain; lightly salt while still warm. Remove steaks from the oven and plate. Spread one tablespoon of butter on each steak and top with Onion Frits. This method results in a steak that is still moist and tender even when well done, and does not have the harsh taste of a grill or open flame. Serves 2.

Porches Bread Pudding with Almond Sauce

This recipe has been featured in Mississippi Magazine *and was recently selected as one of the Top 20 Recipes in their 20th Anniversary Edition. Chris was filmed by Mississippi ETV making this recipe, and this segment is regularly shown.*

6 large eggs	1 quart half-and-half
1½ cups sugar	6 leftover dinner rolls
1½ teaspoons vanilla	(preferably Rich's
extract	frozen dinner rolls)
¼ teaspoon salt	

Preheat oven to 350°. Combine eggs and sugar. Whip until light yellow and sugar is thoroughly incorporated. Add vanilla, salt and half-and-half. Mix thoroughly. Pour into a greased 2-quart shallow glass casserole dish. Break leftover rolls into 4 or 5 pieces each and drop into mixture. Pat rolls down into mixture. Do not let sit too long. It is ready for the oven now. Bake for 35 to 45 minutes or until set. Remove from oven. Let cool 5 to 10 minutes. Slice into serving size and spread Almond Sauce over top.

ALMOND SAUCE:

1 stick butter	1 tablespoon flour
1 cup sugar	1½ teaspoons almond
½ cup canned	extract
evaporated milk	

Bring first four ingredients to a boil. Remove from heat and stir in almond extract.

Clark Creek Nature Area, Wilkinson County

The Pines Region

$\mathcal{F}$rom Civil War grave sites to ancient Native American grounds, from Mississippi's Giant House Party to an original Dentzel carousel, Mississippi tradition is alive and well in the Pines Region. Visit the birthplace of Pulitzer Prize-winning playwright Tennessee Williams which is now home to Colubmus' Welcome Center. While you're there, get directions to Friendship Cemetery and relive some Civil War history. Enjoy Mississippi State University's famous cheese in Starkville. Farther down the road in Philadelphia, join Mississippi's Giant House Party, the Neshoba County Fair, and visit the Mississippi Band of Choctaw Indians' reservation and resort. Learn about Meridian's history at the Jimmie Rodgers Museum and the Peavey Museum, then take a ride on an antique carousel. Make a piece of Mississippi tradition your own in the Pines Region.

The Pines Region Menu

The Pines Region Menu

COTTAGE TEA ROOM

109 East Washington Street
Aberdeen, MS 39730
662-369-1157

The Cottage Tea Room opened in March 1998 in a refurbished 1920s house by mother-daughter team, Sara Gardner and Susan Langford. Sara is a retired nurse and Susan has a degree in fashion merchandising, but both have a real love for cooking. The Tea Room has been featured in several area newspapers. Each year during the spring pilgrimage the Tea Room hosts "A Taste of Mississippi" dinner. They also offer full catering service. In February 2000 they opened "Greensleeves," an 1884 historic Victorian house which is utilized for specal events.

Tea Cakes

1 stick of margarine
  (Parkay recommended)
½ cup Crisco shortening
1 cup sugar
1 egg
2½ cups plain flour
½ teaspoon baking soda
½ teaspoon salt
Dash of vanilla

Cream margarine and shortening until blended; add sugar, creaming thoroughly. Add egg and mix well, then add flour mixed with baking soda and salt. Add vanilla and mix well. Form into small balls and place on well-greased cookie sheet, 3 across and 5 down. Take a glass that has a flat bottom and press on the dough to "grease" bottom, then dip into sugar. Flatten cookie with glass, and repeat until all cookies are flattened. Bake at 350° for no more than 10 minutes. They will continue to brown as they cool. Cool on paper towels. Makes about 60 of the most delicious tea cakes. Recipe by local resident Mrs. Betty Kennedy.

Walnut Torte

COOKIE:
3 cups all-purpose flour
¾ cup sugar
Pinch salt
1 cup butter, softened
1 egg

Mix dry ingredients; using electric mixer, cut in the butter and add egg, mixing well. Divide dough into 7 balls. Roll each ball into 9-inch circle. Invert 9-inch cake pan, grease and flour bottom, and place cookie circle on inverted pan; trim to fit. Bake at 350° for 10 to 12 minutes, until lightly browned. Cool slightly and remove from pan. They are very fragile, save broken pieces; they can still be stacked.

FILLING:
2 cups sour cream
1½ cups confectioners'
  sugar
2 cups chopped walnuts
1 teaspoon vanilla

Mix all of the above ingredients together.

GLAZE:
1 (8-ounce) jar of apricot preserves,
  processed in food processor until smooth

Stack Cookies with Filling between each, then drizzle top with Glaze, allowing it to drizzle over sides. Refrigerate 4 to 5 hours or overnight. Sprinkle with additional confectioners' sugar. To serve, top with whipped cream and glazed walnuts. Serves 12.

Fresh Apple Salad

1 (20-ounce) can pineapple tidbits in own juice	4 medium yellow delicious apples, peeled, cubed
½ cup self-rising flour	1 (8-ounce) carton whipped topping
¾ cup sugar	½ cup chopped pecans
¼ teaspoon salt	8 lettuce leaves
1 tablespoon butter (optional)	8 stemmed cherries

Drain pineapple and reserve juice. Blend flour, sugar, and salt and add to reserved juice, mixing well. Cook over medium heat, stirring constantly until thick and clear, and add butter, if desired. Cool slightly. While cooling, peel and cube apples and mix with pineapple. Mix with sauce and pour into casserole dish; cover with whipped topping. Sprinkle pecans on top, then cover with plastic wrap. This will keep several days in refrigerator. To serve, place on lettuce leaf and top with cherry. Serves 8 to 10.

Overnight Ham or Chicken Casserole

2 cans cream of mushroom soup	2 cups milk
1 can sliced water chestnuts	1 (8-ounce) package macaroni (uncooked)
2 cups chopped chicken or ham	1 teaspoon salt
1½ cups grated Cheddar cheese	1 chopped onion

Combine soup and milk, and mix well. Add remaining ingredients, stirring until well mixed. Pour into lightly greased casserole dish; cover with plastic wrap and refrigerate overnight. Bake at 325° for 1¼ hours or until hot and bubbly. You may add additional grated cheese during the last 10 minutes of baking. Garnish with fresh parsley and chopped pimento. Serves 8.

HARVEY'S

200 Main Street
Columbus, MS 39701
662-327-1639

Harvey's has additional locations in Tupelo and Starkville.

Harvey's Bourbon Pecan-Glazed Grouper

1 cup chopped pecans	4 ounces bourbon
4 tablespoons clarified butter	½ cup whipped butter
¼ cup brown sugar	4 tablespoons chives

TO PREPARE SAUCE:
Toast chopped pecans in dry skillet on medium heat for 3–4 minutes. Add clarified butter and brown sugar, and stir until sugar combines with butter, 2–3 minutes. Carefully (do not stand over skillet or you'll end up with a new hair-do!) add bourbon to pan and flame to burn off alcohol. Finish with whipped butter and chives off the heat. Allow butter to melt on its own. This will make the sauce thicken.

TO PREPARE GROUPER:

4- to 8-ounces grouper	Clarified butter
Buttermilk-egg wash	Olive oil

Portions which have been dipped buttermilk-egg wash may be deep-fried or pan sautéed in a mixture of clarified butter and olive oil. Yields 4 servings.

SERVING SUGGESTIONS:
Harvey's Bourbon Pecan-Glazed Grouper is great served with Creamy Grits or Garlic Mashed Potatoes (see recipes on following page).

Creamy Grits

1 cup heavy whipping cream
2 cups water
3 tablespoons cooking sherry
1 1/2 cups quick grits
3 tablespoons butter
Kosher salt and fresh black pepper to taste

Cook at slow boil, stirring constantly until thick (about 7 minutes). Let stand and allow to thicken more.

Garlic Mashed Potatoes

Mashed potatoes
Roasted garlic, puréed
Heavy whipping cream
Butter
Kosher salt and black pepper to taste

Prepare your favorite mashed potato recipe; add puréed roasted garlic, heavy whipping cream, butter, Kosher salt and fresh black pepper to taste.

Harvey's Broccoli Bites

If you have plastic or latex gloves, this is a good time to put them on.

1 bunch broccoli florets, minced
3/4 cup minced yellow onion
1 cup cooked, chopped bacon
2 tablespoons minced jalapeños
2 cups shredded mild Cheddar
2 cups shredded Monterey Jack
1 cup heavy whipping cream

Place all ingredients into a large mixing bowl and mix thoroughly with your hands. Form mixture into 1-ounce balls, and lay on sheet pan. Cover and refrigerate. Make a wet mixture of egg and buttermilk. Make seasoned flour (flour, salt, black pepper, garlic powder, and cayenne pepper). Heat oil in large pot to 350°. Be sure pot is deep (enough to prevent overflow). Roll prepared balls in seasoned flour, then wet mix, then seasoned flour again. Carefully drop into hot oil, in small batches. Cook until golden; remove and allow to drain on paper towels. Serve with honey mustard dressing for dipping. Yields 40 pieces.

Fettuccine Al Gameri

1 pound wide fettucine noodles
1 tablespoon salt (optional)
6 ounces light olive oil
2 tablespoons minced fresh garlic
1 cup diced green bell pepper
1 cup diced fresh Roma tomatoes
24 large shrimp, peeled and deveined
1/2 bunch fresh parsley, finely minced
1 cup fresh basil, cut into fine strands
Salt and freshly ground pepper to taste
Parmesan cheese (optional)

Boil the pasta with the salt, if desired, in rapidly boiling water until al dente (check package directions for recommended time). Prepare all the other ingredients before putting the pasta in the water. When the pasta is half cooked, place the olive oil in a large skillet over medium heat. When oil is hot, add the garlic, bell pepper and tomatoes to the skillet. Sauté gently for one minute, then add the shrimp. Toss the shrimp and vegetables in the pan for 2 or 3 minutes until the shrimp is just cooked through. Drain the pasta in a colander, and immediately place it into a large serving bowl. Add the parsley and basil to the skillet, and toss for 30 seconds. Season with the salt and pepper and give the pan one more toss. Pour the shrimp evenly over the pasta and top with freshly grated Parmesan cheese, if desired. Serve immediately.

Recipe by Chef John Wilson

Tennessee Williams' Birthplace
Columbus, Mississippi

Portobello Lasagna

RICOTTA FILLING:

1 pound ricotta cheese	1 teaspoon Italian spice
6 ounces (1 box) chopped spinach, squeezed	1 teaspoon Kosher salt
1 egg	½ teaspoon ground white pepper
¼ cup chopped fresh basil	1 teaspoon dried tarragon
2 tablespoons chopped fresh basil	1 teaspoon dried basil

Combine all ingredients well in stainless bowl with wire whip. Reserve under refrigeration until ready to use.

PORTOBELLO FILLING:

2 tablespoons butter	¼ cup chopped fresh basil
½ cup diced yellow onion	
2 tablespoons minced fresh garlic	2 teaspoons dried tarragon
¼ cup white wine	2 teaspoons Italian spice
1 tablespoon lemon juice	½ teaspoon ground white pepper
2 tablespoons minced fresh garlic	
¼ cup white wine	2 teaspoons Kosher salt
1 tablespoon lemon juice	4–5 portobello mushrooms, sliced
2 tablespoons chopped fresh parsley	

Melt butter in large skillet. Add onion and garlic. Sauté 5 minutes. Onions should be soft. Add white wine and lemon juice. Reduce over high heat 2 minutes. Add all spices, herbs and salt. Mix well. Add half of mushrooms, and mix gently with spatula; allow to cook down several minutes. Add rest of mushrooms. Cook until just done. Reserve under refrigeration, if not being used immediately.

LASAGNA ASSEMBLY:

1 pound lasagna noodles	4 tablespoons Parmesan cheese, divided
14 ounces marinara sauce, divided	
1 cup shredded mozzarella, divided	

Prepare your favorite marinara sauce recipe, or purchase a good quality sauce ready made. Cook lasagna noodles according to package directions. Rinse under cold water and reserve. Place 4 ounces of marinara in the bottom of a 3-quart casserole dish. Cover with 4

(continued)

(Portobello Lasagna continued)

lasagna strips. Add 4 ounces of marinara sauce, then top with ½ cup of shredded mozzarella; sprinkle with 2 tablespoons of Parmesan; top with 2 strips of lasagna. Cover sheets with 6 ounces marinara sauce. Cover with remaining ½ cup mozzarella and 2 tablespoons Parmesan. Bake in 350° oven for 25 minutes. Turn pan around and bake for 25 additional minutes. Let lasagna rest for at least 10 minutes before serving.

Recipe by Chef John Wilson

Shrimp and Grits

¼ cup olive oil	¼ teaspoon whole black peppercorns
2 ounces whole butter	
3 ounces chopped shallots	6 ounces chopped tomatoes
1½ ounces chopped celery	
1½ ounces chopped carrots	1½ ounces seafood base
	1 cup white wine
1 ounce chopped garlic	2 tablespoons sherry vinegar
1 small chipotle pepper, chopped	
	½ tablespoon granulated sugar
1 whole bay leaf	½ cup V8 vegetable juice
½ teaspoon whole fennel seed	1½ quarts water
	Cornstarch slurry, as needed
½ teaspoon dried thyme	
½ teaspoon crushed red pepper	6 ounces butter, cut into pats

Heat oil and butter in pan over high heat. Add shallots, celery, and carrots. Cook over medium-high heat until slightly browned. Add garlic and chipotle peppers. Cook for 4–5 minutes. Stir in spices, then add tomatoes and cook until softened. Whisk in seafood baste, then add wine, sherry vinegar, and sugar. Bring to a boil. Reduce heat and simmer for 8–10 minutes. Add V8 juice, and cook for 2–3 minutes. Add water. Bring to a boil. Reduce heat and simmer for 1 hour. Strain through china cap into another saucepan. Use a rubber scraper to push all the liquid out. Bring strained liquid to a boil. Thicken with cornstarch slurry. Remove from heat, and mount with butter. Yields 1 quart.

FOUR SEASONS
Catering and Eatery

307 North Jackson
Kosciusko, MS 39090
662-289-5244

**Linda Reynolds and Ceressa Sims
Co-owners**

Located one block off the north side of the town square, Four Seasons Catering and Eatery is a "small business"—not famous for anything in particular—but everyone brags on their cooking! The business began almost three years ago between two friends who had no money, just lots of encouragement from family and other friends. They offer everything from daily box lunches to full-service catering for wedding receptions or corporate events.

Ranch Pasta Salad

1 (16-ounce) package
  pasta
1/2 cup finely chopped
  celery
1/2 cup diced green
  bell pepper
1/4 cup diced red onion
1 small jar diced pimento,
  drained
1 small can English peas,
  drained
1 (12-ounce) package
  bacon, cooked, drained
  and crumbled
4 boiled eggs, thinly
  sliced and diced
2 teaspoons dried chives
Salt and pepper to taste
1 1/2 cups mayonnaise
1 package dry ranch
  buttermilk dressing

Cook pasta according to package directions. Drain and place in a large bowl. Add remaining ingredients, and mix well. Serve chilled. Serve 12.

Basil Bread

5 1/2 to 6 cups plain flour,
  divided
2 packages yeast
6 tablespoons sugar
1 tablespoon salt
2 cups warm water
1/4 cup margarine, melted
1/4 cup olive oil
1 cup fresh basil, chopped
1/2 cup grated Parmesan
  cheese

Mix 2 cups flour, yeast, sugar and salt in large mixing bowl. Add warm water and melted margarine. Beat with electric mixer, using bread hook, until smooth. Continue adding more flour to make a soft dough. Turn onto a floured surface and knead 8 to 10 minutes. Put into a greased bowl, cover and let rise until double in size. Remove dough from bowl to a lightly floured surface. Punch down and divide dough in half, making two flattened circles. Lightly spread olive oil over dough and then sprinkle chopped basil and Parmesan cheese on top of the olive oil. Roll up in jellyroll fashion, tucking the ends under. Place into two greased loaf pans and let rise until double in size. Bake at 400° for 30 to 35 minutes. Turn onto a cooling rack and rub the tops with margarine.

Roasted Pork Loin

1 (4 1/2- to 5-pound)
  boneless pork loin
3 teaspoons garlic powder
3 teaspoons salt
3 teaspoons black pepper
2 teaspoons dry mustard
2 teaspoons onion powder
2 teaspoon paprika
1/2 teaspoon cayenne
  pepper

Combine dry ingredients. Rub over entire loin. Place loin in a foil-lined pan. Bake, uncovered, at 350° for 2 1/4 to 2 3/4 hours or until inserted meat thermometer reads 160° to 170°. Let stand 10 minutes before slicing. Yields 12 to 15 servings.

J. D.'s Honey Mustard

1/2 gallon mayonnaise
2 cups Dijon mustard
1 (16-ounce) bottle honey
1/2 teaspoon onion juice
1/8 cup apple cider
  vinegar
1/2 cup olive oil

Combine all ingredients in a large mixing bowl, blending until smooth and creamy. Refrigerate in covered container. Yields approximately 12 cups.

OLD TRACE GRILL

719 Veteran's Memorial Drive
Kosciusko, MS 39090
662-289-2652

Cousin's Larry Pickle and Mike England own Old Trace Grill. Glenda Pickle manages the restaurant. Daughters Ginger and McNiell assist in the day-to-day operations. Old Trace Grill is best known for comfort food and homemade desserts—cooked the way Grandma prepared them, such as hamburger steak with grilled onions, smothered in gravy and made-to-order handmade burgers, just the way you like them! Homemade desserts prepared daily include coconut cake, banana pudding, chocolate pie, and coconut pie.

Potato Salad

$\frac{1}{2}$ large onion, chopped
6 large baking potatoes, chopped
$\frac{1}{2}$ large onion, finely chopped
1 cup pickle relish
$\frac{3}{4}$ teaspoon pepper
1 teaspoon salt
$1\frac{1}{2}$ cups mayonnaise
4 green onions, chopped
1 tablespoon chopped pimento

Cook onion and potatoes together in water to cover until barely tender. Drain. Mix potatoes and onions with the remaining ingredients while warm. Chill well.

Buttermilk Coconut Pie

$1\frac{1}{2}$ cups sugar
$\frac{1}{2}$ cup self-rising flour
$1\frac{1}{2}$ cups stick butter, melted
3 eggs, beaten
$\frac{1}{2}$ cup buttermilk
1 teaspoon vanilla
6 ounces coconut, frozen type
1 (9-inch) deep-dish pie shell, unbaked

Mix all ingredients well. Pour into unbaked pie shell. Bake for 10 minutes at 450°, then 35 minutes at 325°. Yields 1 pie.

Chili

1 pound ground beef
$\frac{1}{2}$ cup chopped onion
3 or 4 stalks celery, chopped
$\frac{1}{2}$ cup chopped ground pepper
$\frac{1}{2}$ teaspoon garlic salt
$1\frac{3}{4}$ cup (15 ounces) kidney beans, undrained
4 cups undrained tomatoes
$1\frac{1}{2}$ to $2\frac{1}{2}$ teaspoons salt
2 to 3 bay leaves

Brown meat and onion. Drain grease, then add remaining ingredients. Simmer covered 1 to 2 hours. Serve hot with cheese. Only 156 calories per 1-cup serving.

Chapel of Memories, Mississippi State University
Starkville, Mississippi

LAKE TIAK O'KHATA RESORT

213 Smyth Lake Road
Louisville, MS 39339
TOLL FREE 1-888-845-6151

Lake Tiak O'Khata means "Lake of the Pines" in the Choctaw Indian language.

Two sisters-in-law, Ruby and Catherine Smyth founded Lake Tiak O'Khata. With humble beginnings, the area has been transformed into the tranquil resort that it is now. The heritage at Lake Tiak O'Khata is strong in hospitality, warmth and deep concern for others.

The facilities include 10 dining rooms and a deck that overlooks the 100-acre lake.

Lake Tiak O'Khata has long been an establishment known far and wide for its savory buffet and menu selections. Their chefs specialize in traditional southern delicacies while continuously offering something delicious and different. Just the food makes it worth the trip.

Catfish Orleans

4 boneless catfish fillets
Lemon juice
1/2 teaspoon garlic salt
1/2 cup flour
1/2 cup butter, divided
1 cup heavy cream
Dash Tabasco sauce
1 teaspoon Worcestershire sauce
1/4 cup white wine
1/2 pound shrimp, boiled and peeled
Chopped parsley and lemon twists for garnish

Dip fish in lemon juice; sprinkle with garlic salt, then coat with flour. Melt 1/2 the butter in a cast iron skillet; brown fish on both sides until crisp. Place catfish in pan and put in 350° oven for 15 minutes. Add remaining 1/2 butter, cream, Tabasco sauce and Worcestershire sauce to pan drippings. Stir until heated, then add white wine. To serve, place catfish fillets on platter; top with boiled shrimp. Pour sauce over fish and shrimp and garnish with parsley flakes and lemon twists. Serves 4.

Easy Spaghetti Casserole

1/2 cup chopped green pepper
1/3 cup chopped onion
1 tablespoon margarine
1 (8-ounce) package cream cheese, cubed
1/4 cup milk
1 package spaghetti with meat
1 (3 1/2-ounce) can French-fried onions

Heat oven to 350°. Sauté vegetables in margarine until tender. Add cream cheese and milk, mixing until well blended. Prepare spaghetti as directed on package. Combine half of meat sauce with spaghetti. Place in 10x16-inch baking dish. Top with cream cheese mixture, then remaining meat sauce. Sprinkle with grated Parmesan cheese (usually included in prepared spaghetti box). Bake at 350° for 25 minutes. Top with fried onion rings and bake 5 minutes more. Serves 6 to 8.

Chicken Pot Pie

Salt and pepper
1½ pounds chicken
2 stalks celery
1 stick butter, divided
1 medium onion, chopped
3 cups of chicken broth (from chicken)
¾ cup milk
1 tablespoon flour

Salt and pepper chicken, using pepper generously. Boil in 2 quarts of water with celery stalks until chicken is done. Remove skin from chicken and cut in 1-inch pieces. In saucepan, melt ½ stick butter; add onion and sauté until clear. Add chicken broth (remove celery), milk, and flour. Cook until heated and slightly thickened.

PASTRY:
1 teaspoon salt
3 cups flour
1 cup butter
½ cup cold water

Add salt to flour. Using two knives or a pastry blender, cut butter into flour until particles are the size of peas. Sprinkle water over flour mixture. Mix with fork. Divide into two equal parts and roll onto lightly floured cloth.

Place layer of Pastry on bottom of 9x13-inch casserole dish; prick with fork. Add chicken, top with sauce, and place remaining Pastry on top. Dot with remaining butter. Bake at 400° until crust is golden brown.

Caramel Flan

1 can sweetened condensed milk
1 can evaporated milk
2 large eggs
6 egg yolks
1 cup sugar
1 tablespoon vanilla extract

Preheat oven to 375°. Combine all ingredients and mix in blender until smooth. Yields 1 large flan or 6 ramekins.

CARAMEL SAUCE:
1 cup granulated sugar
¼ cup water

In small pan over medium heat, stir sugar constantly with wooden spoon until lumps are gone and a light amber color is achieved, about 15 minutes.

When sauce is ready, immediately pour into ramekins or pan and coat interior. Sauce will harden immediately. Pour prepared custard mixture into the coated ramekins or pans and cook in water bath at 375° for 15 minutes. Then lower heat to 325° for an additional 20 minutes. If custard is browning, cover with foil. Cook flan until a knife inserted into center comes out clean. Allow to cool for several hours or overnight, then run knife around rim to release edges. Unmold onto serving plate.

WEIDMANN'S

210 22nd Avenue
Meridian, MS 39301
601-581-5770

Opened by Felix Weidmann in 1870, Weidmann's Restaurant was run by their family for 130 years. Weidmann's was purchased by a group of local investors, including hometown celebrity Sela Ward, and re-opened December 31, 2002, as a brand new restaurant with only the name remaining the same, offering Meridian the most unique and innovative dining experience. The menu varies nightly so you will enjoy new delectables with each visit.

Sesame Crusted Tuna

Make sesame mixture. Prepare the grill. Make sauce while grill is heating.

SESAME MIXTURE:

½ cup toasted white sesame seeds	½ teaspoon sesame oil
½ cup black sesame seeds	¼ cup pure olive oil
½ teaspoon minced garlic	2 tablespoons fresh lemon juice
½ teaspoon peeled, minced fresh gingerroot	2 tablespoons soy sauce
1 tablespoon minced fresh chives	1 stick (½ cup) plus 2 tablespoons cold, unsalted butter, cut into 10 pieces

Preheat oven to 375°. On a baking sheet, toast white sesame seeds until slightly golden and aromatic, approximately 5 to 10 minutes. In a bowl, stir together toasted sesame with remaining ingredients.

LEMON SOY BUTTER SAUCE:

1 cup white wine	1 stick (½ cup) plus
2 tablespoons fresh lemon juice	2 tablespoons cold unsalted butter, cut
¼ cup heavy cream	into 10 pieces
2 tablespoons soy sauce	

(continued)

(Sesame Crusted Tuna continued)

In a saucepan, bring wine and lemon juice to boil over high heat until reduced to ¼ to ⅛ cup or somewhat of a syrup consistency. Add cream and simmer, stirring occasionally, until reduced by half. Add soy and reduce heat to low. Whisk in butter, one piece at a time. Keep warm.

ROASTED RED PEPPER-GINGER OIL:

2 cups chopped fresh ginger	2 cups roasted red pepper puree
2 cups pure olive oil	

Add ginger to oil. Bring to boil. Steep 1 hour. Purée with red pepper.

LEMON SCALLION OIL:

2 cups pure olive oil	2 cups chopped
1 cup lemon juice	green onions

Purée ingredients and strain.

SESAME SOY OIL:

2 cups pure olive oil	1 cup soy sauce
1 tablespoon sesame oil	

Purée all ingredients.

6 (½ pound, 1-inch-thick) tuna steaks #1 sushi grade

PREPARE THE TUNA:

Coat both sides of each tuna steak with Sesame Mixture. Grill tuna 2 to 3 minutes per side for medium-rare fish.

Slice and serve over stir-fry vegetables with Lemon Soy Butter Sauce. Garnish with infused oils, pickled ginger and wasabi. Yields 6 servings.

Grilled Georgia Quail with Creamy Grits

8 semi-boneless quail
½ cup pure olive oil
1 tablespoon. chopped fresh garlic
2 tablespoons chopped fresh rosemary
Salt and pepper to taste

Combine all ingredients. Marinate up to 8 hours refrigerated. Cook quail to preferred doneness over high heat on char grill.

CREAMY GRITS:

½ pound unsalted butter
1 quart heavy cream
1 cup grits
1 tablespoon chicken glacé (or 1–2 Herb-Ox chicken bouillon cubes)

In heavy, nonreactive saucepan over moderate heat, melt butter in heavy cream. (Do not boil.) Add remaining ingredients. Cook, stirring constantly, until grits are done.

SAUCE:

2 to 3 ounces pancetta, julienned
¼ cup white wine
¾ cup reduced veal stock
2 tablespoons heavy cream
½ pound unsalted butter
½ teaspoon chicken glacé (or 1–2 Herb-Ox chicken bouillon cubes)
8 shiitake mushroom caps (very fresh), thinly sliced (approximately 2 ounces)
2 dozen sage leaves, chiffonnade

Reduce pancetta, stirring constantly, over moderate to high heat in a heavy-bottom, noncorrosive pan (stainless steel), approximately 3 minutes. Deglaze with white wine. Reduce by ⅔. Add veal stock reduction. Reduce by half, approximately 3 to 4 minutes. Add heavy cream. Reduce 1 minute. Whip in unsalted butter. Add chicken glacé or bouillon cubes, mushrooms and sage.

To serve, ladle Creamy Grits into 4 warm bowls. Place 2 quail on each and top with Sauce. Yields 4 servings.

Chocolate Pots De Crème

½ cup whole milk
3 ounces bittersweet chocolate
¾ cup heavy cream
3 egg yolks
⅓ cup sugar
Boiling water

Line baking pan large enough to hold 6 (½-cup) ramekins with parchment paper with 3 slits cut into it. Place ramekins in it on top of paper; set aside. Scald milk over high heat. Stir in chocolate. Remove from heat and add cream. Stir to blend. Set aside. Combine egg yolks and sugar in bowl. Do not allow foaming. Slowly pour in chocolate mixture, stirring constantly. Strain through fine mesh sieve. Let rest at room temperature for 1 hour. Preheat oven to 325°. Spoon off foam that has risen to the surface. Divide cream equally among the ramekins. Pour boiling water into the pan halfway up the sides of the ramekins. Cover loosely with foil, to prevent skins from forming. Bake until creams are just set at edges, but still trembling in center. Remove from pan and refrigerate from 2 to 24 hours. Serve well chilled without unmolding. Serves 6.

Waverly Plantation
West Point, Mississippi

PEARL RIVER RESORT

Silver Star Resort and Casino
Golden Moon Casino and Hotel

13541 Highway 16 West
Philadelphia, MS 39350
800-557-0711

Restaurants located on the grounds of Pearl River Resort:
Eclipse Restaurant
Galaxy Restaurant

Pearl River Resort is a development of the Mississippi Band of Choctaw Indians. In addition to the hotels, restaurants and casinos, Pearl River Resort's other amenities include Dancing Rabbit Golf Club, The Spa, Geyser Falls Water Theme Park, Startacular, Starcade Arcade plus numerous retail shops.

Tracy Castleman C.E.C., A.A.C.
Executive Chef
Golden Moon Casino and Hotel

Chef Castleman is Chef Grillardin for the Chaine des Rotisseurs and is a member of Euro Toques, the prestigious European Society of Chefs. He graduated from the California Culinary School in 1981.

He won 1st place in the Mississippi State Dessert Championship (1996); 4th place "Taste of Elegance" Award for the National Pork Producers Association in Washington, D.C.; 5th place in the salmon competition (1997) in New York City; and 4th place in beef competition in the National Chefs Championship in New York City (1998).

Scallops in Tequila, Citrus and Chile Dressing

1 pound Nantucket bay scallops, roughly diced
1 teaspoon minced fresh garlic
1 teaspoon minced fresh ginger
1 teaspoon lemon zest
¼ cup tequila
1 teaspoon hot pepper sauce
1 tablespoon honey
½ red bell pepper, minced
1 Serrano chile, minced
⅛ cup extra virgin olive oil
3 tablespoons roughly chopped fresh mint
4 tablespoons roughly chopped fresh cilantro
Salt and freshly ground pepper to taste

Clean muscle off scallops and reserve on ice in refrigerator until needed. Combine remaining ingredients to make marinade and add scallops 15 minutes before serving. Keep scallops in marinade in refrigerator until ready to serve. To serve, fill a glass bowl with crushed ice. Place shells on top of ice and fill with scallops and dressing. Garnish with seaweed and lime wedges. Yields 4 servings.

Recipe by Chef Peter Palisi,
Eclipse Restaurant at Golden Moon

Spicy Tuna Cones
with Ginger-Lime Dressing

SPICY TUNA:

3 tablespoons mayonnaise	2 tablespoons tamari
2 teaspoons Sriracha Hot Chili Sauce	2 tablespoons chopped pickled ginger
1/2 teaspoon sesame oil	2 teaspoons chopped scallions
2 teaspoons wasabi powder	8 ounces fresh sushi-grade tuna, small diced
2 teaspoons water	

In a small bowl, combine mayonnaise, chili sauce and sesame oil; set aside. In another small bowl combine wasabi powder and water; set aside for 5 minutes. Add tamari to wasabi mixture; blend well. In a medium bowl, combine mayonnaise mixture, wasabi mixture, chopped ginger, scallions and tuna. Cover with saran wrap and refrigerate until ready to use. Yields 10 ounces.

GINGER-LIME DRESSING:

3 ounces fresh-squeezed lime juice	2 cups mayonnaise
2 ounces chopped fresh gingerroot	1 cup coconut milk
2 ounces sesame oil	1 ounce red Thai curry paste
2 ounces rice wine vinegar	Salt and white pepper to taste
3 ounces mirin	

In a blender, combine all ingredients for dressing; blend until thick and creamy, then strain and set aside. Yields 4 cups.

SESAME CONES:

2 tablespoons sesame seeds	4 tablespoons unsalted butter
2 tablespoons black sesame seeds	4 ounces light corn syrup
1 1/2 teaspoons ground ginger	1 tablespoon miso paste
1/8 teaspoon salt	1 1/2 teaspoon sesame oil
	1/4 cup all-purpose flour, sifted

Heat oven to 350°. In a medium bowl, combine white and black sesame seeds, ground ginger, salt and pepper. In a medium skillet, heat butter and corn syrup until melted, but not boiling. Remove from heat, stirring constantly, then add sesame mixture and mix well. Using a nonstick baking mat or butter baking pans, drop spoons of 1-teaspoon batter well apart from each other onto baking pans. Bake until discs have browned slightly around edges, about 6 to 8 minutes.

(continued)

(Spicy Tuna with Ginger-Lime Dressing continued)

Remove from pan and form into cone shapes. Let cool until crisp. Yields 30 cones.

FINAL PLATE PRESENTATION:

2 teaspoons Spicy Tuna	1 teaspoon Orange Tobiko Roe
2 each Sesame Cones	
1/8 teaspoon finely minced fresh chives	.25 ounce Daikon Radish Sprout
1 ounce Ginger-Lime Dressing	

Place a teaspoon of Spicy Tuna into each Sesame Cone and sprinkle tuna with chives. Place spicy tuna cones on a square, white oriental appetizer plate. Spot the Ginger-Lime Dressing on opposite ends of plate and top sauce with Orange Tobiko Roe. Sprinkle plate with Daikon Radish Sprouts and serve immediately. Yields 1 serving.

Recipe by Chef Stafford T. Decambra,
Eclipse Restaurant at Golden Moon

Fresh Chilean Sea Bass
with Miso-Hot Sauce Glaze

8 miniature carrots	4 tablespoon hot pepper sauce
8 miniature zucchini	
8 miniature corn	4 tablespoons miso
8 fresh pencil asparagus	8 tablespoons sake
4 tablespoons olive oil	4 tablespoons sugar
Salt and freshly ground pepper	Fresh sea bass fillets

Preheat oven to 400°. In a small roasting pan, combine vegetables with olive oil, salt and pepper, and roast in oven for 45 minutes. Mix hot sauce, miso, sake and sugar until well combined. Set aside 1/4 of marinade for a sauce. Marinate sea bass in remaining marinade for 20 minutes. Remove sea bass from marinade and sear on each side for approximately 7 minutes per side. Discard used marinade. To serve, plate sea bass and pour some reserved marinade on top. Add roasted vegetables on side and serve. Yields 4 servings.

Recipe by Chef Tracy Castleman,
Galaxy Restaurant at Golden Moon Casino and

Lavender Crème Brûlée

2¼ cups heavy cream
½ cup sugar
1½ teaspoons fresh lavender blossoms, or generous ½ teaspoon of dried lavender
½ vanilla bean, split lengthwise
5 large egg yolks
8 teaspoons raw sugar

Preheat oven to 325°. Place cream, sugar and lavender in a medium saucepan. Scrape seeds from vanilla bean. Add bean. Bring to a simmer. Turn off heat. Cover and steep for 30 minutes. Strain through a fine sieve or cheesecloth. Return cream mixture back to a simmer. Remove bean pod. Beat egg yolks in a bowl until smooth. Gradually whip in cream mixture. Divide custard among 6 (6-ounce) ramekins or soufflé cups. Place cups in a large baking pan. Pour in enough hot water to come halfway up sides of cups. Bake until edges are set and 90% of custard jiggles, but is not too fluid, about 40 minutes. Remove from water bath and let cool at room temperature. Cover and refrigerate at least 5 hours or overnight.

Sprinkle 2 teaspoons of raw sugar evenly over each custard cup. Use a torch or your oven broiler to caramelize the sugar. Let stand for 10 minutes before serving. Garnish with candied violets or lavender, if desired.

Recipe by Chef David M. Paul,
Galaxy Restaurant at Golden Moon Casino

ANTHONY'S

116 West Main Street
West Point, MS 39773
662-494-0316

Carter Fraley
Owner

Chef Carter Fraley is a 1994 graduate of the University of Mississippi. He worked in an apprenticeship program at Oxford's City Grocery while enrolled at Ole Miss (1990-1994). Chef Carter worked 2 years at Old Waverly Golf Club before opening Anthony's in 1996.

Murff Row Carbonara Pasta

2 tablespoons diced chicken
2 tablespoons diced ham
2 tablespoons diced bacon
1 tablespoon diced tomato
1 tablespoon sliced mushroom
1 tablespoon sliced green onion
3 teaspoons bacon fat
2½ tablespoons white wine
1 cup quality Alfredo sauce
6 ounces cooked bow tie pasta
⅓ cup asiago cheese
Parsley

Mix first 6 ingredients; sauté in bacon fat in a medium skillet. Sauté until all are hot, then deglaze skillet with white wine. Add Alfredo sauce. Bring to a simmer, then add cooked bow tie pasta. Toss all together and add asiago cheese. Garnish with parsley.

Anthony's Bleu Cheese Stuffed Filet

STUFFING:

2 ounces heavy cream
3 tablespoons cream
  cheese
3 tablespoons fresh
  bleu cheese

1 tablespoon Parmesan
  cheese
1 teaspoon parsley
1 cup bread crumbs

Bring heavy cream to a boil, then add cream cheese, bleu cheese and Parmesan cheese. Heat until all the cheese is melted and incorporated. Add parsley and bread crumbs till nice and thick. Cool mixture until ready to stuff.

1 (8-ounce) beef
  tenderloin
$\frac{1}{3}$ cup sliced
  mushrooms
2 teaspoons butter

$\frac{1}{3}$ cup Marsala wine
1 green onion, sliced
  thin
$\frac{1}{4}$ cup heavy cream

Grill beef tenderloin to desired temperature, then cut a $\frac{1}{2}$-inch slit into top of filet and stuff with Stuffing. Sauté sliced mushrooms in butter, then deglaze with Marsala wine. Add green onion to sauce. Add heavy cream; reduce by half and pour over steak.

THE SAMPLE ROOM

103 Carrollton Avenue
Winona, MS 38967
662-283-2355

Lydia Chassaniol
Owner

Winona native Lydia Chassaniol believes that food is an edible art form. When the opportunity presented itself, Chassaniol combined her love of art and food, and opened The Sample Room in Winona in the former Special Treasures building. As past chairman of the Mississippi Arts Commission, Chassaniol said she had the opportunity to attend many seminars that stressed revitalizing downtown areas through arts and restaurants.

Lydia, a Winona High School and University of Mississippi graduate, catered wedding receptions and rehearsal dinners from her home kitchen from 1982 until 1995. She also served on the State Parole Board, and most recently, used her artistic skills as a designer for the John Richard Collection in Greenwood. Many students have studied art under Chassaniol. Many of their one-of-a-kind art pieces are on display in the restaurant.

The Sample Room is open for lunch Monday through Friday and for dinner Thursday, Friday and Saturday.

Ruby Pittman's Pimiento Cheese Spread

1 pound Cheddar cheese, shredded	Chopped pecans
1 pound mozzarella cheese, shredded	Diced pimiento, drained
	Garlic salt to taste
6 green onions, finely chopped	Sugar to taste
	Mayonnaise

Mix equal quantities of shredded Cheddar cheese and mozzarella cheese. Finely cut up green onions. (Ruby suggests about 6 onions for 2 pounds of cheese.) Add to the mix. Add chopped pecans and enough drained diced pimiento to give it good color. Sprinkle on garlic salt and sugar to taste. Mix in mayonnaise to make a good spreading consistency.

Miss Willie's Apple Cobbler

1 (#10) can (13 cups) sliced apples	2 teaspoons cinnamon
3 cups sugar	2 teaspoons vanilla
1 cup butter	1 cup water

Mix apples with sugar and butter. Set aside. Combine cinnamon, vanilla and water. Pour mixture over apples.

CRUST:

3 cups flour	1 cup milk
½ cup oil	Flour for sprinkling

Combine flour, oil and milk, and mix well. Sprinkle flour on rolling sheet and roll out to ¼ inch thick. Place half of crust in large, greased baking pan. Place in 350° oven and brown for 10 minutes. Remove from oven and cover with apple mixture. Top with a lattice of remaining crust. Return to oven for 50 to 60 minutes or until brown on top.

Mississippi Mud Cake

1 cup vegetable oil	1½ cups self-rising flour
⅓ cup cocoa	2 teaspoons vanilla
4 eggs	2 cups chopped nuts
1¾ cups sugar	

Mix together and bake in a greased oblong pan at 300°. Cover with small marshmallows when removed from oven.

ICING:

1½ sticks butter	⅓ cup cocoa
1 tablespoon vanilla	½ cup evaporated milk
1 box powered sugar	½ cup chopped nuts

Mix ingredients well. Do not cook. Pour over cake while it's still warm.

The Coastal Region

*M*iles and miles of scenic coastline along the Gulf of Mexico from Bay St. Louis to Ocean Springs lay claim to deluxe beach resorts, artists' colonies, fishing villages, and casinos. Take a closer look and you'll see that Bay St. Louis is home to the NASA John C. Stennis Space Center. Keesler Airforce Base, the largest electronics training center in the world, is found in Biloxi. Gulfport boasts the largest tropical fruit port in the Gulf, handling more than 500,000 tons of fruit annually. Travel north to Hattiesburg and visit the University of Southern Mississippi with its beautiful rose garden, then venture on to Laurel where the Laurel Historic District downtown has the greatest number of intact craftsmen architecture examples in the state of Mississippi.

The Coastal Region Menu

(continued)

The Coastal Region Menu

CASINO MAGIC

711 Casino Magic Drive
Bay St. Louis, MS 39520

Chef Troy Meacham

Chef Meacham is a native of the Mississippi Gulf Coast. His career has afforded him the opportunity to work in Louisiana and Mississippi side by side and under the tutelage of renowned chefs such as Joseph Barrale, Paul Prudhomme and John Folse. Among his other accomplishments, he represented the State of Louisiana in the 1992 International Culinary Olympics and at the Washington, D.C. Mardi Gras. Chef Meacham, after completing his apprenticeship in Mississippi, worked as Executive Chef at the Lafayette Louisiana Hilton and Towers. He has spent the last 10 years in the casino industry serving in positions from Executive Chef to Food and Beverage Director.

Crispy Cream Crab Cakes

Unlike Maryland crab cakes, these crab cakes are creamy when you cut into the crispy crust. Mississippi blue crabs are a flavorful staple in the cuisine of the Mississippi Gulf Coast.

4 cups milk, divided	½ cup Parmesan cheese
1 tablespoon butter	2 cups flour
2 tablespoons flour	Italian bread crumbs
1 pound claw crabmeat	1 cup cooking oil (your
2 whole eggs	choice)
Pinch nutmeg	

Scald 2 cups milk in a heavy saucepan over medium heat. Keep it warm over very low heat. Melt butter in a separate saucepan over low heat. When it's bubbling, add flour and whisk until it forms a golden

(continued)

(Crispy Cream Crab Cakes continued)

paste, about 3 to 4 minutes. Whisking constantly, add hot milk in a steady stream. Bring milk to a gentle simmer and continue to whisk until sauce thickens, about 10 minutes.

Add crabmeat and stir until crab is thoroughly mixed into sauce. Remove from heat and transfer into cool dish, then place into refrigerator. Chill for 1 hour. Sauce will thicken into thick paste. Use remaining milk and eggs to make egg wash. Remove crab and cream combination from refrigerator. Flour your hands. Using your hands, form crab and cream mixtures into 2-inch round patties, ¾ inch thick. Dredge patties in flour, then dip them into egg wash, then dredge them in bread crumbs. This should yield 12 patties. Preheat cooking oil in a frying pan. Place crab patties in frying pan and cook for approximately 3 minutes or until golden brown on each side. Yields 6 appetizers or 4 entrées. Place on a plate over a pool of Lemon Butter Cream and serve immediately.

LEMON BUTTER CREAM:

½ pint heavy whipping cream	1 ounce fresh lemon juice, at room temperature
½ pound unsalted, grade A butter	Salt to taste

Using a stainless steel, copper or glass pan (not aluminum), simmer cream on medium heat until it has evaporated to half of its original volume (reduced). Cut butter into small patties. Once cream has reduced, reduce heat to low and gradually add butter one patty at a time, while constantly stirring until the patty has melted, before adding the next patty. Once all of the butter has been incorporated into cream, add lemon juice and salt. Remove from heat and serve immediately or place in a thermos until serving time. Do not allow sauce to cool before serving.

Recipe by Chef Troy Meacham

Flounder Bienville

Mississippi is known for some of the best flounder in the world. Usually caught by spearing them with gigs, flounder is one of the most plentiful and delicate fish readily available on the Mississippi Gulf Coast. Locals go out when the moon is full, the tide is low, and the wind calm, and "gig" for flounder by lantern light.

¼ pound butter, divided	1 cup sliced scallions
1 pound lean smoked ham, cut in small cubes (not honey smoked; hickory would be good)	2 cups cooking oil
	2 eggs
	1 cup buttermilk
2 pounds small shrimp, peeled (no smaller than 110 count per pound)	2 cups corn flour or regular all-purpose flour
	1 cup cornmeal
1 pint heavy cream	2 tablespoons Creole seasoning blend
¼ cup fresh, grated Parmesan cheese	12 (3- to 5-ounce) flounder fillets

In a sauté pan on medium heat, place half the butter. Once butter has melted, add ham. Cook ham until it is browned on each side. Add shrimp and cream. Bring to a simmer. Once shrimp are cooked (test by taking one out and cutting it open; it should be opaque through and through, not translucent), gradually add Parmesan cheese. Once cheese has melted, add scallions. Keep sauce warm while you begin to cook flounder.

Heat oil in a frying pan. Mix eggs and buttermilk. In a separate bowl, mix flour, cornmeal, and seasoning. Dip flounder in milk and egg mixture, then dredge it in seasoned flour mixture. Place breaded fillet directly into hot oil (375°). Keeping heat at this temperature, cook fish on one side about 3 minutes (more or less depending on thickness of fillets) until browned and crispy. Turn fish only once. When fillets are done, drain on paper towels to absorb excess grease.

Gradually add remaining butter to sauce while constantly stirring, leaving a shiny glaze to the sauce; all the butter should be incorporated. Place flounder on serving plate and spoon equal amounts of sauce over each serving. (You can spoon this same sauce over half shell raw oysters and bake in the oven until bubbling and browned for the classic Oysters Bienville.) Yields 6 servings.

Recipe by Chef Troy Meacham

Banana Praline Bread Pudding

This is a perfect dessert for the Mississippi Gulf Coast. One reason is that pecan orchards abound, and Mississippi pecans are some of the best in the world. Two, the Port of Gulfport is the largest entry point for bananas in the United States. Good bananas are always available.

BREAD PUDDING:

1 quart milk	2 teaspoons ground cinnamon
4 whole eggs	
1⅓ cups granulated sugar	1 gallon stale bread cubes
2 teaspoons vanilla extract	1 quart cubed ripe bananas
	¼ cup unsalted butter

Scald milk. Combine milk with eggs, sugar, vanilla and cinnamon. Combine bread and bananas. Pour milk mixture over bread. Dot butter on top of pudding and bake, covered, in water bath at 375° for approximately one hour or until well set.

PRALINE SAUCE:

2 cups pecan halves	¼ cup strong coffee
½ cup butter or margarine	2 tablespoons bourbon whiskey
1 cup heavy cream	
1 cup firmly packed dark brown sugar	

Spread pecans in a small sheet pan and roast in oven. Melt butter in pan over low heat. Add pecans and cook 5 minutes. Add cream, sugar and coffee; slowly bring to a boil, then simmer 5 minutes. Serve warm over Bread Pudding. Serves 12.

Recipe by Chef Troy Meacham

TRAPANI'S EATERY

116 North Beach Boulevard
Bay St. Louis, MS 39520
228-467-8570

**Anthony Trapani, III
Owner**

Established in 1994. Awards: First Place four years in a row in the Annual Red Beans and Rice Cook-off sponsored by the American Cancer Society; Top Bean Award—Judges Choice Award for the best restaurant in Bay St. Louis; 1999 Celtic Festival Culinary Competition—First place People's Choice Award and Second Place Judges' Choice Award, and 2000 First place People's Choice Award. Mentioned in the "Best of the Coast" article in *Southern Living* as having the best po-boys on the Coast.

Grilled Chicken Pasta

2 small onions, minced	Garlic and butter to taste
12 small mushrooms, sliced	Angel hair pasta
3 bell peppers, chopped	4 boneless chicken breasts
10 leaves fresh basil, chopped	Salt and pepper to taste
	Parmesan cheese

Sauté onions, mushrooms, bell peppers, and basil in garlic and butter. Cook until tender.

Prepare angel hair or any pasta you prefer. Grill chicken breasts with Flash Marinade consisting of 1 part soy, ¼ part hot sauce, ¼ part lemon juice and 1 part water. Heat pasta and set on all 4 plates. Place grilled chicken breast atop pasta with no butter or cheese.

Set all 4 plates on table and equally distribute sautéed vegetables on platter. Season to taste.

Save butter in skillet and equally distribute on top of all 4 plates, then sprinkle Parmesan cheese on top and serve. Serves 4.

Stuffed Manicotti with Alfredo Sauce

FILLING:

2 pounds ground lean sirloin, chopped	Garlic to taste
2 onions, chopped	Thyme to taste
1 pound fresh spinach	Oregano to taste
15 leaves fresh basil, chopped	Salt to taste

Thoroughly mix all of the above ingredients; sauté and brown. Drain fat.

½ cup Parmesan cheese	1 pound Ricotta cheese
½ cup Romano cheese	6 manicotti shells

Mix cheeses with Filling mixture. Boil manicotti and stuff. Heat stuffed pasta in microwave. Serve with Alfredo Sauce.

ALFREDO SAUCE:

Simmer garlic and salted butter in skillet. Add onions, salt and pepper (more pepper than salt). Add flour to butter mixture and whip with whisk. Add milk to desired consistency. Sprinkle Parmesan on Alfredo to give cheesy flavor. Garnish with parsley. Serves 6.

BEAU RIVAGE

875 Beach Boulevard
Biloxi, MS 39530
888-567-6667

Restaurants located on the grounds of Beau Rivage:
Anna Mae
Café Jardin
Coast Brewing Company
La Cucina
Memphis Q
Port House

Maki Sushi

CRUNCH ROLL (4 ROLLS):

2 sheets Sushi Seaweed (Nori)	8 ounces fried tempura batter
2 cups Sushi Rice	4 ounces Spicy Mayo
8 ounces crabmeat, drained	4 ounces imitation fish eggs (masago)

OR

SPICY TUNA ROLL (4 ROLLS):

2 sheets Sushi Seaweed (Nori)	4 ounces minced green onions
2 cups Sushi Rice	4 ounces chili oil
16 ounces chopped tuna (raw)	1 teaspoon chili powder

TOOLS:

Bamboo sushi mat	Cold water, small bowl
Knife	Plastic food wrap

It is important to keep hands damp and cool so the rice won't stick to your hands. Lay bamboo mat flat; place ½ nori sheet in center, long side facing you. Dip fingers in cold water. Pick up ½ cup sushi rice, forming it into an oval shape. Place it in center of seaweed.

(continued)

(Maki Sushi continued)

Spread rice evenly, starting from center and working your way towards the edges. Sprinkle masago or chili powder on rice, depending on whether you are making a crunch roll or a spicy tuna roll. Use a spoon to spread as needed. Place a piece of plastic wrap a little bigger than seaweed on top of rice. Flip it over so that plastic ends up on top of sushi mat. Place remaining mixed ingredients on seaweed. If it is the Crunchy Roll, mix Spicy Mayo, crabmeat and batter together and divide resulting mix in 4 parts, 1 for each roll. If you are making the Spicy Tuna Roll, mix green onions, chili oil and chopped tuna. Make sure filling is spread evenly. Holding on to the plastic wrap and mat closest to you, roll sushi away from you until ends meet. Push down firmly. Then push back again onto roll, forming a tighter roll. Unwrap roll and cut into 4 pieces. Serve with Japanese horseradish (wasabi), pickled ginger (gari) and soy sauce (shoyu). Serves 8 people (3 pieces of each roll per person).

SUSHI RICE:

2 cups Japanese sushi rice	2 tablespoons sugar
2 cups water	2 teaspoons salt
4 tablespoons rice vinegar	

Rinse and drain rice. Cook rice and water in rice cooker or 25 minutes on stove at medium-high heat. Do not uncover. Leave rice covered for 10 more minutes. In separate bowl, mix vinegar, sugar and salt until dissolved. Place rice in large bowl and add seasoning mixture. Allow rice to cool to body temperature before using. Makes 4 cups.

SPICY MAYO:

Mayonnaise	Sesame oil
Chili oil	

In a bowl, mix mayonnaise, chili oil and sesame oil until desired degree of spiciness is reached.

TEMPURA BATTER:
Sprinkle previously mixed tempura batter in hot oil to fry. Drain and cool.

Recipe from Anna Mae, Beau Rivage

Shrimp and Crawfish Étouffée

ÉTOUFFÉE SAUCE:

4 ounces butter	1 tablespoon granulated
10 ounces finely diced	garlic
celery	1 tablespoon iodized salt
12 ounces finely diced	4 ounces all-purpose
yellow onion	flour and 4 tablespoons
4 ounces finely diced	paprika (blended
green pepper	together)
1 tablespoon whole	½ gallon crab or
leaf thyme	shrimp stock
1 tablespoon whole	4 ounces tasso sausage,
leaf oregano	shredded
1 teaspoon ground	8 ounces all-purpose flour,
black pepper	and 8 ounces whole
1 teaspoon cayenne	butter (cook together
pepper	until dark brown roux)
1 teaspoon white	
pepper	

Melt butter and sauté vegetables with herbs, peppers, garlic and salt until vegetables are broken down. Add flour/paprika blend, mixing well to form a roux and cook, stirring constantly, for 3 minutes. Add stock, whipping hard to blend roux with stock until smooth. Lower heat and let simmer for 30 minutes, whipping frequently to keep liquid smooth. Cook equal parts of flour and butter over low heat until dark mahogany color is achieved; set aside. Stir in shredded tasso and blend in cooled dark roux, whipping continuously, then low simmer for another 30 minutes, stirring occasionally.

4 ounces olive oil	8 garlic cloves, chopped
1 pound (31–35 count)	1 bunch green onions,
shrimp	chopped
2 pounds crawfish tails	64 ounces Étouffée Sauce

Heat olive oil in large pot and sauté shrimp, crawfish, garlic and green onions until shrimp are pink. Add Étouffée Sauce; stir well and simmer approximately 20 minutes. Serve with hot white rice and garlic bread. Serves 8.

Recipe from Café Jardin at Beau Rivage

Deviled Crab Louis

DEVILED LOUIS DRESSING:

1 cup salsa (your favorite)	2 tablespoons fresh
1 tablespoon minced	lemon juice
chipotle peppers	1 teaspoon sugar
2 cups mayonnaise	¼ cup water or milk

Mix in a blender all the items except mayonnaise until smooth. Pour into a bowl and stir in mayonnaise.

2 large heads romaine	2 pounds jumbo lump
lettuce (reserve a	crab, divided
few leaves)	8 hard-boiled eggs,
1 head iceberg lettuce	cut in quarters
4 red endive, separated	8 Roma tomatoes,
in leaves	cut in quarters
½ bunch parsley,	1 bunch chives, chopped
chopped	Lemon wedges

Shred one romaine and iceberg lettuce. Line each salad bowl with romaine leaves and 5 red endive leaves. Mix shredded romaine, iceberg and chopped parsley with enough Deviled Louis Dressing to bind. Place in center of endive star. Place 4 ounces of picked jumbo lump crab on shredded lettuce. Alternate hard-boiled egg quarters and tomatoes around endive star. Coat crab with 1 tablespoon of Deviled Louis Dressing and sprinkle chopped chives around. Garnish with lemon wedges. Serves 8.

Recipe from Café Jardin at Beau Rivage

Blackened Snapper with Crawfish and Artichoke Cream Sauce

6 ounces Cajun blackening seasoning	4 ounces butter
2 (8-ounce) red snapper fillets	

Lay out Cajun seasoning in a plate. Place fish onto seasoning and coat both sides. Melt butter in a cast-iron skillet. Once butter is hot, place snapper skin-side-up into skillet. Sear until seasoning turns black, about 2 minutes. Flip and repeat. Serves 2.

CRAWFISH AND ARTICHOKE CREAM SAUCE:

2 ounces butter	1/2 cup artichoke hearts
2 shallots, diced	1/4 pound crawfish tails
1 bunch Italian flat-leaf parsley, chopped, divided	1 cup white wine
	1/2 quart heavy whipping cream
1 teaspoon minced garlic	5 nice leaves basil
Salt	1 sprig rosemary, finely chopped
Pepper	
Crushed red pepper	

Melt butter in sauté pan. Add shallots and half of your parsley; cook until shallots are translucent. Add garlic and cook until starting to turn golden brown. Add a pinch of each: salt, pepper and crushed red pepper. Add artichokes and crawfish tails; toss and heat through. Add white wine and reduce by half. Add heavy cream and reduce by half. Stir in the rest of your parsley, the basil, and the rosemary. Serve with blackened snapper. Enjoy.

Recipe from Coast Brewing Company, Beau Rivage

Macadamia Encrusted Mahi Mahi

MANGO CHILI BUTTER:

1 pound butter, softened	$\frac{1}{4}$ cup chili powder
1 mango, diced	1 teaspoon salt

Combine all ingredients in a mixing bowl and whip until fluffy. Roll mixture into logs in parchment paper or plastic wrap and freeze.

SPOON BREAD:

$\frac{1}{2}$ quart polenta	$\frac{1}{4}$ pound butter
2 quarts water	$\frac{1}{2}$ quart jalapeños, chopped
1 quart heavy cream	
1 pound Pepper Jack cheese, grated	Salt and pepper

Combine polenta, water and cream into a large pot. Cook on high heat until mixture starts to boil, then reduce to medium heat. Stir continuously to avoid scorching. Let mixture cook until it becomes a thick consistency. Turn off the heat and stir in butter, cheese and jalapeños. Season to taste. Pour mixture into a 2-inch half pan and cover with foil. Bake in a preheated 300° oven for $1\frac{1}{2}$ hours. Let stand for 15 minutes before serving, or chill for the next day.

SPINACH:

1 teaspoon butter	$1\frac{1}{2}$ pounds cleaned, fresh spinach
1 teaspoon chopped garlic	
	Salt and pepper

Melt butter in a hot pan and add garlic. When garlic begins to brown, add spinach, salt and pepper. Toss until wilted.

MANGO CHILI BUTTER:

4 teaspoons butter	Salt and pepper
1 cup bread crumbs	8 to 10 ounces
2 cups crushed macadamia nuts	Mahi Mahi fillets

Place butter in a hot pan and let melt. Combine bread crumbs, macadamias, salt and pepper to taste, then roll fish in crumbs. Carefully place encrusted fish into hot pan and brown on both sides. Place browned fish on sheet pan and finish in a 500° oven for about 5 minutes.

(continued)

(Macadamia Encrusted Mahi Mahi continued)

GARNISH:

1 flour tortilla   **1 green onion**

Cut flour tortilla into very thin strips and fry in vegetable oil until crispy. Chop green onion.

To serve, cut Spoon Bread into 8 pieces. Arrange each piece in the center of your plates. Top bread with Spinach. Place fish on top of Spinach. Take Mango Chili Butter from freezer and slice into ¼-inch-thick pieces and place 2 on each fish. Top all with fried tortilla and sprinkle with green onion. Serve and enjoy! Serves 8.

Recipe from Coast Brewing Company, Beau Rivage

Caponata

1 cup olive oil
1 large onion, diced
4 tablespoons chopped garlic
1 teaspoon crushed red pepper flakes
2 eggplants, diced
1 tablespoon sugar
1 teaspoon ground cinnamon
½ teaspoon dried thyme
¾ cup tomato sauce
⅓ cup balsamic vinegar
Salt and pepper to taste

Heat olive oil in a large pan. Add onion, garlic and red pepper flakes and heat 4 to 5 minutes until soft. Add eggplants, sugar, cinnamon and cook 5 more minutes, stirring often. Add thyme, tomato sauce and vinegar and bring to a boil. Lower heat and simmer for 5 minutes. Season with salt and pepper. Cool on sheet pans and serve. Serves 8.

Recipe from La Cucina, Beau Rivage

Penne Con Pollo

2 tablespoons extra virgin olive oil
24 ounces boneless, skinless chicken breasts, cut into ½-inch strips
2 cloves fresh garlic, minced
2 tablespoons Kosher salt
2 tablespoons black pepper
8 ounces marinated artichokes
6 ounces roasted red bell peppers
6 ounces cannellini beans
12 ounces chicken broth
2 sprigs fresh basil
2 pounds penne pasta
10 ounces Parmesan Reggiano cheese
1 ounce unsalted butter

Place a large pot of salted water on high heat and bring to a boil. Place a medium-size pot on high heat. Add olive oil. When oil is hot, sauté chicken and garlic, then season with salt and pepper. When chicken is cooked, add artichokes, peppers, beans, broth, and basil; bring to a boil. Place pasta into boiling water and cook 8 to 10 minutes or until tender. Cook sauce for 3 to 4 minutes; slowly add cheese and butter. Season to taste. Drain pasta (do not rinse) and add to sauce; mix together. Serve with fresh grated Parmesan cheese. Serves 8.

Recipe from La Cucina, Beau Rivage

Father Ryan House
Biloxi, Mississippi

Fried Green Tomatoes with a Crawfish Cream

FRIED TOMATOES:

4 green tomatoes, sliced ¼ inch thick	1 quart buttermilk
	4 cups cornmeal

Soak tomatoes in buttermilk overnight.

Heat oil to 350°. Take tomatoes out of buttermilk and place into cornmeal. Coat tomatoes well in cornmeal. Place tomatoes in deep fryer and fry until golden brown. Place tomatoes on plate and pour Crawfish Cream directly on top.

CRAWFISH CREAM:

¼ cup chopped onion	1 pound crawfish tails
2 cloves garlic, minced	Salt and pepper to taste
4 tablespoons butter	1 teaspoon Tabasco sauce
4 tablespoons flour	1 teaspoon Worcestershire sauce
3 cups heavy cream	

Sweat onion and garlic in butter, not browning them. Whisk in flour and cook 5 or 6 minutes, continuously stirring. Once roux is cooked, slowly whip in heavy cream (should be smooth and creamy). Add crawfish tails and juice from the bag and cook a few more minutes. Season with salt, pepper, Tabasco sauce and Worcestershire sauce.

Recipe from Memphis Q, Beau Rivage

Smokehouse Onion Soup

6 yellow onions, cut in half and sliced ¼ inch thick	2 teaspoons chopped fresh oregano
1 leek, white part only, sliced thin	1 pound smoked Boston butt
1 bunch scallions, sliced	1 loaf crusty bread, sliced ¼ inch thick and toasted
2 cloves garlic, chopped	8 slices provolone cheese
¼ cup Jack Daniel's bourbon	Salt and fresh pepper to taste
2 quarts beef stock	
2 quarts chicken stock	

In a hot skillet, caramelize onions, leek and scallions. Once onions are caramelized, add garlic and let it cook for 3 minutes. Deglaze with Jack Daniel's bourbon, scraping the bottom of pan to release all the flavors. Reduce alcohol by half, then add beef and chicken stock. Add oregano and bring to a simmer for about 45 minutes. Add pulled, smoked Boston butt and heat through. Ladle into soup crocks; add a slice of bread, then a slice of provolone and broil until cheese is melted.

Recipe from Memphis Q, Beau Rivage

Beauvoir, Jefferson Davis Home
Biloxi, Mississippi

Crab Cakes

1 small red onion
1 small red bell pepper
1 pound crabmeat
  (works well with jumbo
  lump blue crab)
1 cup bread crumbs
1 tablespoon garlic and
  chili sauce
¼ cup sherry wine
  vinegar
2 tablespoons capers
¼ cup whole-grain
  mustard
½ cup mayonnaise
Butter

Dice red onion and bell pepper very small. Mix with crab and bread crumbs. In a blender, purée garlic and chili sauce, vinegar, capers and mustard until smooth. In a bowl, mix this with mayonnaise until smooth. Add all of this sauce (except for 4 tablespoons) to crab, bread crumbs, pepper and onions. Mold into crab cakes (4 to 8, depending on size needed) and pan-sauté in butter over medium heat until golden brown and hot through. Garnish with leftover sauce and any excess diced bell peppers.

Recipe from Port House, Beau Rivage

Lobster Imperial

1 cup fresh corn
1 medium-size russet or
  Yukon Gold potato
4 cups water
1 shallot
3 tablespoons unsalted
  butter
1 pound lobster meat
2 tablespoons white wine
  or sherry wine
½ pint heavy whipping
  cream
Pinch Kosher salt
Pinch fresh-cracked
  black pepper
½ teaspoon fresh
  rosemary
1 lemon
1 cup bread crumbs
  (pale), divided
2 tablespoons Parmesan
  cheese

Roast corn in a 325° oven on a nonstick pan for 25 minutes, stirring every 5 minutes until golden brown. Peel and dice potato ¼ inch. Boil water and add potatoes for 6 minutes. Strain and cool potatoes; save for later. Dice shallot fine. Dice lobster into ½-inch pieces. Over medium-high heat in a nonstick pan, melt butter. Add shallot and let cook for about 20 seconds or until clear. Add diced lobster meat and sauté for 1 minute. Add sherry or white wine. Add heavy cream. Reduce heat to medium and let simmer for 5 minutes. Remove from heat and add potatoes, corn, salt, pepper, rosemary, juice from half a lemon, and ½ cup bread crumbs. Stir gently and scoop into oven-friendly dish or dishes. Top with remaining bread crumbs and Parmesan cheese. Bake in 400° oven for 10 minutes or until brown. Garnish with remaining ½ lemon. Serves 4.

Recipe from Port House, Beau Rivage

GRAND CASINO
Biloxi

265 Beach Boulevard
Biloxi, MS 39530
1-800-WIN-2WIN (946-2946)

Restaurants located on the grounds of Grand Casino Biloxi:
Murano's
The Sushi Bar

Murano's offers classic Italian favorites and contemporary treasures. It overlooks the beautiful Mississippi Gulf of Mexico and historic Deer Island. Murano's is open for dinner seven days a week and offers upscale service and food at a price that only a casino could offer.

Sushi is the latest craze to enter the Mississippi Gulf Coast, and Grand Casino answered this craze by adding The Sushi Bar. With a nontraditional theme, The Sushi Bar highlights coast cuisine by serving favorites such as blackened shrimp rolls, soft-shell crab rolls and a fresh variety of fish such as red snapper, lemon fish, yellowfin tuna and amberjack caught in our own Gulf of Mexico. Innovative creations from the chef also add to this unique dining experience.

Matthew Meadows C.E.C.
Executive Chef and
Food and Beverage Director

Born in Amsterdam, Holland, Chef Meadows has been working in Mississippi Gulf Coast area kitchens for 20 years. He currently oversees all restaurant operations in the Biloxi Grand Casino. He is the past president of the local American Culinary Federation. He is also an instructor at the University of Southern Mississippi's Culinary Academy in Long Beach. Chef Meadows has won numerous awards in culinary competitions and ice-carving events. He recently received a master's degree from the University of Southern Mississippi.

Chef David Crabtree

Chef Crabtree is a New Orleans-trained chef who has won over 25 medals in food competitions over his 26-year career. He served as an apprentice under renowned chefs William Vrazel, Emeril Lagasse and Gerard Maras and is one of the founding members of the Mississippi Gulf Coast Chapter of the American Culinary Federation. Chef Crabtree is also an adjunct culinary instructor at the University of Southern Mississippi.

He resides in Saucier with his wife Mary, daughter Chantelle, and son Troy. He believes his greatest influence comes from his mother's cooking, Verda Saucier Crabtree.

Chef Joe Randolph C.S.C.

Chef Randolph was born and raised on the Mississippi Gulf Coast. He graduated from the Culinary Academy at the University of Southern Mississippi with honors. Chef Randolph captured top honors in the Mississippi Gulf Coast Culinary Classic with his Royal Red Stuffed Shrimp winning him a gold and best of show! He also won 2nd place in the shrimp festival cook off, 2nd place in the gumbo cook off and a place in the annual ice-carving competition.

Chicken Oscar

6 ounces free-range chicken breast without skin, scaloppine
2 ounces clarified butter
1 ounce seasoned flour
4 asparagus spears, blanched
1 each artichoke heart, quartered
2 ounces blue crab
Splash of white wine
2 ounces Hollandaise sauce
1 teaspoon finely chopped parsley

Lightly pound chicken between two pieces of plastic wrap. Heat clarified butter in a skillet to medium heat. Dredge chicken in seasoned flour and shake off excess. Sauté in skillet for 3 minutes on each side until light brown and crisp. Add asparagus, artichokes and crab to the skillet; toss to warm. Splash in white wine to deglaze. Remove chicken cutlets and place on plate. Top with asparagus, artichokes, crab, and Hollandaise sauce. Garnish with parsley. Serves 1.

Recipe by Chef Matthew Meadows,
Grand Casino Biloxi

Orzo and Fried Angel Hair Pancetta Soup

1 pint orzo pasta
1 tablespoon vegetable oil
$\frac{1}{8}$ cup diced carrot
$\frac{1}{8}$ cup seeded, chopped tomato
$\frac{1}{4}$ teaspoon diced red pepper
$\frac{1}{8}$ cup minced shallots
2 cups chopped cooked Italian sausage
$\frac{1}{2}$ tablespoon thyme
$\frac{1}{4}$ cup Parmesan cheese
1 quart chicken stock
2 cups heavy cream
$\frac{1}{4}$ cup blond roux
1 cup pancetta ham, julienne

Boil orzo in salted water briefly for 8 to 12 minutes or until al dente. Set aside and hold. In soup pot add oil, carrot, tomato, red pepper and shallots. Sweat briefly. Add sausage, thyme, cheese, stock and cream and bring to a simmer. Lightly thicken with roux and allow to simmer briefly. Julienne pancetta and fry until crispy. Add orzo to soup and bring to a boil; serve topped with crispy pancetta ham.

Recipe by Chef David Crabtree,
Murano's at Grand Casino Biloxi

Butternut Squash Cheesecake

CRUST:
2 cups ground pecans
1 egg white
1 tablespoon butter
$\frac{1}{4}$ cup sugar
1 teaspoon cinnamon

Combine all ingredients loosely with a fork. Coat a springform pan with nonstick spray and place crumbs in bottom of pan, patting them down evenly with back of a spoon.

FILLING:
2 pounds cream cheese
2 cups cooked, mashed butternut squash
4 ounces heavy cream
4 ounces dark corn syrup
1 tablespoon cornstarch
6 eggs
1 teaspoon grated gingerroot
1 teaspoon salt

Let cream cheese soften or thaw carefully in microwave. Preheat oven to 325°. Place cream cheese in mixing bowl and whip to creamy with the paddle attachment. Add remaining ingredients and blend until fully incorporated. Pour into pan. Set pan into 1-inch water bath. Place in oven and bake for 45 minutes or until set. Chill cheesecake completely before cutting. Garnish with whipped cream and chopped pecans. Yields 16 servings.

Recipe by Chef Matthew Meadows,
Grand Casino Biloxi

Stuffed Royal Red Shrimp

Deepwater royal red shrimp stuffed with an Italian sausage stuffing, deep-fried, served with grilled potato salad, marinara sauce and seafood bordelaise sauce.

MARINARA:

2 tablespoons butter	1/4 cup dark brown sugar
8 Roma tomatoes, peeled, seeded, chopped	1 cup beef stock
1 large onion, chopped	1/4 cup tomato paste
2 tablespoons Italian seasoning	

In a sauté pan, heat butter; add tomatoes, onion and seasoning. Cook until tomatoes break down and onion is tender. Remove to food processor; add sugar, stock and paste. Blend until well puréed. Return to pan and simmer until thickened. Keep warm for later use.

SEAFOOD BORDELAISE BLANC:

4 cups white wine	1/2 teaspoon black pepper
4 ounces minced shallots	1 cup shrimp shells
1 bay leaf	4 cups heavy cream
2 sprigs lemon thyme	2 ounces butter

In a sauté pan, add wine, shallots, bay leaf, thyme, pepper and shrimp shells. Reduce by three fourths. Add heavy cream and reduce until slightly thickened. Strain through a chinois and finish with butter. Keep warm for later use.

GRILLED POTATO SALAD:

2 cups rice wine vinegar	5 yellow squash, sliced long ways, 2 inches long
4 tablespoons Dijon mustard	5 zucchini, sliced long ways, 2 inches long
1/2 teaspoon salt	5 red bell peppers, roasted, peeled, julienne
1/2 teaspoon pepper	
1 cup olive oil	
1/2 cup chiffonnade fresh basil	1 purple onion, julienne, sautéed
20 small red potatoes, sliced	

In a mixing bowl, place vinegar, mustard, salt and pepper. While whisking vigorously, slowly pour in oil in a small stream until all oil is incorporated and an emulsion has formed. Add basil and mix well. Steam potatoes until they are about halfway done. Place potatoes and all remaining ingredients in vinaigrette

(continued)

(Stuffed Royal Red Shrimp continued)

and marinate for half an hour. Remove vegetables and grill until done. Arrange 4 to 5 potatoes in a circle in center of a plate. Arrange 4 to 5 slices of potatoes on top to complete. Place plate in a warmer until ready to finish plate-up.

STUFFED SHRIMP:

15 ounces Italian sausage	1/4 cup shredded Parmesan cheese
2 tablespoons butter	2 teaspoons thyme
3/4 cup chopped mushrooms	1 tablespoon red wine
1/2 cup chopped onion	30 (10–15 count) royal red shrimp, peeled, butterflied, tail-on
1/4 cup roasted, cleaned and chopped red bell pepper	
2 eggs, beaten	2 cups seasoned flour
3 1/2 cups seasoned bread crumbs, divided	1 cup egg wash
	10 small basil tops for garnish

In a food processor, add sausage and purée until very smooth. In a sauté pan, heat butter and sauté mushrooms, onion, and pepper until tender. Add this to food processor with sausage and blend until evenly incorporated. Remove to a mixing bowl. Add eggs, 1/2 cup bread crumbs, cheese, thyme and wine. Mix well. Place 1 teaspoon of stuffing in each shrimp. Arrange 3 shrimp tails up, stuffing together, so sides of shrimp meet and enclose stuffing. Roll each shrimp cluster in flour, then dip in egg wash, then roll in remaining bread crumbs. Deep-fry shrimp to a golden brown. Remove plates from warmer and place 1 shrimp cluster in center of each potato. Spoon 3 tablespoons of each sauce on either side of potatoes. Garnish with basil leaves. Serves 10.

Recipe by Chef Joe Randolph,
Murano's at Grand Casino Biloxi

Grilled Red Drum Ancona

SAUCE:

½ teaspoon Tabasco sauce	2 cups V8 vegetable juice
2 tablespoons Worcestershire sauce	1 pint seafood stock
	¼ teaspoon basil
	¼ teaspoon oregano
1 teaspoon lemon juice	1 cup beef stock
2 tomatoes, seeded and chopped	1 cup heavy cream
	¼ cup cornstarch

Bring all items except cornstarch to a light simmer. Make slurry by adding a little water to cornstarch. Once Sauce is simmering, add slurry and allow to thicken slightly.

2 pounds red drum or any mild-flavored fish	1 cup Italian dressing

Trim fish fillets, removing blood line, and portion into 6-ounce fillets. Place fish in Italian dressing and allow to marinate 3 to 4 hours.

1 pound fresh linguini pasta	1 cup Roma tomatoes
1 tablespoon olive oil	1 cup mushrooms

Cook pasta in boiling salted water and drain well. In sauté pan, heat olive oil, Roma tomatoes, and mushrooms, and toss with pasta.

Grill fish and set aside. (Do not overcook fish; cook just until done and serve immediately).

To assemble, place pasta on plate with fish over top. Drizzle Sauce over fish and sprinkle 1 cup of crispy fried leeks over the top.

Recipe by Chef David Crabtree,
Murano's at Grand Casino Biloxi

Chilled Asian Cucumber and Sake Soup
with Marinated Red Snapper and a Spicy Mango Relish

MARINATED RED SNAPPER:

4 oranges, juiced	¼ cup diced peeled cucumber
2 lemons, juiced	
1 tablespoon sriracha chili sauce	¼ cup diced fennel
	2 tablespoons chopped mint
1 teaspoon honey	
Pinch of sea salt	1 tablespoon chopped cilantro
1 pound red snapper, diced	
	1 teaspoon grated ginger

In a small bowl, whisk together orange juice, lemon juice, chili sauce, honey, and salt, and pour this marinade over diced red snapper. Cover and refrigerate for 15 minutes. Strain liquid and add to red snapper the remainder of ingredients. Gently toss to incorporate all ingredients and chill until ready for use.

SPICY MANGO RELISH:

1 cup plus 2 tablespoons peeled and diced mango	2 tablespoons fresh chopped cilantro
¼ cup seeded, minced jalapeños	1 tablespoon mirin rice wine
¼ cup chopped green onion	1 teaspoon orange marmalade
2 tablespoons fresh chopped mint	1 teaspoon grated ginger
	Salt and pepper (optional)

In a small bowl, add all ingredients and gently toss to incorporate. Season with salt and pepper, if necessary, and chill until ready for service.

2 quarts chicken stock	1 orange, juiced
1 cinnamon stick	¼ cup yogurt
1 star anise	¼ cup mirin rice wine
2 cloves	2 tablespoons grated ginger
2 English cucumbers, divided	
1 cup high quality sake	1 tablespoon sriracha chili sauce
½ cup chopped fresh mint	Salt and pepper
½ cup chopped fresh cilantro	Fresh mint leaves to garnish (optional)

In a medium stockpot, add stock, cinnamon stick, star anise and cloves and bring to a boil. Reduce heat and

(Chilled Asian Cucumber and Sake Soup continued)

let simmer for about 30 minutes. Strain and chill. Meanwhile, roughly chop 1½ cucumbers, and leaving skin on, submerge cucumbers in boiling salted water for about 30 seconds. Remove and shock immediately in ice water. In a food processor, place chilled stock, cucumbers, sake, mint, cilantro, orange juice, yogurt, mirin, ginger and chili sauce and purée until very smooth. Season to taste and strain through a fine mesh sieve; chill. Serves 10.

Ladle 1 cup of chilled soup into 10 chilled shallow bowls. Mold Marinated Red Snapper into quenelle dumpling shapes using 2 teaspoons. Peel and thinly slice remaining ½ cucumber and fan out 5 slices of cucumber in center of each bowl. Arrange 5 Marinated Red Snapper quenelles around cucumbers and finish soup by placing 2 tablespoons of Spicy Mango Relish in center of cucumbers. Garnish with fresh mint leaves, if desired, and serve immediately.

Recipe by Chef Bryan Pisarich,
The Sushi Bar at Grand Casino Biloxi

The Lighthouse
Biloxi, Mississippi

IMPERIAL PALACE

850 Bayview
Biloxi, MS 39530
228-436-3000

Restaurants located on the grounds of Imperial Palace:
The Crown Room
Embers Steak House

Ed Glaser, Food Director
Aston Johnson, Executive Chef

The Crown Room is situated at the pinnacle of the hotel tower and dramatically captures the extraordinary views of the bay and coast as customers dine in an environment that can only be described as exquisite. The Crown Room serves extravagant and mouth-watering dishes. Appetizers include Jumbo Lump Blue Claw Crab Cake, and Lobster Bisque en Crute. Entrées include Filet Mignon, and Cammarones Con Baccio—"Shrimp with a Kiss." Desserts include Chocolate Decadence and the Banana Tower. James "Forrest" Hall is Chef de Cuisine, Crown Room.

Known for its steaks cooked perfectly to your order, wine selection, exceptional service, friendly staff and unique environment, **Embers Steak House** serves American, Continental and Southern dishes. Appetizers include Baked Oysters Embers and Gulf Blue Fried Crab. Entrées include Crawfish Stuffed Pork Chops, and Filet Mignon and Steamed Lobster Tail. Desserts include Black Forest Cake and Pecan Pie. Jeffery Cayouette is Specialty Chef, Embers Steak House.

Snapper Angelique

Our chef's signature dish of pan-broiled red snapper fillet covered with sautéed mushrooms, sweet peppers, green onions, Gulf shrimp, and jumbo lump crabmeat. Topped with a ribbon of rich Hollandaise sauce. Serves 4.

SNAPPER:

4 (8-ounce) snapper fillets, dressed	Clarified butter
Flour seasoned with salt and freshly ground white pepper	

Dredge snapper fillets in seasoned flour and sauté in clarified butter in an ovenproof skillet until golden brown. Drain excess butter and place skillet in 400° oven for 5 to 8 minutes until done. Keep warm until service.

TOPPING:

1 ounce clarified butter	2 ounces green onions, chopped
2 ounces white wine	16 ounces large shrimp, cleaned
8 ounces sliced jumbo mushrooms	8 ounces jumbo lump crabmeat
2 shallots, chopped	1 level tablespoon Spice Mixture
2 ounces red bell pepper, chopped	2 tablespoons chopped parsley
2 ounces green bell pepper, chopped	
2 ounces yellow bell pepper, chopped	

Add clarified butter to clean skillet and sauté shallots, mushrooms and shrimp until done. Add Spice Mixture and stir. Deglaze with white wine. Add chopped bell peppers, crabmeat and green onions and carefully mix together, taking care not to break up jumbo lump crabmeat. Heat until warmed through. Divide into 4 portions and keep warm until service.

HOLLANDAISE SAUCE:

12 egg yolks	Salt and cayenne pepper to taste
24 ounces clarified butter	Juice of 2 lemons

Whisk egg yolks in top of double boiler until thickened. Gradually add clarified butter while whisking continuously until sauce is smooth and creamy. Add salt, cayenne and lemon juice to taste. Keep warm until service.

(continued)

(Snapper Angelique continued)

SPICE MIXTURE:

8 tablespoons sweet paprika	2 teaspoons ground white pepper
2 tablespoons dried dill weed	1 teaspoon ground ginger
1 tablespoon dried sweet basil	1/2 teaspoon ground cinnamon
1 tablespoon onion powder	1/4 teaspoon ground cloves
2 teaspoons dried oregano	1/2 teaspoon salt
2 teaspoons dried marjoram	1/2 teaspoon Accent (optional)
2 teaspoons ground allspice	1/2 teaspoon light brown sugar

Mix together and store in airtight container. Makes approximately 1 cup.

TO ASSEMBLE DISH:

Place cooked Snapper fillet onto plate. Cover with Topping mixture. Top with ribbon of Hollandaise Sauce and garnish with chopped parsley.

Note: Spice Mixture can also be used as a general seasoning for vegetables, poultry, seafood and as a dry rub marinade for meats.

Recipe by Chef J. Forrest Hall, Crown Room at Imperial Palace

Blackened Chicken Linguine

As prepared at Embers Steak House

Blackening seasoning to taste	½ ounce olive oil
8 ounces chicken breast	1 ounce chopped garlic
1 red bell pepper	5 ounces heavy cream
1 green bell pepper	Linguine pasta (or pasta of your choice)
1 yellow bell pepper	½ ounce Parmesan cheese
½ purple onion	
4 ounces button mushrooms	Salt and pepper to taste

With your favorite blackening seasoning, sear off the chicken breast in strips; set aside. Julienne the trio of bell peppers and onion. Quarter the button mushrooms. Add oil to sauté pan; add the trio of bell peppers and mushrooms and sauté until tender. Add garlic and blackened strips and cook until garlic starts to brown. Add heavy cream and reduce heat until thick. Toss in pasta of your choice and Parmesan cheese until pasta is heated. Season to taste. Single serving.

*Recipe by Chef Jeffery Cayouette,
Embers Steak House at Imperial Palace*

MARY MAHONEY'S
Old French House Restaurant

Highway 90 and Rue Magnolia
Biloxi, MS 39531
228-374-0163

"Built 1737"

Mary Mahoney's Old French House is one of the few restaurants that successfully re-creates the lavish atmosphere of the pre-Civil War period in the South. The restaurant itself is housed in a building that dates from 1737 and at one time served as the residence for the first governor of the Louisiana Territory. The menu is varied, with an emphasis on French food; however there is a good sampling of Creole cooking, and many of the dishes show the influence of the Italian-born chef.

Seafood Gumbo

6 tablespoons flour	1 teaspoon pepper
5 tablespoons bacon drippings	2 pounds shrimp (fresh or frozen)
2 onions, chopped fine	2 pounds crabmeat (fresh or frozen)
1½ cups finely chopped celery	1 package cut okra (frozen)
1 garlic pod, chopped	3 tablespoons Worcestershire sauce
1 large can tomatoes	
1 can tomato sauce	1 pint oysters (optional)
5–6 cups water	
3 teaspoons salt	

Brown flour in bacon drippings to make roux. Add onions, celery and garlic and brown for 5 minutes. Add tomatoes, tomato sauce, water, salt and pepper and boil for one hour over medium fire. Add shrimp, crabmeat and okra and cook 20 minutes longer. Add Worcestershire sauce and oysters, if desired. Stir well and serve over steamed rice.

Irish Coffee Balls

2 cups vanilla wafer crumbs	1 tablespoon cocoa
1 cup chopped pecans	1 tablespoon instant coffee
2 tablespoons white Karo syrup	1 cup powdered sugar
	$\frac{1}{3}$ cup Irish whiskey

Mix all of the above ingredients. Take about 1 teaspoon of mixture and roll into a ball. Roll in powdered sugar. Makes about 50 balls.

Mary Mahoney's Pralines

2 cups sugar	1 teaspoon vanilla
1 can evaporated milk	$1\frac{1}{2}$ cups pecan halves or chopped pecans
3 tablespoons butter or margarine	

In a heavy saucepan, stir together sugar and evaporated milk. Bring to a boil over medium heat, stirring constantly. Cook to 234° (soft-ball stage), stirring to prevent candy from sticking. Add butter or margarine and vanilla while continuing to stir candy mixture. Add pecans and beat candy for 2–3 minutes or till candy begins to feel thick. Drop candy from tablespoon onto wax paper or aluminum foil. Let candy cool before removing from paper.

BACK DOOR CAFÉ

705 Beef Alley
Columbia, MS 39429
601-736-1734

Fran Ginn, Chef/Owner
Deborah Myers, Chef de Cuisine

The original business, In Good Taste Catering, was founded in 1984. Since that time, we've taken the catering company to Tennessee, Louisiana, Arkansas, Georgia, Florida and all over Mississippi. We've served governors, U.S. senators and representatives and other dignitaries. The fewest number we've served is two (and there is a precious little boy as the result of that dinner) and the greatest number is 5,000, which we've done several times. We have been featured in *Southern Accents, Southern Living* (several times) and in the special publication *Southern Living Brides, Mississippi Magazine* (several times) and *Alabama Bride*.

We opened The Back Door Cafe in 1996 in a 130-year-old building (which is on the National Register of Historic Places) in Columbia. Our building has been featured in a documentary on small town business filmed by the BBC. We are open "lunch only" and have an eclectic menu with our specialty being our "world famous chicken salad."

Unrolled Cheeseball

2 cups grated sharp
  Cheddar cheese
1 cup grated Monterey
  Jack cheese
¼ cup chopped green
  onions (or more to taste)
¼ cup chopped toasted
  pecans (or more to taste)

¼ cup chopped green
  olives (or more to taste)
Mayonnaise, enough to
  bind
Black pepper to taste

Mix together either by hand or with the paddle attachment of a mixer. (Do not try to do this in a food processor or you will get mush.) Pack into a container. This will keep for weeks in the refrigerator (or as long as you can resist eating it).

Marinated Olives Muffaletta Style

DRESSING:

⅓ cup red wine vinegar
⅓ cup olive oil
¼ cup dry onion flakes
1 tablespoon dry Italian
  seasoning

1 teaspoon fennel seed
3 garlic cloves, minced
Salt and pepper to taste

Put all Dressing ingredients in a small saucepan and bring to a boil (this is to soften the onion).

½ pound provolone
  cheese, cubed
½ pound ham, cubed
½ pound salami, cubed
1 green bell pepper, cut
  into pieces about the
  size of the cheese cubes

1 (14-ounce) can
  quartered artichoke
  hearts, drained
1 (16-ounce) jar Queen
  olives, drained
1 (16-ounce) jar Kalamata
  olives, drained

Let Dressing cool and pour over cheese, meats, vegetables and olives. This can be made up to 2 days before serving. Just before serving, stir in some freshly chopped parsley.

Butterbean Crostini

1 loaf baguette French
  bread, sliced diagonally
  about ½ inch thick)

Seasoned olive oil (or
  plain olive oil)

Brush bread lightly with olive oil and place on a baking sheet. Bake in a 200° oven until bread is golden and crisp.

BUTTERBEAN TOPPING:

¼ cup sliced green
  onions
4 tablespoons olive oil,
  divided
8 ounces frozen green
  butterbeans or lima
  beans
1 bay leaf
2 cups chicken stock
  (or enough to cover)
2 tablespoons roasted
  garlic purée
Zest of 2 lemons, grated

Kosher salt, freshly
  ground black pepper
  and Creole seasoning
  to taste
2 tablespoons lime juice
¼ cup chopped fresh
  herbs: parsley, thyme
  and rosemary, mixed
2 tablespoons finely
  chopped red onion
  and lemon zest
  to garnish

In a medium saucepan, sauté green onions in 2 tablespoons olive oil. Add butterbeans, bay leaf and enough stock to cover them. Bring to a simmer, then reduce heat and cook till beans are tender, adding more stock if needed. Cool in cooking liquid over an ice bath.

Remove bay leaf and pulse in a food processor with garlic purée, lemon zest, 2 tablespoons olive oil, salt, pepper, Creole seasoning, lime juice, and fresh herbs. Don't over process. This is ideally made the day of the party. Let the lima mixture come back to room temperature before serving. We like to garnish the crostini with chopped red onion and lemon zest. This can also be served as a dip with the crostini surrounding it.

—adapted from Ben Barker's Not Afraid of Flavor

Uptown Winery Caviar Spread

28 ounces cream cheese, softened
½ cup sour cream
2 tablespoons finely chopped white onion
Juice of half a lemon
2 tablespoons finely chopped fresh parsley
2 (3-ounce) jars red caviar

In a mixer—not a processor—combine all ingredients except caviar. While mixture is very soft, gently fold in caviar, being careful not to break eggs too much. Let this stand in refrigerator for about 4 hours or overnight to blend flavors. Bring out of the refrigerator at least 30 minutes before the party. This is especially pretty presented in the center of a head of Boston lettuce.

PETIT BOIS CAFÉ
and Catering

1115 Highway 90
Gautier, MS 39553
228-497-7005

Michael and Dee Anne Majure worked together to open the Petit Bois Café in the summer of 1997. The café features fresh local seafood dishes and many specialty chalkboard items. In the five years since opening, the Petit Bois Café has become one of the favorites of the locals and travelers alike.

Fried Green Tomatoes

¼ pound butter
½ cup all purpose flour
1 pint half-and-half
½ tablespoon thyme
½ tablespoon basil
Dash of Tabasco sauce
½ tablespoon salt
1 pound crawfish meat, drained
6 slices green tomatoes, fried

On low heat in a medium pot, melt butter, and then add flour. Sauté until lightly brown. Next add half-and-half and sauté. Add the thyme, basil, Tabasco sauce and salt. Sauté until mixture is thick, then add the drained crawfish meat and stir for 2–5 minutes. Remove from heat and place the fried green tomatoes on a round plate. Add sauce and serve.

Recipe provided by Michael C. Majure

Shrimp and Sausage Jambalaya

2 slices bacon
¼ cup cooking oil
½ cup diced celery
½ cup diced green bell
  pepper
½ teaspoon chopped
  garlic
½ cup diced onion
2 cups diced tomatoes
2 cups sliced sausage
1 tablespoon basil

1 tablespoon thyme
1 tablespoon oregano
2 tablespoons Old Bay
  seasoning
2 tablespoons Tabasco
  sauce
3 tablespoons
  Worcestershire sauce
7 cups water
3 cups rice
2 pounds shrimp

Cut bacon into small pieces; put in large cooking pot with oil and sauté for 1 minute. Add celery, bell pepper, garlic, and onion and cook for about 3 minutes on medium heat. Next add diced tomatoes, sausage, and the spices and cook for about 5 minutes; then add water. Cover and let boil. When the mixture boils, add rice and stir. Reduce heat to low and cover. Bring to a boil again, then add shrimp; stir and cover. Turn off heat and let it sit until rice has risen. Serves 10.

Recipe provided by Ferney "Antonio" Ayala

BBQ Shrimp

12 ounces beer
1 tablespoon thyme
1 tablespoon basil
1 tablespoon oregano
2 tablespoons lemon juice
2 tablespoons
  Worcestershire sauce

2 tablespoons olive oil
1 tablespoon salt
1 tablespoon chopped
  garlic
Pinch of cayenne pepper
12 jumbo shrimp
  (heads on, still in shell)

Combine all ingredients except shrimp in skillet. Sauté on medium heat until hot. Add shrimp and turn to high heat. Sauté again for 3–5 minutes. This can be served over rice or pasta. Also great to just peel and eat.

Recipe provided by Michael Majure

Butterscotch Pecan Pie

3 eggs
1 cup sugar
1 cup Karo syrup
1 tablespoon vanilla
1 tablespoon melted butter

Pinch of salt
¾ cup pecans
½ bag of butterscotch
  morsels
1 deep-dish pie shell

In a large bowl, mix eggs and sugar in blender for about 1 minute. (If you don't have a blender whip until ingredients are combined.) Next, add syrup, vanilla, butter and salt, and blend well. Add pecans and butterscotch morsels. Be sure that all the ingredients have been blended well together. Pour mixture into pie shell and bake for about 45 minutes at 350° or until top of pie starts turning a golden brown. Let it sit until the pie has become firm. Makes 1 pie.

Shrimp Boats

GRAND CASINO
Gulfport

3215 West Beach Blvd.
Gulfport, MS 39501
1-800-WIN-7777

Restaurants located on the grounds of Grand Casino Gulfport: LB's Steakhouse Market Place Buffet

B. J. Creswell, Kitchen Manager

Chef Creswell was born and raised in Memphis, TN. He started his cooking career at the age of 17 working at Western Sizzlin Steak House in Memphis. After working there for four years, he went to work at Fitzgerald's Casino and Hotel in Tunica, MS. There he was promoted to Sous Chef. He arrived on the Mississippi Gulf Coast in March 2000 and began employment with the Grand Casino, Gulfport. He was first employed as a production cook for the Market Place Buffet, and shortly was promoted to lead cook, then as assistant kitchen manager. He presently holds the position as kitchen manager at the Market Place Buffet.

Chef Eoin Redmond

Originally from Dublin, Ireland, Eoin Redmond began cooking at an early age and has traveled throughout the U. S. learning different styles of cooking. Among his many achievements, Chef Redmond completed The Greenbrier Culinary Apprenticeship course in 1997.

Red Snapper with Andouille and White Bean Ragout

1 (8 ounce) portion snapper, skinned and descaled
Salt and white pepper to taste
Olive oil
1 ounce diced white onion
1 ounce diced red pepper
½ ounce chopped garlic
2 ounces shiitake mushrooms
2 ounces andouille sausage
4 ounces white beans
2 ounces white wine
1 ounce Pernod
2 ounces chicken stock
½ ounce chopped basil
2 ounces arugula (for garnish)

Fillet and portion snapper into 8-ounce pieces. Descale by running a knife parallel along skin. Score the fish by scratching 3 small lines in the skin. Season fish on both sides and sauté in olive oil. Make sure to crisp skin a light brown color. Finish fish in the oven for about 6 minutes. Serves 1.

FOR THE RAGOUT:
Dice onion, pepper, chop garlic and sliced mushrooms. Sauté vegetables in olive oil, until tender but not brown. Add sausage and cooked white beans. Sauté for 1 minute. Deglaze pan with white wine and Pernod. Add chicken stock and finish with basil. Serve snapper on top of bean ragout in a entrée size bowl and finish with arugula just before serving.

Recipe by Chef Eoin Redmond,
LB's Steakhouse at Grand Gasino Gulfport

Chicken Penne Pizza Pasta with Tomato Alfredo Cream Sauce

4 (6-ounce) boneless, skinless chicken breasts
32 ounces penne pasta, cooked
1½ cups chopped fresh broccoli
1 cup sliced (¼-inch-thick) mushrooms
3 tablespoons pesto
1 (9-inch) pizza crust (Boboli)
1½ cups shredded mozzarella, divided
4½ cups Tomato

Cut chicken into bite-size pieces and cook until no longer pink inside. Put in a bowl and set aside. Cook pasta. Drain and rinse with cold water and set aside. Lightly blanch broccoli and slice mushrooms and set aside. Preheat oven to 350°. Spread pesto on top of pizza crust, then sprinkle 1 cup cheese on top of crust. Bake until cheese is melted. Remove from oven and slice crust into six or eight slices. Set aside. Sauté sauce in saucepan. Add chicken, broccoli and mushrooms. Simmer 2 to 3 minutes. Add pasta mix well. Pour mixture in middle of pizza crust and sprinkle remaining cheese on top. Cook in oven 3–5 minutes. Remove and serve.

TOMATO ALFREDO SAUCE:

1½ quarts heavy cream
½ cup grated Parmesan cheese
1 tablespoon salt
1 teaspoon white pepper
½ tablespoon minced fresh garlic
1 tablespoon thyme
1 teaspoon basil
¼ teaspoon cayenne pepper
14½ ounces diced tomatoes in juice
2 teaspoons margarine
1 tablespoon flour

To make sauce combine all ingredients except margarine and flour in saucepan. Reduce cream down. In a separate pot, melt margarine and add flour and cook 2 to 3 minutes over medium heat. Add to sauce mixture and simmer to desired consistency.

Recipe by B. J. Creswell, Kitchen Manager,
Market Place Buffet at Grand Gasino Gulfport

Crusted Venison Tenderloin with Mustard Sauce

¼ cup vegetable oil
2 pounds venison tenderloin
¼ teaspoon salt
½ teaspoon pepper
2 cups bread crumbs
½ cup white wine
½ cup heavy cream
1 ounce Creole mustard

Heat oil in pan. Season roast with salt and pepper. Lightly brown on all sides. Cool roast and coat in bread crumbs. Preheat oven to 325° and roast until well done. To prepare sauce take remaining juices from roast and heat over direct heat; pour off fat. Deglaze roasting pan with white wine. Stir in well and let simmer for 2 to 3 minutes. Strain sauce into saucepan and add heavy cream and mustard. Simmer until reduced. Adjust seasoning with salt and pepper to taste. Slice roast and serve with 1 ounce of mustard sauce on top.

Recipe by B. J. Creswell, Kitchen Manager,
Market Place Buffet at Grand Gasino Gulfport

CRESCENT CITY GRILL

3810 Hardy Street   519 Azalea Drive
Hattiesburg, MS 39402   Meridian, MS 39305
601-264-0657   601-553-3656
www.nsrg.com

New Orleans . . . the name itself exudes a quality that at best can be described as completely unique and exotic. The very same holds true for the Crescent City Grill. At the Crescent City Grill, every selection we offer is made from scratch daily and from only the very finest ingredients. From our garden fresh salads to our seafood that is caught daily in Gulf waters, you can be assured that painstaking care has gone into the preparation and presentation of each dish.

Robert St. John

Robert St. John, a native of Hattiesburg, is a 21-year veteran of the restaurant business. For the past 14 years, he has served as Executive Chef/Owner of Purple Parrot Company, Inc., which operates the Purple Parrot Café, Crescent City Grill, and the Mahogany Bar. Since 1997, he has served as owner and president of New South Restaurant Group, LLC. He is a graduate of the University of Southern Mississippi.

St. John was chosen Mississippi Restaurateur of the Year for 1996 by the Mississippi Restaurant Association.

St. John hosts a monthly-televised cooking show and writes a syndicated weekly food column. He is author of *A Southern Palette*, a coffee-table-style cookbook released in 2002 and now in its third printing.

Creole Cheese Fritters

¾ cup freshly grated Parmesan cheese	¼ teaspoon crushed red pepper
3 eggs	1 cup flour
¼ cup finely chopped parsley	½ tablespoon Crescent City Grill Cayenne and Garlic Sauce
¼ cup diced green onions	10 ounces Pepper jack cheese, grated
¼ cup horseradish	6 ounces Mozzarella cheese, grated
¼ cup sour cream	6 ounces Cheddar cheese, grated
1½ tablespoons minced garlic	
1 tablespoon Crescent City Grill Creole Seasoning	

Place Parmesan cheese, eggs, parsley, onions, horseradish, sour cream, garlic, Creole Seasoning, red pepper, flour and cayenne and garlic sauce in an electric mixer and combine at medium speed. Add the three cheeses and continue mixing until well blended. Heat vegetable oil to 350° in a cast-iron skillet. Drop golf ball-size spoonfuls of cheese fritter mixture into hot oil, making sure not to cook too many at once. Serve with Comeback Sauce for dipping. Yields 24–30.

*Administration Building, University of Southern Mississippi
Hattiesburg, Mississippi*

Pumpkin Cheesecake

CRUST:

3 cups graham cracker crumbs
⅓ pound butter, melted

½ cup sugar
⅛ teaspoon nutmeg
¼ teaspoon cinnamon

Combine all ingredients and press Crust along bottom and up sides of a springform mold. Refrigerate until Filling is ready.

FILLING:

2 pounds cream cheese, softened
¾ cup sugar
¾ cup brown sugar
4 eggs
4 egg yolks

1 (12-ounce) can pumpkin pie filling
1 tablespoon vanilla
1 teaspoon cinnamon
½ teaspoon nutmeg
½ cup whipping cream

Preheat oven to 300°. In a mixer, using the whip attachment, combine cream cheese and sugars and whip until smooth. Add eggs one at a time until completely incorporated. Add pumpkin, vanilla and spices and beat until smooth. Turn mixer to low speed and add cream. Mix until cream is incorporated. Pour cream cheese filling into springform mold and bake for 1 hour and 30 minutes. The cheesecake should jiggle just slightly when done. Cool for 24 hours. Use a hot, wet knife when cutting to get nice, smooth pieces. Yields 12–16 servings.

PURPLE PARROT CAFÉ

3810 Hardy Street
Hattiesburg, MS 39402
601-264-0656
www.nsrg.com

**Robert St. John
Executive Chef/Owner**

Rich, deep-toned woods, grand bouquets of fresh-cut flowers, crisp white linens and beautiful presentation of original southern art all come together to create an elegance for this culinary gem as noted for ambiance and style as it is for contemporary seasonal southern cuisine.

The Purple Parrot Café offers the flavors, culture and warmth of the seductive South while using only the freshest ingredients and cooking techniques. As our artfully prepared delectables start to arrive, you begin to understand why this is one of the most praised and awarded restaurants in the region. Your meal is nothing less than a feast for the senses. Purple Parrot Café was recently awarded the Wine Spectator Award of Excellence.

Eggplant Dauphine

18 eggplant rounds
1 cup seasoned flour
1½ cups eggwash
1½ cups seasoned bread crumbs
Vegetable oil, enough to deep fry in
½ cup clarified butter
1 pound (31-36 count) shrimp, peeled, deveined
2 teaspoons Old Bay Seasoning
3 tablespoons minced garlic
1½ cups sliced mushrooms
1 pound crawfish tail meat
½ cup white wine
1 cup crawfish cream
1 cup Parmesan cream sauce
1 cup Romano cheese, divided
Fresh parsley for garnish
½ cup chopped green onion

Peel eggplant and cut into round slices ¼-inch thick and 3 inches in diameter. Marinate eggplant in salted ice water. To prepare eggplant wheels, dust wheels with seasoned flour, shake off excess flour, then dip them in eggwash and coat with bread crumbs. Fry, a few at a time. (Be careful not to overload the oil.) Drain on paper towels. Hold in a warm oven while you prepare seafood mixture.

In a large skillet, heat butter over medium-high heat. Season shrimp with Old Bay Seasoning and sauté 3–4 minutes. Add mushrooms, garlic and crawfish meat and continue to cook for another 4–5 minutes. Deglaze with white wine and reduce by half. Add crawfish cream and Parmesan Cream Sauce and bring to a simmer. Stir in ¾ cup of the Romano cheese and green onions. On serving plates, layer eggplant wheels with seafood mixture and garnish with parsley and remaining Romano cheese. Yields 6 servings.

Crawfish Madeline

6 puff pastry shells
2½ cups crawfish cream
½ cup heavy cream
1 pound cooked crawfish tail meat
¾ cup sliced green onions
¾ cup grated Romano or Parmesan cheese
4 tablespoons chopped chives

Follow baking instructions on puff pastry shell box. While shells are baking, bring crawfish cream to a simmer over medium-high heat in a large skillet. Once it begins to simmer, add heavy cream and crawfish tails. Return to a simmer and allow mixture to cook for 3–4 minutes until it is thoroughly hot. Stir in green onions and once again bring it up to a simmer. Remove from heat. Place puff pastry shells on serving dishes and evenly divide the mixture over top of pastry. Top each one with grated cheese and chives; serve immediately. Yields 6 servings.

Chocolate Volcano

CHOCOLATE CAKE:
1½ cups unsalted butter
10 ounces chocolate (chips or block cut into small pieces)
4 eggs
4 egg yolks
¾ cup flour
1½ cups powdered sugar
12–16 fresh raspberries

Over a double boiler, melt butter and chocolate and mix well. Using a wire whip of an electric mixer, incorporate eggs and yolks one at a time. Add flour and powdered sugar and beat until smooth.

Lightly flour and butter the 6-ounce gelatin molds. Preheat oven to 375°. Fill mold halfway with batter and place 2 raspberries in the center. Fill molds the rest of the way with batter (leaving ¼ inch from the top unfilled) and bake for 12 minutes. Allow them to sit for 2–3 minutes, then carefully unmold them onto serving dishes. Yields 6–8 servings.

LAUREL INN
Bed and Breakfast

803 North Second Ave.
Laurel, MS 39440
601-428-8773

Peggy O'Connell
Innkeeper

At the Laurel Inn Bed and Breakfast, a typical breakfast consists of cheesy garlic grits, grilled vegetables, scrambled eggs, honey-cured bacon, biscuits and preserves. You will not be disappointed.

Cheesy Garlic Grits

1 cup grits	4 ounces half-and-half
3½ cups water	2 cloves garlic, freshly
2 ounces fresh Parmesan	pressed
cheese	Salt

In a saucepan, slowly stir grits into boiling water. Reduce to medium to low heat; cover. Cook grits until thickened; stir in cheese, half-and-half, garlic and salt to taste. Reduce heat; blend ingredients and simmer. Serves 8.

Heirloom recipe handed down by Peggy O'Connell's mother, Hazel Lambert Smith

Grilled Tomatoes

4 medium tomatoes	¾ cup Italian bread
5 tablespoons extra	crumbs
virgin olive oil	2 tablespoons Cavender's
2 tablespoons balsamic	Greek seasoning
vinegar	

Preheat oven to 375°. Rinse tomatoes and halve. Place cut-side-up in baking dish. Mix olive oil, balsamic vinegar, bread crumbs and Greek seasoning. Spoon mixture over tomatoes. You might need to add a wee bit more oil. Bake for 30 minutes and serve right away. This is a delicious side dish for breakfast, lunch or dinner. Serves 4 .

Recipe by Peggy O'Connell

Morning Cakes

Years ago when my mom, my sister and I made these "breakfast cakes," ready-made pastry was not available, so our pastry was made from scratch. Thank goodness with the passage of time we do have ready-made pastry of all forms.

½ pound ready-made	2 tablespoons sliced
puff pastry	almonds
1 small egg, beaten	4 tablespoons heavy
6 tablespoons of any	whipped cream
preserves	
2 tablespoons superfine	
sugar	

To make this delightful dish, preheat oven to 425°. Roll out pastry dough on a lightly floured surface. Cut into 2 identical pieces. Place one piece of pastry dough on a baking sheet that has been sprayed or dusted with vegetable oil. Brush edges of pastry with a portion of beaten egg. Add your favorite fruit preserves. Place second pastry sheet over fruit preserves. Gently cut openings in top pastry for steam to escape. Press pastry edges together to seal. Scallop edges. Brush pastry with a small amount of beaten egg; sprinkle with the sugar and almonds. Bake for 25 to 30 minutes until golden brown. Cool. Top with whipped cream. Serves 4.

Heirloom recipe handed down from Hazel Smith

CHAPPY'S SEAFOOD RESTAURANT

624 East Beach
Long Beach, MS 39560
228-865-9755

Chappy's Seafood Restaurant opened its doors in December of 1984 and has become one of the premier restaurants on the Gulf Coast today. Chappy's is open 7 days, 11:30 a.m. until 10 p.m.

John Chapman was born in Mobile, AL, where his father was the British Consul. Later after his father's death, John and his family moved to New Orleans, LA, where he graduated from Loyola University of New Orleans with a degree in Business. Learning his cooking techniques from his mother, Chappy always dreamed of owning and operating his own family-style restaurant. John received his nickname "Chappy" from his wife, Starr, while they were courting. "Chappy" was also his father's nickname.

Oysters Bienville

24 raw oysters, their juices, and their cleaned shells
1/4 pound butter
1 bunch chopped green onions
12–15 chopped mushrooms
1/2 cup white wine
1/2 cup boiled and chopped shrimp
1/2 teaspoon basil
1/2 teaspoon oregano
1/2 teaspoon thyme
1/2 teaspoon salt
1/2 teaspoon white pepper
2 teaspoons Chappy's Garlic Spice
1/2 cup evaporated milk
1/2 cup bread crumbs
1/4 cup shredded Cheddar cheese

Heat oyster juices until boiling. Place oysters in juice until edges begin to curl. Remove and place on cleaned oyster shells or oyster dish. Keep warm.

Melt butter in skillet on high heat. Sauté green onions and mushrooms together. Add white wine. Add cooked shrimp and spices. Mix well. Stir in evaporated milk slowly. Add bread crumbs. Mix gently. The mixture will congeal nicely. Turn heat down and simmer for 3 minutes. Remove from stove. Place 1 teaspoon mixture upon each oyster until all mixture is evenly divided. Top with Cheddar cheese. Melt cheese in oven for 3–5 minutes. Serve immediately. Serves 6.

Mardi Gras Mambo Punch

After the first drink, you will be yelling "Throw me something, mister!" and diving for beads. That's Mardi Gras.

1 pint freshly squeezed lemon juice
1 fifth dry white wine
1 1/2 cups granulated white sugar
1 fifth dark rum
1 fifth light rum
1 fifth brandy
1 1/2 cups peach schnapps
1 1/2 cups apricot brandy

Heat lemon juice and wine; add sugar and stir well. Add remaining ingredients and let stand at room temperature for two hours. Chill well. Pour into punch bowl and add ice ring that contains lemon slices. If the alcohol content is too high for you, omit 1 fifth of light rum and 1 fifth brandy, add equivalent of 2 fifths of Hawaiian Punch. Serves 1 small crowd.

Crayfish Zydeco Soup

Cajun music is from southern Louisiana. It is a blending of French and Acadian culture sautéed together with strong accordian overtones. Zydeco is a blues version of Cajun music. This music is the base of the Mardi Gras music. Crayfish Zydeco Soup is my soulful tribute to the Mardi Gras every year. If you ever attend the Bacchus Parade, yell for me, Chappy. Better yet, make a sign. Good Luck!

½ cup chopped onion
½ cup chopped green
  pepper
½ cup chopped celery
½ cup oil or butter
½ cup flour
1 teaspoon Chappy's
  Garlic Spice
1 teaspoon Chappy's
  Zydeco Spice
1 quart to ½ gallon milk
½ cup chopped carrots

½ cup chopped purple
  cabbage
½ cup chopped green
  cabbage
½ cup little purple
  Bermuda onions,
  halved (optional)
4 cups peeled, cooked
  crayfish tails
1 dash cayenne pepper
  or Tabasco to taste

Sauté onion, pepper, and celery in oil or butter over medium-high heat. Add flour and make a roux. Continue stirring. Add spice and seasonings. Add milk and bring the roux up (by that, I mean to gradually add the milk until the roux actually rises). Do not boil. The amount of milk added depends on desired consistency. In other words, how thick or thin you want the soup to be. Reduce heat to low. Add chopped veggies for color. After 10 minutes, add the crayfish. Simmer for 2–3 minutes longer. Add cayenne pepper or Chappy's Pepper Sauce for spice. Serves 6–8.

Chappy's Pepper Steak

The sauce is a great accent to the meat. That's why I call it a dipping sauce. For a nice twist to the sauce, add sugar or honey for a unique sweet and sour taste.

¼ pound butter
4 thin New York strips;
  remove the fat
3 turns cracked black
  pepper per steak
1 yellow pepper, julienned
1 red pepper, julienned
1 green pepper, juilenned

1 teaspoon Chappy's
  Garlic Spice
3 dashes Lea & Perrins
  Worcestershire Sauce
1 teaspoon chopped fennel
  or ½ teaspoon dried
  fennel leaves

Melt butter in skillet on a medium-high heat. Place steaks in skillet and sauté for 5 minutes. Add the cracked pepper. Add peppers, garlic, and Lea & Perrins. Flip steaks when browned. Add fennel and cook to desired doneness. Arrange peppers on a plate and top with steaks sliced into strips and Dipping Sauce. Serves 4.

DIPPING SAUCE:
¼ cup horseradish sauce   ¼ cup sour cream

Mix together in a bowl. Place a dollop in the center of each pepper steak. Serve immediately. Serves 4.

STEVE'S MARINA RESTAURANT

213 E. Beach Blvd.
Long Beach, MS 39560
228-864-8988

**Steve and Shandell Pucheu
Owners**

Steve's Marina Restaurant is located overlooking the beautiful Long Beach Harbor on the Gulf of Mexico. The spectacular waterfront location facing the Long Beach Harbor allows diners to enjoy the scenery whether they choose to dine on the deck overlooking the water, or whether they choose the comfortable indoor dining area with the same spectacular view. There isn't a seat in the restaurant that doesn't allow the customer to enjoy the waterfront experience.

Steve has developed his menu as a result of 18+ years experience in restaurants along the Coast. He has owned and operated a very successful restaurant for more than 8 years. This experience has paid off with some of the most outstanding dishes found anywhere on the Coast. Steve's love for cooking and his love for Long Beach have been instrumental in making his childhood home the location of his new restaurant.

Steve's Red Snapper Cat Island

1 stick butter	Shrimp
1 medium onion, chopped	Salt and pepper to taste
	Juice of 2 lemons
1 pound sliced mushrooms	½ pound jumbo lump crabmeat
1 can artichoke hearts, quartered	4 fresh snapper fillets (or any fresh fish)

Melt butter in sauté skillet. Sauté onion and mushrooms till tender, about 5 minutes. Add artichokes and shrimp and sauté another 5 minutes. Add salt, pepper, lemon juice, and crabmeat. Sauté until crabmeat is warmed throughout, being careful not to break up crabmeat. Turn off heat for the crabmeat mixture while you cook the fish. Cook fish anyway that you prefer: fried, grilled, broiled or blackened. (We prefer grilled or blackened.) Place fish on serving plate and top with generous amount of Cat Island sauce. Serve over pasta or rice. Enjoy! Serves 4.

Steve's Shrimp Diane

3 pounds sliced mushrooms	Salt to taste
2 sticks butter	Cayenne pepper to taste
1 cup dry white wine	1 bunch green onions, rough chopped
3 pounds jumbo shrimp, peeled and cleaned	2 pounds cooked pasta
¼ cup fresh basil or ⅓ cup dry	2 cups grated Parmesan cheese

In a large skillet, sauté mushrooms in butter and wine for about 6 minutes. Add shrimp, basil, salt and pepper. Sauté another 5 minutes or until shrimp are cooked, then add green onions. Place pasta in a large bowl or serving platter. Pour shrimp and mushrooms over pasta and top with Parmesan cheese. Enjoy! Serves 4 to 6 people.

GERMAINE'S FINE DINING

Highway 90
1203 Bienville Boulevard
Ocean Springs, MS 39564
228-875-4426

Jack Gottsche, Owner

Gypsy Oysters

1 gallon fresh oysters
3 to 4 lemons, juiced
2 tablespoons
  Worcestershire sauce
2 tablespoons Creole
  seasoning
1 teaspoon Tabasco sauce
1 tablespoon granulated
  garlic
Salt to taste

Drain oysters and place in a heavy-duty, heat-resistant pan. Add all ingredients, including lemon rinds, and combine with oysters. Place open pan over a medium heat charcoal fire and cover the grill so oysters absorb smoke. For best results, add wood chips to fire to increase smoke flavor. Pecan wood is recommended for best flavor. Remove from grill when oysters just begin to curl. Do not overcook. Remove lemon rinds and serve immediately. Serves 8.

Note: The quantities of all the ingredients may be varied according to taste.

Chicken Gee-Gee

2 tablespoons butter
1 tablespoon all-purpose
  flour
4 or 5 chicken tenderloins
  (about 5 ounces)
1 teaspoon Cavender's
  seasoning
5 julienne strips each:
  red and yellow bell
  peppers
2 tablespoons finely
  chopped white onion
1 clove garlic, minced
¾ cup whipping cream
2 teaspoons white wine
Rice or angel hair pasta

Place butter in small skillet over medium heat; add flour and mix well. Do not brown. Season chicken strips with Cavender's seasoning. Add chicken to pan and cook on both sides until chicken is about half done (about one minute). Add peppers, onion and garlic to sauté. Add cream and cook until the sauce thickens. If sauce gets too thick, add more cream until you reach the desired consistency. Continue cooking until chicken is done, about another two minutes. Add wine and serve over rice or pasta. This makes one generous serving.

Note: You can substitute whole chicken breasts for the tenderloins, but they will cook more slowly.

Oysters Kelon

½ cup whipping cream
½ teaspoon butter
Salt and pepper to taste
1 cup grated Parmesan
  cheese
3 canned artichoke hearts,
  quartered
1 medium white
  mushroom, sliced
5 to 6 oysters, depending
  on size
Cracker crumbs
2 tablespoons finely sliced
  green onions

Over medium heat, reduce cream by half. Add butter, salt, pepper and cheese. Cook until consolidated, then add artichokes and mushroom. Cook for one minute. Add oysters and cook for another minute or until oysters just begin to curl. (Do not overcook oysters.) Transfer ingredients to ovenproof dish. Top with cracker crumbs, and place under broiler to brown lightly. Top with green onions and serve. Makes one individual serving.

SCRANTON'S
Downtown Plaza

623 Delmas Avenue
Pascagoula, MS 39567
228-762-1900

Richard Chenoweth, Jack Pickett, and Merle Ivy established Scranton's Restaurant in 1982. The building, built in 1924, is on the National Register of Historic Places. It formerly housed the fire station, city hall, city jail and the civic center. Rooms are filled with memorabilia that depict the history of Pascagoula's bygone days. The engine room lounge still has the original fire door that had to be lifted up to let the fire truck go out!

Spinach and Artichoke Dip

This recipe is designed for restaurant use but can be portioned down.

1 (#10) can of artichoke hearts	4 cups sour cream
1 (3-pound) package chopped spinach	2 cups Parmesan cheese
2 cups chopped red onion	3 tablespoons Italian seasoning
1½ cups mayonnaise	2 tablespoons black pepper
	1 tablespoon salt

Mix well. Portion into serving cups and refrigerate. May be microwaved or baked at 350° until bubbly.

Shrimp Louisiane Casserole

1 cup chopped onions	3 cups cooked rice
¾ cup chopped green pepper	1 tablespoon chopped parsley
1 clove garlic, minced	1½ tablespoons lemon juice
2 tablespoons butter or margarine	1½ teaspoons salt
1 pound raw shrimp, peeled, deveined, or crawfish tails	¼ teaspoon ground black pepper
1 (10¾-ounce) can condensed cream of mushroom soup	¼ teaspoon red pepper
	2 slices white bread
	½ cup milk
	Paprika

Cook onions, green pepper and garlic in butter until tender-crisp. Add shrimp and continue cooking 3 minutes longer. Stir in soup, rice, parsley, lemon juice and seasonings. Add bread, which has been soaked in milk; mix well. Spoon into a buttered, shallow 2-quart casserole. Sprinkle with paprika. Bake at 350° for 30 minutes. Yields 6 servings.

Shrimp and Rice Rockefeller

1 cup chopped onions	1 (8-ounce) can water chestnuts, drained and sliced
2 tablespoons butter or margarine	2 (10-ounce) packages frozen, chopped spinach, cooked and drained
12 ounces, raw shrimp, peeled, deveined, and sliced in half lengthwise	
1 (10¾-ounce) can condensed cream of mushroom soup	1 tablespoon lemon juice
1 cup grated Swiss cheese	¼ cup grated Parmesan cheese, divided
¼ cup sherry	Salt and ground black pepper to taste
3 cups cooked rice	

Cook onions in butter until tender, but not brown. Add shrimp and continue cooking until slightly pink, about 2 minutes. Stir in soup, Swiss cheese, and sherry, and heat until soup is warm. Add rice, water chestnuts, spinach, lemon juice, and 2 tablespoons Parmesan cheese. Season to taste. Turn into a buttered, shallow 2-quart casserole. Sprinkle with remaining Parmesan cheese. Bake uncovered at 350° for 25 minutes or until hot and bubbly. Makes 6 to 8 servings.

MERRY WOOD

26 Dillons Bridge Road
Tylertown, MS 39667
866-222-1415 (toll free)
www.merrywoodcottages.com

Merry Wood is a vacation hide-a-way bed and breakfast located in a 300-acre private preserve on the Bogue Chitto River. The owners of Merry Wood, Merry and Ryck Caplan, have combined their desire to provide an experience of beauty, luxury and relaxation with their commitment to ecological responsibility. The staff is dedicated to providing quality, individual attention and professional service. You can select one of three unique houses for your private use. Each is furnished with country antiques, and situated to provide complete privacy and seclusion. The number of guests is limited, so attention to detail can be assured. Although each house has a full kitchen, the rate includes a hardy country breakfast delivered to you. Each stay at Merry Wood reflects the individual interests of guests; at this magical oasis you can plan time completely undisturbed, or days filled with activities. Choose from selected professional services to create an individual stay that meets your specific needs. These services include private dinners, selected spa services, and sessions in yoga, tai chi or meditation. On the grounds enjoy a library, exercise room, conference room, hidden ponds, river beach, three miles of groomed trails, organic garden and 130-foot labyrinth. Surrounding activities include antique shops, flea markets, festivals, town museums, canoeing and biking.

Lentil Salad

$1\frac{1}{2}$ cups small lentils
$\frac{1}{2}$ cup diced roasted red peppers
2 garlic cloves, minced
$\frac{1}{2}$ small mild onion, minced
1 bay leaf
2 teaspoons chopped fresh mint
1 tablespoon chopped fresh parsley
1 tablespoon chopped fresh marjoram
1 tablespoon chopped fresh oregano
5 ounces Lemon Vinaigrette
Sea salt and freshly ground pepper, to taste
1 small head of frise (or baby mixed greens), remove core, rinse in cold water, dry

Rinse lentils and cover with cold water. Add garlic, onion, and bay leaf and bring water to a boil; reduce to simmer and cook until tender, but firm. Drain lentils, cool, and remove bay leaf; fold in fresh herbs, Lemon Vinaigrette and half of the roasted peppers. Season with salt and pepper. Keep at room temperature. Toss greens with Lemon Vinaigrette, salt and pepper. Taste lentils and adjust seasoning, if needed. Arrange greens around small plate. Place lentils in center; spread with spoon and top with remaining peppers.

LEMON VINAIGRETTE:
1 lemon, juiced
$\frac{1}{4}$ teaspoon paprika
Pinch cayenne pepper
1 clove garlic, minced
$\frac{1}{4}$ teaspoon sea salt
6–8 tablespoons olive oil

Mix above ingredients. Adjust seasoning if needed. Serves 4–6.

Madeleinies

5 tablespoons butter
$\frac{1}{2}$ cup sugar
3 eggs
$\frac{1}{2}$ teaspoon almond extract
$\frac{1}{2}$ teaspoon vanilla extract
$\frac{3}{4}$ cup all-purpose flour
$\frac{1}{2}$ teaspoon baking powder

Cream butter and sugar until light; add eggs, and beat 2–3 minutes after adding each egg. Add almond and vanilla extract. Sift flour and baking soda together and fold into mixture.

Butter molds, then fill each mold about $\frac{2}{3}$ full. Bake in preheated 400° oven until golden brown, about 10 to 20 minutes. Turn out and cool on wire rack.

MAGNOLIA RESTAURANT

Highway 63 South
Waynesboro, MS 39367
601-735-5231

The Magnolia Restaurant is owned and operated by Bobbie Henderson on Highway 63 South in Waynesboro. Bobbie has 20 years experience in the restaurant business. For the last 9 years, she has enjoyed serving the locals and visitors to this area. They have enjoyed her fine style of country cooking served buffet style. The buffet is open Monday through Friday, 11 a.m. until 2 p.m. Private parties available.

Chicken Breast with Dried Beef Sauce

6 boneless, skinless
  chicken breasts
Black pepper to taste
1 can of cream of
  chicken soup
1 cup sour cream
1 jar dried beef (chopped
  fine in food processor)
¼ cup margarine, melted

Wash chicken well and drain. Place in casserole dish. Lightly sprinkle with pepper. Mix cream of chicken soup, sour cream, dried beef and margarine together. Spoon over chicken. Bake at 350° for 45 minutes or until chicken is done. Serves 6.

Mixed Vegetable Casserole

1 large package frozen
  mixed vegetables
  (broccoli, cauliflower
  and carrot mix)
1 cup grated cheese
½ cup sour cream
1 can cream of chicken
  soup
½ cup margarine
1 sleeve of crackers
  crushed

Cook vegetables according to package directions until just tender. Drain well. Mix cheese, sour cream, and soup together. Pour over drained vegetables into casserole dish. Melt margarine; mix with crackers and sprinkle over top. Bake approximately 30 minutes at 350° or until done.

Squash Casserole

2 cups fresh squash,
  chopped
1 medium onion
2 eggs
½ cup milk
1 cup grated cheese
¼ cup margarine
1 tube Ritz crackers,
  crushed
Salt and pepper to taste

Cook squash and onion until tender; drain off all liquid. Mash. Beat together eggs and milk; add to squash. Mix cheese, margarine, and cracker crumbs. Add ½ to squash mixture. Season to taste. Pour into buttered casserole dish. Sprinkle remaining crumbs on top. Bake 20 to 30 minutes at 400°.

THE ROUNDTABLE
Restaurant and Catering

103 Mississippi Drive
Waynesboro, MS 39367
601-735-2819

The Roundtable Restaurant is a family-owned restaurant owned and operated by Tim and Kim Williams and Kim's mother, Marvie Giles. We have been serving locals and tourists down-home southern cooking for 15 years in Waynesboro. Some of our most famous dishes are our Baked Chicken and Banana Pudding, and don't forget the yeast rolls. The *Wayne County News* and its readers voted us the Best of the Best Caterers!

Baked Chicken
(House Recipe)

2 whole chickens, cut up
4 tablespoons seasoned
  salt
1 large bell pepper
1 large onion
2 tablespoons black
  pepper

Wash chicken. Place chicken in a 4-inch deep baking dish. Sprinkle with season salt and black pepper. Slice bell pepper and onion. Layer bell pepper and onion evenly over chicken. Cover with foil. Bake in a 450-degree oven for 20 minutes then reduce heat to 350° and bake for another hour and a half. Makes 12 servings.

Baked Catfish

12 catfish fillets
2 tablespoons seasoned
  salt
$1\frac{1}{2}$ tablespoons garlic
  powder
$1\frac{1}{2}$ tablespoons lemon
  pepper seasoning
2 tablespoons melted
  butter

Wash catfish fillets. Layer catfish in a single layer in a shallow baking dish. Sprinkle with seasoned salt, garlic powder, and lemon pepper. Pour melted butter over each fillet. Cover with foil, and bake 20 minutes in a 350° oven. Uncover and bake for another 10 minutes. Serves 12.

Roundtable Yeast Rolls

2 cups very warm water
2 tablespoons active dry
  yeast
$1\frac{1}{2}$ sticks butter, melted
$\frac{1}{2}$ cup sugar
1 egg, beaten
4 cups sifted self-rising
  flour

Pour 2 cups warm water in a large mixing bowl. Add yeast and mix until yeast dissolves. Let stand for 5 minutes. Add butter, sugar, egg and flour to yeast. Mix well (it will be a little lumpy). Let stand for another 10 minutes. Spoon mixture into greased muffin tins. Bake for 10 minutes or until golden brown. Brush with melted butter. Serve hot. Yields 24 rolls.

Special Section

Special Section Menu

THE BAILEY HOUSE

Recipes submitted by
family and friends of the author.

Ann Freeman Bailey, Executive Chef
John M. Bailey, Sous Chef and Author

Potato Casserole

6–8 large potatoes	1 bunch chopped green
1 stick butter	onions (tops and
2 cups grated Kraft Old	bottoms)
English cheese	2 cups sour cream
¼ cup whole milk	Salt to taste

Boil potatoes in jackets in salted water; chill. Peel when cold and grate potatoes. Melt butter and cheese in skillet with milk. Add onions and sour cream. Mix in potatoes. Season to taste. Put in large buttered casserole dish. If possible, chill several hours or overnight. Bake at 350° for about 45 minutes or until hot. Serves 6.

Italian Spinach

3 boxes frozen leaf	3 eggs, beaten
spinach	Parmesan cheese
Salt to taste	2 slices mozzarella
¼ cup olive oil	cheese
2 or 3 cloves fresh garlic,	
minced	

Cook spinach (salt to taste) and drain very well (press water out with a paper towel). Heat olive oil in skillet with garlic (don't burn the garlic). Add spinach and three beaten eggs to oil. Stir (over low heat) until the eggs are cooked. Add Parmesan and mozzarella cheese to spinach. Stir until cheese melts. Ready to serve. Great as side dish with pasta or steak. Serves 4.

Hot Fudge Pie

1 stick butter	¼ teaspoon salt
3 ounces chocolate squares	1½ cups sugar
4 eggs, beaten well	1 tablespoon vanilla
3 tablespoons white Karo syrup	1 pie shell, unbaked

In double boiler or pan, melt butter and chocolate over low heat. Mix eggs, Karo syrup, sugar, salt, and vanilla together. Mix well, then add to chocolate mixture. Stir and pour in unbaked pie shell. Bake at 300° until firm to touch. Serve hot with vanilla ice cream.

Recipe by Gertrude Freeman

Chicken and Dumplings

1 whole chicken (Mom always said a large fat hen)	2 celery stalks, chopped
	2 bay leaves
Water to cover	1 teaspoon black pepper
2 teaspoons salt	½ teaspoon ground cumin
1 large onion, chopped	

Cover chicken in pot with water. Add remaining ingredients and simmer covered about 1 hour or until chicken is done. Remove chicken to cool. Strain broth and set aside for cooking Dumplings. Debone chicken when cool.

DUMPLINGS:

1½ cups flour	Dash of pepper
2 teaspoons baking powder	2 tablespoons vegetable oil
½ teaspoon salt	Water to mix

Mix flour, baking powder, salt and pepper. Cut in oil. Add water to make a soft dough. Roll dough very thin and cut into 1x2-inch strips. Add Dumplings to boiling broth a few at a time. When all have been added to broth, add chicken on top of Dumplings and cover. Simmer about 45 minutes or until tender. Leftovers can easily be reheated by placing in a 350° oven with a little milk. Serves 6 to 8.

Submitted by Ross Herrin and Ralph Forrey

Chicken Tajine

Vegetable oil	½ teaspoon black pepper
4 large split chicken breasts (preferably with skin on)	½ Preserved Lime or Lemon, chopped
2 onions, finely chopped	3 tablespoons chopped parsley
3 cloves garlic, chopped	1 cup green olives
Pinch of saffron	
1 tablespoon grated fresh ginger	

Oil large frying pan. Brown chicken lightly. Coat with onions, garlic, saffron, ginger and pepper. Cook covered on medium heat for about ½ hour, turning occasionally. Add a little broth or water if it becomes too dry. Add Preserved Lime or Lemon, parsley and olives. Continue cooking, turning occasionally, until chicken is done. Usually there is enough salt in the lime and olives so that more salt is not needed. Transfer chicken to oven-proof pan and place under broiler until nicely browned. Serve with rice. Serves 4.

PRESERVED LIMES OR LEMONS

Limes or lemons	Salt

Wash and dry fruit. Cut in quarters from one end, leaving the quarters attached at stem end. Do not separate quarters. Open quarters slightly and stuff with 1 tablespoon salt. Pack in clean, dry jar as each fruit is done. Cover jar tightly (if using a metal lid, use plastic wrap underneath metal lid) and place in sun every day for three weeks. Press fruit down as juice forms so that all fruit will eventually be covered with juice. Store preserved fruit in a dark place and it will keep almost indefinitely.

Submitted by Ross Herrin and Ralph Forrey

Beans with Masa Cornbread

1 pound pinto beans	1 (14-ounce) can diced
Water or stock for cooking	tomatoes
1 teaspoon cumin	6 jalapeño peppers (fresh
2 bay leaves	or canned)
1 large onion, chopped	Salt to taste
4 slices thick-sliced bacon,	2 tablespoons chopped
chopped	fresh cilantro (optional)
6 cloves garlic, chopped	Sour cream for garnish

Pick and wash the beans. Place beans in a large pot and cover with water or stock. Add bay leaves and cumin. Cover and simmer about 3 hours or until tender. Add more hot liquid as needed to cook beans. Cook bacon in a skillet until browned. Add onion and garlic. Cook until tender. Add tomatoes and jalapeños. Simmer for a few minutes. Add mixture to bean pot. Salt to taste. Continue cooking till very tender. Add fresh cilantro, if desired, the last 15 minutes of cooking. Serve topped with sour cream. Serves 6 to 8.

MASA CORNBREAD:

6 eggs, separated	½ cup sugar
1 cup masa harina	10 tablespoons butter,
(Spanish for corn meal)	softened
½ teaspoon salt	½ cup cold water
1½ teaspoons baking	
powder	

Preheat oven to 375°. Butter standard loaf pan (9x5x 3-inch). Fit bottom of loaf pan with wax paper; butter the wax paper. Beat egg whites until stiff and set aside. Mix masa harina, salt, baking powder and sugar in mixer bowl. Cut in butter. Add water and beat well. Beat in egg yolks. Beat well. Fold in beaten egg whites. Pour into prepared pan and cook 45 minutes. When done, run knife around edge of pan and unmold. Remove wax paper and serve hot.

Submitted by Ross Herrin and Ralph Forrey

Smoked Portobello Salad
with Mixed Greens and Balsamic Vinaigrette

MUSHROOMS:

1 teaspoon salt	1 ounce chopped fresh
1 teaspoon black pepper	garlic
2 tablespoons sugar	1 large portobello
2 teaspoons	mushroom
Worcestershire sauce	
3 ounces olive oil	
1 teaspoon chopped	
fresh rosemary	

Mix all but mushroom very well. Clean "gills" from mushroom and marinate in mixture for at least 2 hours. Remove from the liquid (reserve the liquid) and smoke for 1 hour at 150°. Remove from smoker and place back into liquid. Chill.

DRESSING:

1 teaspoon chopped garlic	2 ounces Dijon mustard
1 teaspoon chopped	2 ounces balsamic vinegar
shallots	3 ounces olive oil
1 teaspoon salt	1 teaspoon fresh basil,
1 teaspoon black pepper	julienne

Mix garlic, shallots, salt, pepper, and mustard in a bowl or blender. Slowly add vinegar and oil, alternating between them. When all are incorporated and well blended, remove and stir in fresh basil. Chill.

ASSEMBLY OF SALAD:

Place your favorite salad greens on a chilled plate. Remove portobello mushroom from liquid and slice it very thinly. Place it atop salad greens. Garnish with Kalamata olives, sliced Roma tomatoes and fresh croutons. Finish it with Dressing.

Recipe by Chef Robert L. Bellew, Jr.

Crab, Brie and Avocado Spring Rolls with Roasted Red Pepper Sauce

1 pound jumbo lump crabmeat	¼ cup sliced roasted almonds
1 tablespoon salt	6 spring roll wraps
1 tablespoon freshly ground white pepper	½ pound Brie, thinly sliced
3 tablespoons chopped green onions (tops only)	2 avocados, pitted and scooped out of skin

Place first 5 ingredients in a mixing bowl; mix well, then place about 3 ounces of mixture in center of a spring roll wrap. Place 2 slices of Brie and a small amount of avocado in the very center, and wrap spring roll up.

TO SEAL SPRING ROLLS WRAPS:

1 egg	1 tablespoon
1 tablespoon water	cornstarch

Beat ingredients together for egg wash. Cover the outside of the spring roll to seal it.

PEANUT OIL FOR DEEP-FRYING:

Heat frying oil to 350° and deep-fry spring rolls until golden brown (about 3 minutes). Slice lengthwise, diagonally, and serve with Red Pepper Sauce atop a bed of greens.

RED PEPPER SAUCE:

6 roasted red peppers, chopped	8 ounces seafood stock
1 small clove garlic, peeled and minced	¼ cup white wine
	1 quart heavy cream
2 shallots, minced	Salt and pepper to taste

To roast peppers, place whole uncut peppers over an open flame until skins begin to blister and turn black, turning to get all sides. Take roasted peppers off flame and put immediately into a mixing bowl and cover with plastic wrap to steam them. Let them remain in bag for approximately 10 minutes, then remove from bag. The blackened skin should peel right off the peppers. Sauté first 5 ingredients until peppers are soft. Remove from heat and add heavy cream, then stir gently to warm. Put mixture into blender or food processor and purée. Season to taste. Strain and set aside.

(continued)

(Crab, Brie and Avocado Spring Rolls continued)

ROUX:

1 stick unsalted butter	1 cup flour

Combine butter with flour in a saucepan and cook over heat until mixture combines and turns a golden brown. Add Roux to Red Pepper Sauce a teaspoon at a time to thicken, being careful not to add too much.

Submitted by Jay Villarraga

Pan-Seared Duck Breast with Persimmon and Ginger Glaze

GLAZE:

4 cups cut persimmons, seeds removed	1 tablespoon cleaned fresh thyme
1½ tablespoons finely chopped garlic and shallots	1 cup water
	1 teaspoon salt
1 tablespoon ground ginger	½ teaspoon black pepper
	Honey to taste

Blend persimmons, garlic, shallots, ginger, thyme and salt until smooth. Place this mixture into a saucepot with the water and heat to a boil. Reduce heat, add salt and pepper, and let simmer until sauce is thick (similar to marmalade). Stir in a little honey to taste.

½ teaspoon olive oil	2 tablespoons soy sauce
2 duck breasts with skin on	

Heat sauté pan and add olive oil on medium-high heat. Sear each side of the duck breasts until brown. Slice; drizzle soy sauce over the breasts, then cover with Glaze.

Submitted by Thomas Blackledge

Glossary

aïoli ~ A garlic mayonnaise from France usually served with seafood.

al dente ~ An Italian phrase used to describe pasta or vegetables cooked just until firm, not soft or overdone.

ancho ~ A fairly mild red chile pepper.

andouille ~ A thick Acadian sausage of lean smoked pork, ranging from bland to very peppery.

anise ~ An herb that tastes like licorice. It is often used in pastries, cheeses, etc.

antipasto ~ An appetizer that is generally served before pasta.

appareil ~ A mixture of ingredients already prepared for use in a recipe.

Arborio rice ~ An Italian medium-grain rice that is used frequently for risotto.

arugula ~ A leafy salad herb that has an aromatic peppery flavor.

baguette ~ A French bread that's been formed into a long, narrow cylindrical loaf.

bain-marie ~ (Water bath) consists of a bowl placed over a bowl of boiling hot water to gently cook the sauce, etc., without overcooking.

balsamic vinegar ~ A very fine, aged vinegar made in Modena, Italy, from white Trebbiano grape juice.

basil ~ An aromatic herb widely used in Mediterranean cooking. It is used in pesto sauce, salads and cooking fish.

basmati rice ~ A long-grain rice with a nutty flavor.

bay leaf ~ This aromatic herb comes from the evergreen bay laurel tree, native to the Mediterranean. Dried bay leaves are used frequently in poultry, fish and meat dishes as well as stocks and soups.

béarnaise ~ One of the classic French sauces. It is made with emulsified egg yolks, butter, fresh herbs and shallots. It is often served with meat, grilled fish and vegetables.

béchamel ~ One of the basic French sauces. It is a sauce made from white roux, milk or cream, onions and seasonings.

beignet ~ A French word for batter-dipped, fried fritters, usually sweet like a doughnut, and dusted with confectioners' sugar.

beurre blanc ~ A white butter sauce made from shallots, white wine vinegar and white wine that has been reduced and thickened with heavy cream and unsalted butter.

beurre manié ~ A paste of flour and butter used to thicken sauces.

bisque ~ A thick, rich soup usually made from puréed seafood (oysters, shrimp or lobster) and thickened with cream.

blanch ~ To plunge fruits and vegetables into boiling water briefly, then into cold water to stop the cooking process.

bon appétit ~ Literally, "good appetite" or "enjoy your meal."

boudin blanc ~ A peppery, pale-brown link of pork meat, liver, onions and other seasonings. Rice is usually what binds the fillings of this richly seasoned sausage.

braise ~ The slow cooking of food in a tightly covered container with a flavoring liquid equal to about half the amount of the main ingredient.

Brie ~ A soft cows' milk cheese made in the French region of Brie.

brûlé ~ A French word for "burnt" and refers to a caramelized coating of sugar, such as a topping for crème brûlée.

bruschetta ~ Toasted bread slices rubbed with garlic and drizzled with extra virgin olive oil.

café au lait ~ Coffee and chicory blend with milk; usually a half-and-half mixture of hot coffee and hot milk.

Cajun ~ Slang for Acadians, the French-speaking people who migrated to South Louisiana from Nova Scotia in the 18th century. Cajuns were happily removed from city life, preferring a rustic life along the bayous. The term now applies to the people, the culture and the cooking.

cannelloni ~ Large, round tubes, typically stuffed then baked with a sauce.

caper ~ The pickled bud of a flowering caper plant. It is found on the Mediterranean coast. Capers are often used as a condiment in salads, in making tartar sauce and as a seasoning in broiling fish.

capon ~ A castrated young male chicken, fed a fattening diet and brought to market before it is ten months old.

caramel ~ Sugar that has been cooked until it melts and becomes a golden brown color.

cardamom ~ A member of the ginger family. It has a spicy flavor and is used in Indian and Middle Eastern dishes.

cayenne pepper ~ Red chile pepper that is dried and ground fine for home use.

chaurice ~ A highly spiced pork or beef sausage used in Cajun cooking.

chervil ~ An herb belonging to the parsley family. It is best used fresh because of its delicate flavor.

chicory ~ An herb, the roots of which are dried, ground and roasted and used to flavor coffee.

chiffonnade ~ Leafy vegetables such as spinach and lettuce cut into thin strips.

Chinese five-spice powder ~ Used extensively in Chinese cooking, this pungent mixture of 5 ground spices usually consists of equal parts of cinnamon, cloves, fennel seed, star anise and Szechuan peppercorns.

chipotle ~ A brownish-red chile pepper that has been dried and smoked and sometimes canned. This chile pepper has a smoky flavor and is very hot.

chives ~ A member of the onion family used in flavoring foods.

chutney ~ A sweet and/or sour seasoning that can be made from fruits and vegetables and flavored with many kinds of spices.

ciabatta ~ Italian bread named for its slipper shape.

cilantro ~ A fresh coriander leaf.

clarified butter ~ Butter that has been heated to remove the impurities.

clarify ~ To remove all impurities.

condiment ~ Any seasoning, spice, sauce, relish, etc., used to enhance food at the table.

consommé ~ A clear strained stock, usually clarified, made from poultry, fish, meat or game and flavored with vegetables.

coriander ~ A member of the carrot family. Fresh coriander is also called cilantro. This herb is prized for its dried seeds and fresh leaves and is used in similar ways to parsley.

coulis ~ A thick sauce or purée made from cooked vegetables, fruits, etc.

court-bouillon ~ A rich, spicy soup, or stew, made with fish fillet, tomatoes, onions and sometimes mixed vegetables.

couscous ~ Traditional couscous is generally made from coarsely ground semolina, a wheat flour used for pasta. It is popular in the Mediterranean areas of Morocco and Algeria. It is often served over vegetables or meats along with sauces.

crème brûlée ~ A custard made from eggs and covered with a "burnt" layer of sugar which has caramelized in the oven.

crème fraîche ~ Made from un-pasteurized cream with an additive such as yogurt which gives it a distinctive flavor.

Creole ~ The word originally described those people of mixed French and Spanish blood who migrated from Europe or were born in southeast Louisiana. The term has expanded and now embraces a type of cuisine and a style of architecture.

crevette ~ The French word for "shrimp."

cumin ~ A spice from the seeds of the cumin plant. It is often used in making pickles, chutneys and, especially, in curries.

currant ~ A fruit used to make jams and jellies. It is also used as a glaze for meats. The red variety is widely used.

curry powder ~ A mixture of spices widely used in preparing and cooking meats and vegetables. It is often used in Indian cooking.

daikon ~ A large radish.

deglaze ~ A process of dissolving cooking juices left in a pan where meats or poultry have been cooked. This is achieved by adding liquids such as stock or wines to the sediment and then reducing it to half the volume. The sauce is the strained and seasoned.

demi-glace ~ A brown sauce boiled and reduced by half.

Dijon mustard ~ Mustard made from a white wine base.

dill ~ An herb used with vinegar to pickle cucumbers. It is also used to flavor foods.

dirty rice ~ Pan-fried, leftover cooked rice sautéed with green peppers, onions, celery, stock, liver, giblets and many other ingredients.

dredge ~ To coat food with a dry ingredient such as breadcrumbs, cornmeal or flour.

Dungeness crab ~ A large rock crab found in the Pacific Northwest.

espagnole sauce ~ A rich, reduced brown stock containing herbs, tomato purée or fresh tomatoes and a mixture of browned vegetables, all thickened by brown roux.

étouffée ~ A succulent, tangy tomato-based sauce. Crawfish étouffée and shrimp étouffée are delicious New Orleans' specialties.

fagioli ~ The Italian word for "beans."

fais do-do ~ The name for a lively party where traditional Cajun dance is performed.

farfalle ~ "Butterfly"-shaped pasta.

fennel ~ A vegetable bulb or herb with a spicy flavor. It is often used in soups and salads.

feta cheese ~ A soft and crumbly goat's milk cheese often used in salads and Greek dishes.

filé powder ~ Sassafras leaves that have been dried and used in the final stages to thicken and flavor gumbo. Okra can also be used to thicken gumbo instead of filé powder.

filo (phyllo) ~ A very thin dough that contains little fat and is used for strudel, baklava and other pastries.

flan ~ An open custard tart made in a mold. Caramel cream custard is a popular flan dessert.

foie gras ~ The enlarged liver of a fattened or force-fed goose.

frais, fraîche ~ Fresh.

fraise ~ Strawberry.

free-range ~ Poultry or animals allowed to roam and feed without confinement, as opposed to commercially bred animals, which are caged.

fumet ~ Liquid that gives flavor and body to sauces and stocks. Fish fumet is used to poach fish fillets. It is made from dry white wine, fish stock, and bouquet garni.

garde manger ~ Pantry area where a cold buffet can be prepared.

garnish ~ A small amount of a flavorful, edible ingredient added as trimmings to complement the main dish and enhance its appearance.

ginger ~ A spice from a rhizome of a plant native to China. It is used fresh in Chinese cooking, but can also be used dried or ground.

glace ~ Ice cream; also used for cake icing.

glaze ~ It is used as a coating to give a shiny appearance to roasts, poultry, custards, jams and jellies.

glutinous rice ~ Sticky rice used by the Japanese to make sushi and rice cakes.

Gorgonzola ~ A strong Italian blue cheese.

gratons ~ The Acadian-French word for fatty pork skins fried in lard (also known as cracklings).

grillades ~ Squares of braised beef or veal. Grillades and grits is a popular local breakfast.

guava ~ A tropical fruit shrub. It makes delicious jellies.

gumbo ~ A Cajun or Creole soup thickened with okra or filé powder. Gumbo is an African word for okra.

habanero ~ An extremely hot chile pepper, oval-shaped and smaller than the jalapeño. The color changes from green to orange and red upon ripening. It is used in stews and sauces.

haddock ~ Closely related to a cod but smaller and thin-skinned. It is excellent broiled in butter.

halibut ~ The largest member of the flounder family. It can be smoked, broiled or grilled.

haricot vert ~ Green string beans.

Herbsaint ~ Anise liqueur—tastes like licorice.

hoisin sauce ~ Used in Chinese cooking to flavor sauces and marinades. It is a thick brown sauce made from soybeans, garlic, sugar and salt.

hollandaise ~ One of the classic sauces in French cooking. It is made from an emulsion of hot clarified butter and eggs lightly heated until it begins to have the consistency of a smooth custard. It also contains lemons and shallots.

infuse ~ To soak spices, herbs, or vegetables in a liquid to extract their flavor.

jalapeño ~ A very hot green chile pepper generally used fresh, but also available canned.

jambalaya ~ A Cajun dish of rice, shrimp, crawfish, sausage, chicken and beans, seasoned with Creole spices.

julienne ~ Vegetables cut into thin strips.

kalamata olive ~ Large, black Greek olive.

kale ~ A frilly, leafy vegetable of the cabbage family.

King Cake ~ A ring-shaped pastry decorated with colored sugar in the traditional Mardi Gras colors, purple, green and gold, that represent justice, faith and power. A small plastic baby is hidden inside the cake and the person who finds it must provide the next King Cake.

lagniappe ~ This word is Cajun for "something extra," like the extra doughnut in a baker's dozen. An unexpected nice surprise.

leek ~ A member of the onion family. Leeks are used in soups, casseroles, etc.

loganberry ~ Similar to a blackberry and raspberry. It can be served with cream as a dessert, a filling for tarts or as a cream pudding.

mandoline ~ A tool use to cut vegetables evenly into thick or thin slices.

mango ~ A delicious, sweet tropical fruit served alone as a dessert and also used in cooking preserves and chutneys.

marinade ~ A liquid, including seasonings, to flavor and tenderize fish, meat and poultry before cooking.

marinara ~ A tomato sauce flavored with herbs and garlic, usually served with pasta.

Merlot ~ A red-wine grape that produces a fruity flavor.

mesclun ~ A mixture of wild salad leaves and herbs. They are generally served with dressing containing walnut or olive oil and wine vinegar.

mirepoix ~ A mixture of cut vegetables—usually carrot, onion, celery and sometimes ham or bacon—used to flavor sauces and as a bed on which to braise meat.

mirin ~ A sweet and syrupy Japanese rice wine used for cooking.

mirliton ~ A hard-shelled squash.

miso ~ A soybean paste.

Mornay Sauce ~ A classic French sauce; béchamel sauce to which egg yolks, cream and cheese are added.

muffuletta ~ This huge sandwich is made up of thick layers of several different types of Italian meats, cheeses and a layer of olive salad. Served on special Muffuletta bread.

oregano ~ Oregano is an herb very similar to marjoram but more pungent. It is widely used in Greek and Italian cooking.

orzo ~ Rice-shaped pasta.

panache ~ French to describe something mixed or multicolored such as salads, fruit or ice cream.

panéed ~ Breaded and pan-fried.

pancetta ~ Italian bacon that is sometimes rolled into a solid round.

paprika ~ A variety of red bell pepper that has been dried and powdered and made into a cooking spice. It is used in making Hungarian goulash, etc.

penne ~ Tube-shaped pasta cut on the diagonal.

peperonata ~ An Italian dish of bell peppers, tomatoes, onions and garlic cooked in olive oil. It can be served hot or cold.

peperoncini ~ A hot red chile pepper served fresh or dried.

pepperoni ~ A Italian salami of pork and beef seasoned with hot red peppers.

phyllo ~ See filo.

piccante sauce ~ Hot spicy tomato-based sauce.

piccata ~ Veal scallop.

plantain ~ A tropical fruit similar to the banana.

po-boy ~ A type of sandwich which started out as an inexpensive meal. There are fried oyster po-boys, shrimp po-boys and others. All are served on French bread.

poisson ~ French for "fish."

poivre ~ French for "pepper."

pomodoro ~ Italian for "tomato."

porcini ~ Italian for "wild mushrooms."

portobello mushroom ~ A large cultivated field mushroom which has a firm texture and is ideal for grilling and as a meat substitute.

praline ~ A sweet candy patty. The main ingredients are sugar, water and pecans.

prawn ~ A large shrimp.

prosciutto ~ Italian ham cured by salting and air drying.

purée ~ Food that is pounded, finely chopped, or processed through a blender or strained through a sieve to achieve a smooth consistency.

quiche ~ A custard-filled tart with a savory flavor.

radicchio ~ A reddish member of the chicory family used as a garnish or for salad.

ratatouille ~ A mixture of tomatoes, eggplants, zucchini, bell peppers and onions cooked in olive oil. It can be served hot or cold.

red beans and rice ~ Red beans cooked in seasonings and spices and usually with chunks of sausage and ham—served over a bed of rice.

reduce ~ To boil down a liquid to thicken its consistency and concentrate its flavor.

relleno ~ Stuffing.

rémoulade ~ One of the classic French sauces. It is made from mayonnaise seasoned with chopped eggs and gherkins, parsley, capers, tarragon and shallots. It is served with shellfish, vegetables and cold meats.

rice wine ~ Distilled from fermented rice.

ricotta ~ The word ricotta means "recooked" in Italian. It is a soft cheese made from whey. It has a slight sweet taste.

rigatoni ~ Italian macaroni.

riso ~ Italian for "rice." A rice-shaped pasta; used to make risotto, an Italian rice dish.

risotto ~ An Italian arborio rice dish simmered slowly.

roghan josh ~ A spicy lamb dish from India, red in color and served with rice.

rosemary ~ A shrub with aromatic needle-like leaves. It is used fresh or dried as an herb, especially with lamb, pork and veal.

rouille ~ A spicy red pepper and garlic mayonnaise.

roulade ~ French for a rolled slice of meat or piece of fish filled with a savory stuffing.

roux ~ A mixture of flour and fat (usually butter or shortening) cooked together slowly to form a thickening agent for sauces, gumbos, and other soups.

sec ~ Means "dry."

scaloppine, scaloppina ~ An Italian term for a thin scallop of meat. The meat is dredged in flour, then sautéed and served variously.

shallot ~ A sweet member of the onion family. It has a more delicate flavor than regular onions. It is used extensively in French cooking.

shiitake ~ A dark brown mushroom with a meaty flavor. It is available both fresh and dried. It was originally from Japan but is now cultivated in both America and Europe.

slurry ~ A thin paste of water and flour (or cornstarch), which is stirred into hot preparations (such as soups, stews and sauces) as a thickener. After the slurry is added, the mixture should be stirred and cooked for several minutes in order for the flour to lose its raw taste.

sommelier ~ Wine steward.

sorrel ~ A leafy plant often used in salads, soups, omelets, purees and sauces. It has a distinct lemon taste.

sweat ~ To cook in a little fat (in a covered pot) over very low heat, so that the food exudes some of its juice without browning: used especially with vegetables.

tamari ~ Similar to but thicker than soy sauce, tamari is also a dark sauce made from soybeans.

tapenade ~ A thick paste made from capers, anchovies, ripe olives, olive oil, lemon juice, seasonings and sometimes small pieces of tuna.

tartar ~ A sauce made with mayonnaise, egg yolks, chopped onions, capers and chives. It is often served with fish, meat and poultry.

tasso ~ A highly seasoned Cajun sausage made from pork.

thyme ~ An herb with a pungent smell that belongs to the same family as mint. It is used in soups, stocks, casseroles and stews.

timbale ~ Metal mold shaped like a drum.

tofu ~ A white Japanese bean curd made from minced soy beans boiled in water then strained and coagulated with sea water. It is soft and easily digested.

tomatillo ~ Mexican fruit related to the tomato. It is often used in salsa, salads, sauces, etc.

tournedo ~ A trimmed cut of beef or veal fillet.

U10 or U12 jumbo shrimp ~ 10 or 12 shrimp to a pound.

veal ~ The meat of milk-fed baby calves.

vermicelli ~ A thin Italian pasta.

vinaigrette ~ A basic dressing of oil and vinegar with salt, pepper, herbs and sometimes mustard.

white sauce ~ Béchamel or velouté sauce, both made from roux.

yuca ~ (Cassava) A root that ranges from 6–12 inches long and 2–3 inches in diameter. Peeled, grated white flesh can be used to make cassareep (a West Indian condiment found in Caribbean markets) and tapioca.

zabaglione ~ A rich Italian custard made of egg yolks beaten with Marsala wine and sugar until very thick.

zest ~ The outer skin of citrus where the important oils have accumulated.

Recipe Index

Restaurant Index

Fine Dining Series

**Fine Dining
Mississippi Style**

**Fine Dining
Louisiana Style**

**Fine Dining
Tennessee Style**

*W*e hope that you have enjoyed *Fine Dining Mississippi Style.* Each book in the FINE DINING SERIES collects signature recipes from the very best restaurants, chefs, and bed & breakfast inns in each featured state.

Dedicted to Preserving America's Food Heritage for twenty-five years, Quail Ridge Press is nationally renowned for the acclaimed BEST OF THE BEST STATE COOKBOOK SERIES and RECIPE HALL OF FAME COOKBOOK COLLECTION as well as the FINE DINING SERIES.

All of our cookbooks are available in bookstores, gift and kitchen shops nationwide. They can also be ordered directly from Quail Ridge Press. To place an order or to request a free catalog, call 1-800-343-1583 or visit us on the web at **www.quailridge.com** where you'll also find special offers, free recipes, and more.

QUAIL RIDGE PRESS
Preserving America's Food Heritage

P. O. Box 123 • Brandon, MS 39043 • 1-800-343-1583 • www.quailridge.com

Wilkinson County Museum
Woodville, Mississippi

Stanton Hall
Natchez, Mississippi